# JOURNEY WITH CARAVEL

Every land, every parish has a tale to tell.
*Sir Winston Churchill*

# Journey with Caravel

Fred Carlisle

## We ran away to sea

With an appendix on celestial navigation

CLARKE, IRWIN & COMPANY LIMITED  Toronto Vancouver

© 1971 by Clarke, Irwin & Company Limited

ISBN    0-7720-0505-2

Printed in Canada

1  2  3  4    JD    74  73  72  71

To the men and women of many nations
whom we met along the way and who
welcomed us onto their boats and into their
homes. They made our voyage easier by
their hospitality, happier by their friendship,
and safer by their help. Yet they asked
nothing in return.

# ACKNOWLEDGEMENTS

The author and publisher thank the following persons and organizations for permission to use the photographs acknowledged here:

Ardmore Studio: Arriving at Mount Sinai

Bermuda News Bureau: Carlisle family on board *Caravel II* at St. George, Bermuda; Kitty in the galley; Nora and Mary doing lessons

George W. F. Ellis: *Caravel* greeted by Mrs. Carlisle at Padstow

*Hamilton Spectator: Caravel* is launched

Hal Kelly: Mary and Nora on their fo'c'sle bunk

A. W. Stubbs: Tied up at the Sussex Yacht Club

Toronto Star Syndicate: *Caravel* at the foot of Bay Street

United States Coast Guard: *U.S.S. Androscoggin*

Donald W. Young: Author and family plot position in cabin; Author in chart-house; Carlisle family on deck

# CONTENTS

Prologue / xi
Let's run away to sea / 3
Of lakes and locks / 11
Bascule ahead, believed hostile / 19
Red nun and black can / 25
Flight from Cape May / 32
The forest primeval / 40
Caravel Island / 48
Of palms and pelicans / 56
Inez and Dolores / 63
Trouble at Gun Cay / 72
Chopper to Mount Sinai / 81
Of conchs and coves and coral reefs / 93
Texas Tower / 102
*Echo* and Pico Gorda / 111
Doom Bar / 122
Longships and Portland Race / 136
The Rock / 144
Costa del Viento / 155
Of mosques and minarets / 163
Night on Bald Mountain / 175
Search for *Beyond* / 183
In the wake of the buccaneers / 194
The sea was meant for sailing / 207
Appendix: celestial navigation
               the easy way / 212
Glossary / 226

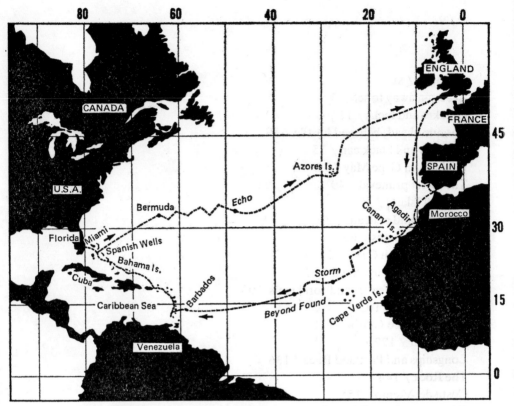

*The North Atlantic, showing the two crossings of* Caravel

# MAPS

The North Atlantic / viii
Accommodation layout / 8
Gun Cay and Cat Cay (Bahamas) / 76
Central Bahamas / 89
Land's End and the Scilly Isles / 132
Strait of Gibraltar / 149
Islands of the Caribbean / 196
Southern Bahamas / 202

# PROLOGUE

It is fashionable, these days, to argue that the spirit of Cook and Eric the Red, of Drake and Magellan, of the explorers of the Middle Ages and the Sea Dogs who came after them, is dead. We are told that twentieth-century man is too concerned with his grey flannel suit existence, his mortgage payments, a second car for his wife and his pension plan, ever to risk his neck or credit rating by doing anything dangerous or unconventional.

And it is, of course, true that life in the seventies does exercise a tight control over us, that it is difficult to break the shackles of the sales conference and the monthly car payments. Society pressures us to conform in matters of dress, habits and speech, as well as in political, economic and religious thought. If born north of a line on a map, you are expected to salute this flag, cheer this leader, take up arms to support this political ideal. If born south of the same line, it is another flag, another leader, and a different set of values that you must accept.

But the human animal is still an individual, and the human male especially so. He resists these pressures, in varying degree, according to his personality. Why else does he take up his gun in the fall and go off into the bush, in response to some hunter instinct within him? Why else does he prefer a tent under the stars or a canoe on a northern lake to a room at the Waldorf? Why else does he respect the astronaut and secretly despise the hair stylist? What else can explain the fact that he spends his spare time building a cottage in the forest, sailing a boat or taking flying lessons?

And for every one who succeeds in breaking the bonds that confine him to the computer, the lathe or the desk, there are fifty others who would dearly love to break them, who yearn for the freedom that they surrendered as part of the price they paid for their home, their car, and their child's ballet lessons.

We cannot, of course, all be astronauts, or Eisenhowers, or even join the Peace Corps. But still there exists in the hearts of many men and women a deep desire to break these bonds, to get away from the rat race, to do something that seems different and worthwhile, something that can be remembered for the rest of one's life with nostalgia, and maybe a touch of pride.

Many readers will already have decided to cruise the seven seas in their own boat, and if they know as little about it as I did, they are now reading everything they can find by others who have trodden the path before them, in the hope that they can learn something and even avoid one or two of the pitfalls. This book is addressed to them, for although I am far from being an experienced sailor I hope that I have learned a few of the basics, and that I have developed the ability to avoid some of the mistakes. It may be that something I have written, some stupid blunder that I shamelessly recount, may help them to avoid a similar mistake, or even save a life.

But there are probably far more readers who, while they would love to sail down the trades and cruise the islands, are under no illusions that life will be that generous to them. The bonds are too strong. This book is addressed to them too. For it is surely no disgrace to curl up with a book and to enjoy vicariously the peace of the Great Dismal Swamp, the beauty of a sunset over a Bahamian lagoon, the awesome fury of a Force 10 storm off Bermuda, and the joy of a landfall after many weeks at sea.

As I write this book, I am conscious of its dual role. To the reader who intends, or even hopes, to do the same thing himself, I say, "This is the way we did it. In many ways we made a mess of things, but I hope that our mistakes will help you to avoid stubbing your toe on the same cleat."

And to the reader who knows that his dream can never come true, I say, "This is what it is like. I was fortunate enough to be able to do it. I have a wife who was willing to go along with it, for without that I could never have got to first base. This is how we, as a family, tackled the problem. We hope that the narrative will entertain you. If you really can't make it yourself, we hope that you will enjoy reading about the way our efforts turned out."

This book is in no sense a manual of cruising, for I am far from qualified to write one. If you want to learn to tie a bowline, or protect your bronze fittings from electrolysis, or design self-steering twin jibs, there are excellent books to help you. All I can do in this field is to note a few of the things we discovered as we went along, which are not normally found in any cruising guide.

Kitty, for instance, has learned that preparing for a dinner party at home and keeping a hungry crew fed in a gale in the Bay of Biscay (with only one burner working on the kerosene stove, and with dried food that turns out to be full of weevils) are not quite the same thing. But if you buy right, stow right, and spice it up right, you can whip up a surprisingly good meal under pretty awful conditions.

Similarly, I have discovered, to my surprise, that it is possible to pinpoint one's position in mid-ocean, to within two or three miles, with a cheap, plastic sextant and a $15 wrist watch, without first taking a Ph.D. in advanced mathematics—in fact, without doing anything more difficult than adding and subtracting. Later on I'll explain how!

And if you are using your children as an excuse for not going to sea, forget it! While you are biting your nails in the middle of an Atlantic gale and wondering whether you will ever live to see tomorrow's dawn, they will be playing with their toys, completely oblivious to you and your old double-reefed main.

But what surprised us most of all were the friendships we made, deeper and more sincere than most of those on land. When you make friends with another boat—and it doesn't matter whether they are Americans or Swedes, Frenchmen or Australians—and then sail into some port 3,000 miles away and six months later to see the familiar hull and rig at anchor there, you hail them, and wave to them, and call them over for drinks before you have even got your anchor down. Nobody is trying to sell anything to anyone, or to impress them. You just want to hear of their adventures, and to relate your own, since you last saw them in Miami, Gibraltar or Martinique. It's so darned *good* to see them again.

These are just a few of the things which we have learned, and which have made life in *Caravel* so rewarding. I hope that some of what I shall write will be helpful, and that it will raise the occasional smile.

SOUTHWARD BOUND

# LET'S RUN AWAY TO SEA

The decision to retire was, as I recall, originally taken some fifteen minutes after I left school and started work, in a dingy wholesale grocery office in Liverpool, England, back in the depths of the depression. But, brilliant though the plan seemed at the time, it had to be tabled for a while, for I was at that point earning fifteen shillings a week, payable two weeks in arrears, and was a mite shy on risk capital.

The decision to retire down south was not reached until much later. After living in Toronto for twenty years, I discovered that I was allergic to snow.

The decision to retire down south in a boat was actually a recurring one, taken about May 10th of each year, when the real estate tax bill arrived. I would pay this legalized extortion with a bad grace, fully determined to move to a place where such taxes didn't exist. This seemed to spell B-O-A-T.

Being a realist, I could foresee problems. For one thing, although I had managed to acquire a house, a reasonable bank account and a moderately successful general insurance agency, I wasn't sure how long these assets would last in the Caribbean.

Secondly, I had also acquired a wife and two small daughters, and while Kitty usually went along with most of my plans, she shared neither my wanderlust nor my distaste for snow shovelling and taxes. In addition, although Mary and Nora were still babies, they would tend to grow, and Kitty kept bringing up the apparent lack of good high schools in the Galápagos Islands. She also mentioned the fact that my total sailing experience, as Master under God, consisted of puttering around some of the smaller lakes in Haliburton in a 12-foot runabout. Women, I find, often adopt a somewhat negative approach in such matters.

At this point the project sort of bogged down, until I was snapped out of my lethargy by an event which occurred at about 2:30 on a morning in January 1964. With the outside temperature about 10 below, the furnace went on the blink. By 9 a.m. a bathroom pipe had burst and flooded the front hall closet, the living room fireplace was smoking badly,

3

and I had lost 45% of a night's sleep, to say nothing of being cold, sooty and fed up. As we sipped coffee in our dressing gowns, I made a snap decision.

"This settles it. This is the living end. I've had it up to here. I quit. I'm going to buy a boat and go down south. Want to come?"

I had never put it to her quite this bluntly before, and the reply came as a bit of a shock.

"When?"

"Oh, as soon as we can buy a boat I guess, and rent the house, and sell the business, and the car, and a few things like that."

Even as I said it, it sounded quite an undertaking. But if I did have any misgivings they were dispelled a week or so later, when the National Boat Show came to Toronto. As I ducked in from the 12-degree wind whistling across Lake Ontario I saw a sleek-looking trimaran.

Now when Man hollowed out his first log, paddled it into mid-stream, and promptly capsized, he learned his first lesson in naval architecture—that a boat has to have a built-in stability to keep it right side up and the skipper dry. He first achieved this by filling the bottom with rocks, and as technology improved he changed over to pig iron or lead.

Out in the Pacific the Polynesians, with no iron or lead deposits handy, had developed another theory. Stick two boats together, side by side, and they'll hold each other upright. Presto, the catamaran! They made some long trips in this kind of boat, although one suspects that the casualty rate may have been rather high, for if you were a bit careless in a stiff wind over they went.

Further west still, the Indonesians were hard at work on the Mark II version, with three hulls—a big one in the middle and a smaller outrigger on each side. They were fast, and they stayed right side up.

Meanwhile, designers on this side of the world were still plugging the "rocks-in-the-bottom" theory, until one Arthur Piver, of San Francisco, decided that if you used plywood and fibreglass instead of hacking out logs, you might produce a fine cruising boat. And the trimaran, as we know it, was born.

Like every other type of vessel, it has its good points and its bad. On the credit size is its amazing roominess, both on deck and below—quite a point if you have young children and propose to live on board, year in and year out. Secondly, being built of wood, with no lead or pig iron, it will continue to float, even if holed in all three hulls, a feature which,

4

because of my well-developed sense of self-preservation, held for me an instant appeal. Thirdly, even a 40-footer draws a mere three feet, so you can get into the shallows where other boats can't go, such as in many of the Bahamian lagoons. It also has a reputation for speed, although I would prefer to describe it as potentially fast, for speed is largely a function of nerve. Keep your weight down and your genoa up, and a trimaran will really fly . . . until something lets loose!

The disadvantages of the trimaran are that, being light, with a buoyant bow, it doesn't like bashing into head seas, and under heavy conditions is slow going to windward. But while this makes for a hard ride, it also keeps the boat dry, and green water on deck is a rarity. In a short, beam sea there is an unpleasant, jerky motion, but down-wind, even up to Force 6 or 7*, the trimaran is a dream, fast and comfortable, with no sign of roll. Every boat is a compromise, but as a family cruising boat this type seems to have more good points than bad.

Many of these technicalities I was to discover only in the fullness of time. At the 1964 Boat Show I was concerned mainly with the gleaming fibreglass and stainless steel, the hatches, winches, blocks, cleats and rigging. I could already see myself in spotless white ducks, with just a touch of gold braid around my hat and a pair of binoculars on my chest, giving brisk orders as we glided into the calm waters of the lagoon at Tahiti.

During the next few days we kicked around the pros and cons of "Operation Palm Tree," as the project now became known, at great length.

For a start, I was crowding fifty, and had already seen too many friends, neighbours and business clients keel over with a coronary, ulcers, or an unexpected cancer. They had worked to achieve success, a good home, the pleasures of suburbia, only to be cut off at an early age. Why shouldn't we enjoy the results of our own hard work now, while we still had a few years left?

Then too, the world seemed to have shrunk in the jet age, to have developed a drab "sameness" all over. The desert island of yesterday was now an expensive resort, and the exotic cities of the Orient were growing more like New York and London. When I had been a boy it had taken weeks to cross an ocean. Now it took a few hours but no

---

*See Beaufort Scale of Wind Speeds in glossary.

longer meant very much. I wanted Mary and Nora to grow up with the memory of having seen the world while it was still worth seeing, not as tourists but as travellers.

What better education, in the widest sense of the word, could we give them? They would have to learn the three R's, of course, from books and a correspondence course. But in addition they would learn geography from seeing the world as it was, history from visiting the places where it was made, languages from playing with the children of other lands, sociology from seeing how other people lived, biology from observing the fish, animal and plant life around them, and science and mathematics from sailing, plotting a course and taking a sunsight. They would live in the open air and swim like fishes. They would develop tolerance from seeing other cultures. And they would become more creative and self-reliant from playing games, reading and doing things for themselves, instead of merely watching cartoons on TV.

I should have to sell the business, of course, and this would mean getting along on a much reduced income. But our expenses would drop, for there would be no need for such things as a car, a telephone, winter clothes for four people, heating oil, electricity or vacations. We should have to eat and to maintain the boat, but that would be about all. Our tastes would be simple, and we could come and go as we pleased. It would be perpetual summer.

Where, I wondered, was the catch?

At the time, I remember wondering why Kitty didn't oppose the whole thing more forcefully than she did, for had she exercised her right of veto at the outset, I should probably still be peddling insurance instead of writing this saga of the sea. But she didn't, and it wasn't until much later that I learned the reason. She had already decided that if this was what I really wanted, then she would rather live in a boat with a happy husband than in a house with a miserable one.

What do you do with a wife like that?

Gene Bucci was an Italian-Canadian who, like his father and grand-father before him, had been a master boat builder in Trieste. He was a perfectionist, and to him a boat was a work of art, or it was nothing. His skill with the English language, however, was something else again. In general, I found it wise to go along with his ideas, but on the occasions when I did pull rank on him over some point, he would shrug his shoulders, stare at the ceiling, mutter something in Italian that sounded

6

like a prayer, and sulk for hours. As the vessel developed, based on the lines of her designer Arthur Piver, but modified internally to suit our requirements, she grew into a thing of beauty, with easy, flowing lines and graceful proportions.

Her name was to be *Caravel II*.

We chose the name *Caravel*, partly because it was euphonious and easy to spell in most languages, but also for historical reasons. For the caravel had been an extremely successful type of sailing craft in the Middle Ages, making possible the exploration of the Americas, the Pacific and the Orient by Columbus, Da Gama and Magellan. But somewhere there was another British ship registered as *Caravel*, so we had to accept *Caravel II*.

She was 40 feet long (38 feet, 6 inches on the waterline) with an overall beam of 22 feet, 6 inches, so that her deck looked like that of an aircraft carrier. Her main mast stood 44 feet above the deck (51 feet above the water), and with her 28-foot mizzen she was ketch-rigged. The working sails of just under 600 square feet were not enough for racing, but enough for a middle-aged couple to handle in a 3 a.m. squall.

In the choice of auxiliary power we faced problems. Piver was a purist, stressed lightness, and didn't like engines at all. A real sailor shouldn't need a "stink-pot." I didn't feel that I could go quite this far, so I compromised on the matter of weight and installed a pair of Johnson outboard motors on brackets. These, I felt, would provide a high power-to-weight ratio and good manoeuvrability. They would also be easy to maintain. The manufacturer claimed fitness for salt water, so I ordered them with long shafts, electric start, remote controls, the works!

The accommodation, starting at the bow, consisted first of a triangular bunk in the fo'c'sle, large enough for two small children if they didn't fight, or one large adult. There was also a small section, right up in the forepeak, which in most boats serves as a chain locker. In *Caravel* it became a dolls' house.

Then came the washroom, comprising a washbowl, head (marine toilet), and various hanging lockers, cupboards and shelves for clothes, linen and bathroom supplies.

The main cabin, amidships, had a long, folding table down the centre, with seats along each side. To port and starboard of these were two large double bunks, sitting on the "wings" which joined the main hull to the outriggers. Aft of the main cabin was the galley, with sink, stove, cupboards, drawers and a Propane refrigerator.

1. Pulpit
2. Forepeak
3. Fo'c'sle & children's bunk
4. Forward hatch
5. Safety nets
6. Shelves
7. Hanging locker
8. Forward wing deck
9. Forward cross-arm
10. Position of main mast
11. Starboard bunk (double)
12. Starboard outrigger
13. Bunk hatches (port & starboard)
14. Refrigerator
15. Galley
16. Bosun's cupboard
17. Work table (shelves under)
18. Steering wheel
19. After cross-arm
20. Position of mizzen mast
21. Propane tank
22. Fantail
23. Boarding ladder
24. Chart table
25. Chart-house hatch
26. Covered sunken cockpit with Diesel under
27. Windshield over
28. Fuel tanks (port & starboard)
29. Stove
30. Sink
31. Cupboards
32. Seats (port & starboard)
33. Port outrigger hatches
34. Folding table
35. Windows
36. Dinghy stowed here
37. Washbowl
38. Head

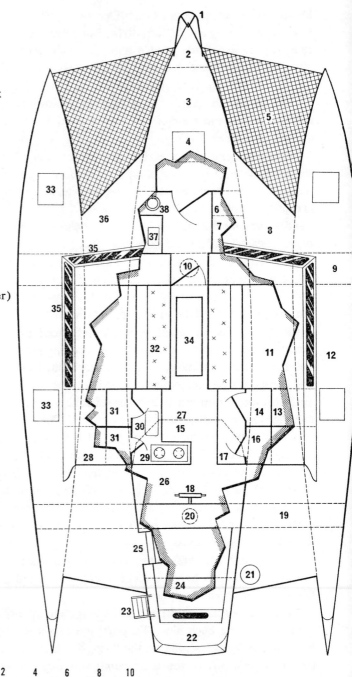

Scale of feet

Caravel II. *Deck plan and cutaway showing accommodation below*

8

Two steps up from the galley, and cut off by a louvred door, was the cockpit or wheelhouse. This was roofed over, and canvas dodgers could be clipped in place to enclose it completely. Aft of this again was a small cabin which we called the chart-house, although it was actually a sort of office-cum-cabin, with a single bunk that could be rigged up to take an extra guest or crewman, or removed to convert the place into an office. It also made an excellent music room for any child who wanted to practise her recorder.

The outriggers contained no accommodation at all, for with room in the main hull to sleep nine, this was hardly necessary. But they did provide almost limitless stowage, with access through two deck hatches in each, for sails, rope, bulk food supplies, spare clothes, garbage, soiled laundry (when we hadn't been ashore lately), and 1,001 other items that we didn't want in the main cabin.

Under the cabin sole, and in the seats, was still more stowage space for such heavier items as fuel, batteries, water tanks and canned food, for we tried to keep most of the weight in the main hull.

The enclosed cockpit was a sore point with Gene, who felt that its height would spoil the lines and create windage. He was probably right, too, but I was thinking ahead of those long, cold, wet, windy nights at sea. All this jazz about fighting the wheel and staring stoically into the teeth of a nor'wester looks fine in rotogravure, but I'm all for my creature comforts. Also, that roof kept us cool in the tropics, for we could leave the cabin door open all night without fear of being drowned in a rainstorm.

The dinghy was a problem, for it had to be:
1. Big enough to carry four people plus groceries, laundry, etc.
2. Seaworthy enough to weather a nasty chop
3. Unsinkable
4. Light enough to be hauled on deck by one person
5. Proof against sun, gasoline, concrete pilings, and being dragged over rocks, coral and broken beer bottles
6. Free from maintenance requirements
7. Cheap.

Unable to find a design that met all of these specifications, we settled for a little plastic job that was rather tippy and which punctured when it sat on anything sharp. We later changed to a plywood one, which could at least be repaired with fibreglass. Many cruising boats carry an inflatable dinghy, but while convenient, these tend to deteriorate in the sun, are unmanageable in a high wind, and have very little tolerance for broken bottles.

On the subject of where to stow a dinghy we have, after five years' study of the matter, reached the conclusion that there is no suitable place on any craft of under 15,000 gross registered tons. Some yachts tow it behind, but on the one occasion that we tried that it filled with water and nearly sank. We ended up storing ours on deck.

There is the additional problem that when you take the dinghy ashore and beach it, you are liable to return three hours later to find that the tide has either:

A. Come in, so that the dinghy is now floating gently 200 yards out to sea, or

B. Gone out, in which case you have to carry both dinghy and groceries a similar distance across wet, slippery rocks or deep, slimy mud, usually in the rain.

By late summer *Caravel* was ready, even if we were not. There were a million things to do at home, not the least of which was to go through all the items that we owned and divide them into three categories, namely:

1. Can't possibly do without, so pack in cardboard boxes, list, weigh, identify and put away for stowage on board.

2. Can't justify taking, but want to keep, so pack separately and arrange with tenant to leave in basement.

3. Everything not included in 1 and 2 above. Put out as garbage or burn at bottom of garden. (People were not worried about air pollution in 1965.)

It is only when faced with the task of sorting, evaluating, listing, weighing, packing, labelling and stowing every single item you possess that you realize why you "can't take it with you." The logistical problems would be immense.

The launching was set for October 7th, and was attended by a great many friends and neighbours. A heavy crane lifted *Caravel* into the water while cameras clicked, and then everyone trooped on board, examined her vital parts, and made two cases of beer seem rather inadequate. It was a moment of emotion, a turning point in our lives.

As *Caravel* was the first of her class, the *PI-40*, Arthur Piver himself flew to Toronto to try her out. He took the wheel on Lake Ontario, and was well pleased with her performance.

He was a delightful character, with a wonderful sense of humour and an endless fund of sailing anecdotes. He had crossed both the Atlantic and the Pacific in small trimarans when they were mere experimental types. As he was leaving, Kitty buttonholed him and told him of our plans, our lack of experience, and her fears. Did he think us foolish for taking such chances?

"The first time you hit really bad weather," he replied, "you'll be scared silly and wish you had stayed home. But you'll find that *Caravel* can take it a lot better than you can, and when it's all over you'll feel wonderful, just knowing that by your own efforts you have lived through an experience that few of your friends have ever known. Next time you won't feel quite so scared."

We were to remember those words many times, and find them prophetically true. It is ironic that we were never to see him again. For with all his skill and experience it was he who was to perish at sea, while we, so far at least, have survived.

During the spring of 1968, while sailing down the California coast on a 500-mile qualifying run for the Trans-Atlantic Solo Race that summer, he simply vanished. No bad weather was reported and no wreckage ever found. It remains a sea mystery as baffling as that of the *Marie Celeste*, although the most likely explanation seems to be that he was run down by a freighter while he slept, for he was in the coastal shipping lanes. He could not possibly keep a 24-hour watch, and may have paid the ultimate price for sailing alone.

The world lost a fine man and the yachting fraternity lost one of its great pioneers.

*Caravel* lost a friend.

<br>

♈♈♈

## OF LAKES AND LOCKS

Our departure date was to be November 4th, and events were moving to an inevitable climax. We packed things and made arrangements at the bank. We bought medical supplies and got our inoculations. We sent for passports and arranged to rent the house and sell the car. We disposed of the business and we had *Caravel* registered, documented, insured, watered, fuelled and victualled. We stopped newspapers, magazines and milk, and we left a forwarding address for mail. We commuted daily between Scarborough and Bronte with loads of cardboard boxes, suitcases, bundles and bags. And we learned to take the boat in and out of harbours with fewer and fewer bumps.

It was after one of these trips out on the lake, while we were chatting in the cabin with some friends, that Nora poked her head in and interrupted. I brought her up short, for there was a standing rule that she wait until grown-ups had finished and then ask permission to speak. With a six-year-old you have to be firm. She waited patiently, and I finally told her to go ahead.

"I'm sorry, Daddy! But Mary fell into the water, and I can't find her."

In three seconds flat we were all on deck, and Nora was pointing to the spot, between the stern and the quay, where Mary had last been seen. My heart went cold as I stared into the black, dirty water that I knew to be ten feet deep.

While I was trying to decide whether the most logical course was to dive in blindly, or try to think of something more constructive, somebody let out a shout.

"There she is!"

A faint splashing came from between the hulls, and we saw that Mary was alive and swimming towards the pilings. A dozen hands hauled her out, and she stood on the quay, her dress clinging pathetically to her little body. She shivered violently, and coughed up some water. Lake Ontario in November is cold.

In front of a hot stove a few minutes later, we learned what had happened. They had been running round the deck and Mary, in leaping for shore, had tripped and gone straight in. Her Red Cross swimming course paid instant dividends, but her navigation was poor, and when she came to the surface she simply struck out blindly for Olcott, N.Y., 40 miles across the lake. It wasn't until she saw an empty horizon ahead and heard voices astern that she changed direction.

They were sadder and wiser children, with badly scared parents. And they now knew the reason for the rule, "No Running On Deck!"

On the evening of the 3rd, things seemed to have shaken into place,

12

although it was past midnight before we finally fell into bed, and even then I couldn't sleep.

This was our last night in the big house that we had built with our own hands, inch by painful inch over the years. It was the only house we had ever owned, the only home the children had known. We had set every block, driven every nail, hung every door. We had started the business in this house, from nothing, and had slowly built it up into a thriving enterprise that had fed and clothed us all. We had raised a family under this roof. For years these walls had echoed to the sound of Christmas festivities, and the noisy laughter of children's birthday parties, and of countless evenings before the fire, listening to music or watching TV. So much had happened in this house: so much laughter, so many tears! And now I was dragging them all away from it—to live in a boat!

I must be crazy!

Suddenly the alarm was ringing. It was 6 a.m. and we were grabbing toast and coffee on the run. No time for regrets now! We bundled things into the station wagon, turned off the water and electricity, took photographs of each other closing the front door, and then, before anyone could ask me why, we drove off. The house grew smaller in the rear-view mirror, and disappeared round the bend.

At Bronte the quay was crowded with friends and relatives, and we formed a bucket brigade to load the last of the cargo, throwing it below to be sorted out later. The waterline sank ominously.

For the first part of the voyage we had two experienced sailors as volunteer crew, Bill Hibbard for the week-end and Mike Covell as far as New York. But with one thing and another, it was mid-afternoon before we were ready to go. Good-byes were said and motors started. Cameras clicked as lines were cast off, and at 4:09 *Caravel* slid away from the quay and out into the lake. It was sunny and warm, for November, and the water sparkled as we raised the sails in a light westerly breeze and switched off the motors. We waved to the tiny figures on the distant harbour wall.

As the sails filled and the bow-wave gurgled and hissed, we all felt better. The doubts and the tensions were behind us. Operation Palm Tree had begun. We could relax.

But we forgot Murphy's Law!

For the benefit of the uninitiated, Murphy's Laws of Sailing control

13

all aspects of life afloat in much the same way that Newton's Law of Gravity controls the physical universe. They are:

1st. What can happen will happen.

2nd. What has happened will get worse.

3rd. What can't happen will occur when you least expect it.

The inevitability of the first law was brought home to us very early in our nautical careers.

The strategy was to reach Oswego, N.Y. the next day (Friday), in time to enter customs and take down our masts (because of low fixed bridges on the Erie Canal), and enter the canal before the weekend. With the present fair wind, we expected to make it.

But a fair wind, like a vacuum, is something that nature abhors, and within the hour it had not only gone round through 180°, but had also perked up to 20 knots plus. Pretty soon we were faced with a nasty, steep slop. In her overloaded state *Caravel* was plunging into it and shipping water over the bow, which, I had been led to believe, doesn't happen in a trimaran. The time had obviously come to shorten sail, and foul weather gear was indicated.

According to the cargo list, this was in box 59. I knew its dimensions, weight and complete contents, but not its location. So I went out in a sports jacket and got soaked.

Without the mainsail we made little headway, so we turned on the motors. The port started all right, but the starboard was dead. Murphy's 2nd Law! Furthermore, the port one was doing little except pushing us round to starboard. The screw kept breaking the surface, producing a lot of froth and a wail like a banshee, but very little thrust. Pretty soon it got discouraged, spluttered and died, probably from water in the ignition.

Under jib and mizzen *Caravel* pitched, tossed, wallowed and heaved, and one by one everyone on board except Bill and the children made a dash for the head where we, too, wallowed and heaved. Fortunately, we had plenty of Dramamine. In simple pill form, this is supposed to be taken thirty minutes before throwing up, but under actual field conditions I defy you to time things to such fine limits. As the therapeutic value of any anti-nausea drug is much reduced if it goes down and comes straight back up again, we also carried the suppository type, which you take from the other end. This calls for a degree of anatomical skill, especially in the dark in a heaving boat and with your head in the

14

toilet, but once in it does work, and I was soon back at the wheel while Mike took his turn at the head.

He came out looking ten years older, and reported a perfect manifestation of Murphy's 3rd Law. The self-locking, waterproof forward hatch had failed to lock and had let in enough water to drench all of Mike's clothes, several of our cardboard boxes, and the bedding on the forward bunk. Morale sagged.

Meanwhile, Kitty was struggling valiantly with the Primus stove, and somehow managed to produce hot soup and coffee for those who still had any stomach lining, and some dry crackers for those who hadn't.

All in all it was a miserable night, and by dawn it was obvious that we weren't going to make Oswego that afternoon. The weather was cold and windy, with low scudding cloud, and we were all suffering from seasickness and lack of sleep. But I refused to let my mind dwell on the house back at Scarborough, with its central heating, its dry, cosy beds and, most of all, its solid, horizontal foundations. This was neither the time nor the place to judge the merits or otherwise of the whole undertaking.

Throughout the day we tacked along the shore of New York State, gaining a few hundred yards a time. The wind eased a little, and with four adults to share the steering we were able to get some rest, if not actual sleep.

Darkness came early, and at the same time the condensation started to drip from the deck-head. Soon our clothes and bedding were saturated. But a reluctant dawn found us off Oswego at last, and by 8 a.m. Mike was coaxing *Caravel* into the narrow entrance against a stiff wind, without power. By 9 a.m. we were alongside, cold, wet, tired and fed up. But then our luck changed, for not only could the marina unstep our masts at once, but a customs and immigration man appeared and offered to clear us, which was most hospitable of him.

Meanwhile, Mike was sitting on deck, surrounded by bits of outboard. With 150 miles of canal ahead of us and no masts, we either got those motors going or we rented a horse. He adjusted the throttles, cleaned the plugs, and we had two motors again.

Unstepping the masts, however, was another matter, and I found myself faced with one of those nasty little surprises that occur from time to time. For the benefit of those readers who did not serve time before the mast of a windjammer, perhaps I should explain this unstepping bit.

First of all, a trimaran's masts do not go through the deck, but sit on it, being held upright by what is called standing rigging. This consists of stainless steel cables from the deck, where they can be adjusted or released by turn-buckles. To unstep a mast you attach a sling from a crane at the halfway point, take the strain, release all the turn-buckles, and lower away.

The snag is that one of these cables, called the triatic stay, doesn't come down to the deck at all, but joins the top of the main mast to the top of the mizzen mast, and the turn-buckle is at the top of the main. Some poor sucker has to go up there in what they laughingly call a bosun's chair, 51 feet away in outer space, to disconnect the thing.

The term "bosun's chair" is a complete misnomer, for it isn't a chair at all. It is a piece of half-inch plywood, about 16 by 8 inches, with a hole through each corner, through which ropes are threaded and knotted to prevent them from coming out again. These ropes join at a point three feet higher up, and are shackled to the main halyard, a cable normally used to haul up the sail. You sit on the thing, which would be deemed far too hazardous an item ever to market as a kitchen stool, while someone winches you slowly into orbit, with frequent pauses to get his breath back. Viewed from any angle, the procedure is extremely distasteful.

The crane operator took the strain and looked around.

"Who's going to let go the triatic?"

As nobody volunteered for the job—though during the long silence that followed they had all sorts of opportunity to do so—there seemed little alternative but to go up myself.

While 51 feet may not sound much if you say it quickly and measure it horizontally, it's the height of a five-storey building, and seems a lot more when you look down than it does when you look up.

In addition, what may appear to be a flat calm on deck can be quite a swell up on the end of a long pole.

Also, if the man below happens to lose sight of the fact that a human life (yours), depends on his maintaining a good grip on the winch handle, things are liable to happen quickly. For when a winch handle starts to spin, with the weight of a man behind it, it does so at an alarming speed, and any attempt to slow it down results in an instantly shattered wrist.

And although the main halyard consists of ⅛th-inch diameter, 7 by

16

19 stainless steel wire, the breaking strain of which is quoted in the engineering manual as 1,760 pounds, when you see it a mere inch in front of your nose, and realize that you are hanging from it, ⅛th of an inch seems totally inadequate for the purpose.

Bill started to winch me up, with much puffing and grunting, and eventually, as I clung affectionately to the mast, I felt the spreader above me. This was discouraging, for it meant that I hadn't yet reached the halfway point, and already the harbour was beginning to look like an aerial photograph. But eventually I reached the top, and by feeling above my head could actually touch the triatic.

It was impossible to look up without tipping back at a sickening angle, and the only alternative was to stare, cross-eyed, at the shackle in front of my face and grope above my head with one hand while hanging on to the port shroud with the other. The old adage "One hand for the ship and one for yourself" suddenly made a lot of sense.

It wasn't easy to straighten out and remove the cotter pins with one hand, blind, and without pliers. (I had dropped them during the first few seconds aloft, and as a result the audience below was now standing well back.) But I found that the whole process was made more acceptable if I kept my eyes closed and pretended that I was doing it all on the back lawn at home.

The job was eventually done, and after a brief delay when the winch jammed and had to be dismantled, they got me down again. We lowered the masts, lashed them onto the deck, and were ready for the 31 locks of the Erie Canal.

Inside the locks, going up, the incoming water produces considerable turbulence, and you have to hang on tight to avoid being swept out of control. On the other hand, if you don't release your lines in time as the boat rises, you are liable to disappear in a welter of bubbles. Coming down, the opposite holds true, and you either let go on time or find yourself hanging from your own dock warps. Incidentally, it takes over five million gallons of water to raise a boat the 40 feet of the highest lock.

Even in November the countryside was lovely, and as we rose in each lock we could see the canal ahead, meandering between the hills. We were too late for the fall colours, but on the other hand we did have the water almost to ourselves, for most of the pleasure boats had gone either south or into winter storage. Sometimes we passed through villages and towns, entering not down the main street with its gas stations and used

17

car lots, but through the older and quieter parts, where lawns and gardens ran down to the water's edge. If there was any industry at all, it was usually an old sawmill or textile factory from the last century, to remind us why the town happened to grow there in the first place.

The motors were still acting up, due to fouled plugs, and one or the other would always cough and die at the wrong moment, so that we seemed to spend half our time changing, cleaning and drying spark plugs.

Also, the condensation problem was getting worse. No matter how warm and dry the cabin was at 7 p.m., with stove and catalytic heaters going full blast, by midnight the deck-head was dripping all over the bedding, which would stay wet until we reached the next town with a laundromat.

Bill had now returned home, so that we were short-handed in the locks. However, they were downhill by this time, and easier to manage. By the 11th we were at Troy, where we entered the Hudson, tieing up for the night a mile or so down-stream at the Albany Yacht Club. We had intended to restep the masts at Matton's yard, at Troy, where the charge was $20, but missed the place and had to do it at Rondout Marine in Kingston instead—for $53! Other yachtsmen using the canal might care to note this.

Down the Hudson, autumn was less advanced than in Ontario, and the Catskills were ablaze with colour as we slid between the majestic hills. Beautiful old houses sat high on the bluffs, including the Roosevelt home at Hyde Park. Then came the narrows, near West Point Academy, and on past Sing Sing prison, where it began to widen again. The occasional train on the left bank showed where the then New York Central tracks hugged the shore. Signs of activity increased as we came closer to the metropolis itself.

One morning, very faintly through the mist and smoke haze, we could make out the silhouette of Manhattan. After 450 miles we were beginning to feel like travellers, if not actual sailors.

It was with Mike at the wheel—for I still turned it over to him when things got sticky—that in a fresh wind, a following current, and with a stuttering port motor we turned in to the 79th Street Marina on the afternoon of the 15th. Next day Mike left for home, and we were completely and irrevocably on our own.

We were held up for several days in New York, due to a strong west wind, and to make matters worse the charge was $9.50 a day.

18

The wind created another problem, too, albeit a minor one. I discovered that the various lines that ran up the masts, known collectively as the running rigging, can set up an awful din in a wind, all through the night. The stainless steel ones go "Kerprang, Kerprang" as they slap against the mast, while the Dacron ones go "Therumph, Therumph." You put up with this until 2 a.m., and then struggle into your foul-weather gear (It will be raining.) and go out with a flashlight. The solution is to slack off each line in turn, flick the middle of it out and around the spreader, halfway up the mast, and then haul it tight again and cleat it. This quietens things down.

**ᐁᐁᐁ**

## BASCULE AHEAD, BELIEVED HOSTILE

Finally, on the morning of the 19th, the wind dropped, and there was no longer any valid excuse for staying in the comfort of New York harbour at $9.50 a day. The Hudson wasn't any more crowded than usual, and down-river the black and red funnels of the Queen Elizabeth had disappeared from the Cunard pier. This was encouraging, for I didn't fancy a discussion with her over the right of way!

Now taking a boat—any boat—out into the Hudson River, especially if it happens to be your first time alone at the helm, is not something to be undertaken lightly and with reckless abandon. I felt rather like a learner-driver on his first solo, who had somehow wandered onto the Indianapolis Speedway in the middle of the Memorial Day "500."

We topped up water and fuel tanks, studied the charts of New York harbour until we could have redrawn them from memory, got a radio weather report, started both motors to make sure they were running, and discussed last-minute strategy over a cup of coffee. At 11 a.m. we cast off the lines and eased cautiously into mid-stream. Nobody hooted at us, or flashed any red lights, or wanted to know where we thought we were going, or showed the slightest interest in us at all. As we drifted crabwise in the slow current, I turned to port with a little more confidence.

19

"You take the wheel," I suggested. "I'll get some sail on her."

Kitty looked dubious, but I reassured her and went forward to look after the sails.

The mainsail was furled along its boom, and as I let go the lashings it collapsed over the deck and cockpit, completely obscuring Kitty's view. There was a howl of protest, and her head appeared from under the endless folds of Dacron. I could see her problem, and promptly grabbed the winch handle to wind up the sail. But after a couple of feet or so, it jammed. The halyard was all fouled up in the topping lift, up by the spreader. Ah, yes, of course! The slapping lines, three nights ago! Pity I hadn't remembered that little rat's nest before we left the quay. Still, a fellow can't think of everything.

Taking a quick look ashore, I noticed that Kitty seemed to be steering a direct course for Pennsylvania Station.

"Come over to starboard," I yelled, waving an arm in the general direction of Elizabeth, N.J. "Okay. Hold that course till I can sort out this mess."

Her head disappeared as she changed course, but soon popped out again.

"CAN'T HEAR YOU! MOTOR'S TOO LOUD!"

"HOLD THAT COURSE!"

"HOW CAN I? CAN'T SEE WHERE I'M GOING!"

She had a point, I supposed, and the obvious answer was to give her a compass course that she could follow from below. Trouble was, I had taken the compass in at Oswego, and stowed it in the bosun's cupboard, in case of theft. Frankly, it hadn't occurred to me that we were going to need the thing this morning, not in brilliant sunshine and within 200 yards of 12th Avenue. It just shows that you can't take a darned thing for granted in a boat. I mounted the compass, gave her a course of 210°, and returned to the mast.

It was going to be a slow business, staring up into the sun and trying to disentangle all those lines, for I couldn't remember which I had wrapped round the spreader first, and if I guessed wrong, it just made things worse. Every few minutes there would be a cry for help from Kitty, who had aged visibly since 79th Street, and who kept pointing at real or imagined hazards on the river. First it was a freighter being eased into a dock by a tug, and then it was a buoy that we hadn't expected, but which turned out to be on the chart after all. Then came

20

a Liberian tanker, a string of barges carrying crushed stone, a liner with a West German flag, and the Statten Island Ferry, all of which she regarded with deep suspicion and a baleful eye, as though they had no right to be in her river at all. By the time we reached the Narrows, she was a nervous wreck. As she plaintively mentioned later, her education at Malvern Collegiate hadn't included taking a trimaran down the Hudson River—blindfolded!

Fortunately, by this time I had the rigging sorted out and the sails up, and as we switched off the motors the silence was like the loss of an aching tooth. I was photographing points of interest and explaining the sights to the children, who seemed less interested in the history of the Statue of Liberty than in a seagull which was perched on top of our mast. They wanted to feed it crusts.

Kitty gave up the wheel with obvious relief, and as *Caravel* lifted gently and easily to the incoming swell, we sailed under one of the most spectacular structures in the world, the huge Verrazano bridge, spanning the Narrows in long, graceful curves. If man's most beautiful creation is, in fact, the sailing ship, then the suspension bridge must surely come a close second.

Yet as we approached, camera at the ready, I felt sure that we would hit the steelwork of the high, central span. It was an optical illusion, but looking up, from the deck, all sense of perspective goes, and one is convinced that the mast will touch.

South of the bridge the Ambrose Channel sweeps away to the east, to the open Atlantic, but we carried on south across Lower Bay towards Sandy Hook, that long spit of land on the New Jersey shore. A Coast Guard helicopter flew several curious circles around us, and then we had the bay to ourselves.

At 4 p.m. we slid into the little harbour at Atlantic Highlands, behind Sandy Hook, and dropped anchor 100 yards from shore. We were a tired, but happy family. We had taken *Caravel* to sea, alone, for the first time. Under the light of a gently swinging hurricane lamp we opened a can of chicken and celebrated our "first" in style, while the boat drifted contentedly at her drooping anchor line.

Boy, did we sleep!

Down the east coast of the United States runs the Intra-Coastal Waterway, a sheltered route for barges and pleasure craft. Yet sur-

21

prisingly, except for the relatively few who sail on it or live along its banks, it is largely unknown. This situation, however, has already changed somewhat since we first travelled there, as more and more people discover it.

The fact is that the east coast of the U.S. is not, as one might expect, 1,500 miles of commercial waterfront property, but rather, for the most part, a series of low, sandy islands, separated from the mainland by anything from a few yards to a few miles of tidal flats, swamp or clear water, usually quite shallow. None of the major ports are on the actual coast, but are some miles up a sound or river, for the coastal area has, in most cases, proved too difficult and expensive to drain and develop.

The result is that even today it is possible to travel down whole sections of the east coast and to see it as it was before the white man arrived. But you can't do it by car, or even on foot. Do it by boat, and a rare pleasure awaits you as you pass through absolute wilderness for mile after mile.

In some places it is swamp, with islets covered with coarse grass, where water birds nest and breed by the million. In others you glide over still, black water, while the forest presses in from both sides.

To one part of the North Carolina coast Sir Walter Raleigh, some 350 years ago, brought a shipload of settlers from England. They were never seen again, and the place is still referred to as the Lost Colony. The Indians may have massacred them, or they may have survived, for the exact location was never recorded. But it is known that in a lonely part of this coast, near Cape Hatteras, the families who have lived there for generations still speak a strange dialect which is very like that spoken in parts of southwestern England—in the sixteenth century!

I can think of no other coastline, anywhere in the world, where nature has created such a perfect waterway for small boats. To turn it into a navigable channel has required only limited dredging and cutting. In places this work was started nearly two centuries ago, and is being continued today by the U.S. Army Corps of Engineers, with the Coast and Geodetic Survey and the Coast Guard entering the picture by charting it, supervising it, and maintaining the buoys and markers. The end result is one of the most useful, interesting and picturesque waterways anywhere, available without charge to all who will take the trouble to explore it.

There are bridges at intervals, and even two locks. As you approach

22

a bridge you give three blasts on your air horn and the keeper stops the road traffic and raises the bridge for you, even if you happen to be a 16-foot sailboat.

The Intra-Coastal Waterway, or I.C.W., actually starts about 30 miles south of New York, at an otherwise rather insignificant place called Manasquan. You have to go outside at Sandy Hook, and down the coast, before entering the Waterway itself. And it was upon this short ocean passage that we embarked on the morning of November 20th.

The marine forecast was for settled weather, the glass was steady, and the sky cloudless. At 10:15 a.m. we raised both anchor and sails, rounded Sandy Hook and headed south. By 11:30 we were becalmed, our sails drooping sadly, so we dropped them and purred along at 4 knots under the motors.

Highlands, Monmouth Beach and Asbury Park drew abeam, but it soon became apparent that we weren't going to reach Manasquan before dark, which posed a problem. I had never entered an inlet before, but I had read about them, and wasn't amused. It sounded a frightening enough prospect in broad daylight, let alone in the dark.

Fortunately, Shark River is only 3 miles beyond Asbury Park, and from the chart the entrance didn't seem too gruesome, except for a wiggly river and several bridges. It would make a nice haven for the night, so I broke out the airhorn and turned in for the shore.

As we approached, sure enough, there was the town, the river, and the first bridge—in the "down" position. I slowed down in the river mouth and gave the usual three blasts.

Now Shark River has a narrow entrance, but inside it widens considerably, so that the tidal flow at the mouth is fast, a fact which any experienced sailor would have realized at once from the chart. But at this point I was a little short on experience, although I was due to get quite a lot of it in the next few minutes. I hadn't thought to check the tide tables, and had no idea whether it was ebbing or flooding. As a matter of fact it was flooding—but good! In fact the water was doing about 6 knots. Add to this the 3 knots that we needed to steer, and that gave us 9 knots, or about 10½ miles an hour over the bottom.

At 300 yards, there was no sign of life on the bridge, and the channel was getting narrower and the current faster. It was no longer possible to turn *Caravel* around and claw our way out again, so I began

23

to worry a little. Nine knots may not sound fast to you folks who are used to freeways, but in a narrow channel, with a bridge looming up, and with no brakes, it's a fair turn of speed, believe me.

At 250 yards the bridge was still down, and the girders looked quite capable of decapitating a battleship. I gave four long blasts, the signal that an emergency existed, which it did. At 200 yards I forgot all about the International Code of Signals, and just blasted away in sheer panic, remembering only that Gene had mentioned, in passing, that our beautiful gold-anodized aluminum masts by Proctors of England had cost $2,000 plus air-freight.

Then I noticed that the traffic over the bridge had stopped, and at 150 yards one end started to go up. For a moment I stopped breathing, for we seemed to be leaping forward at an alarming rate.

At 100 yards, Kitty was staring in horror at the slowly-moving bridge, and chewing on a dishtowel.

"We're not going to make it," she moaned.

I eased *Caravel* over to port where the height of the bridge was greater. With both motors going astern, I gave them a little throttle, for too much would have made her yaw sideways. The water under the bridge boiled and eddied as it swept through the narrow gap.

Slowly, and with a ponderous grinding of heavy gears, the bridge inched up, while *Caravel* shuddered as I opened the throttles a little more. I tried to hold her back and also to steer her by sheer will power, but the bow swung too far to port, and I had to slam the starboard engine into full reverse to pull her away from the pilings.

The huge, steel girders under the roadbed rushed at us, and I knew we weren't going to clear. There just wasn't room. The mast would slam into it and there would be a sickening crunch and a jolt.

Kitty muttered, "Oh, dear God!"

Now we were actually under the roadbed, and the mast was still moving—silently! My heart stopped.

Daylight! We could see daylight behind the top of the mast. We were *through*! I looked down at the pilings and they, too, were rushing by without a sound. We hadn't even scraped the paint. As I went into full ahead again, to get steerage-way, I had a fleeting glimpse of white faces staring down from the roadway by the bridge. Old buildings, black wooden fences, the backs of garages, railway tracks, another bridge—this one open—a factory chimney, and suddenly we were in

24

the broad placid water of the inner estuary, with all the room in the world. There was nothing but acres of still water, and mud flats, and a few rowboats with men fishing.

Over to port was a marina, and my legs felt like jelly as we tied up for the night. A little later I was discussing the matter with one of the locals.

"Yes, he's been a bit slow lately. Course, he's getting on, you know. Should have retired him years ago, I guess, but they were sorry for him."

In the morning we went out dead on slack water, timing it to seconds. The bridge went up like clockwork, and we slipped out with no trouble at all. Sometimes it happens that way.

The weather was still calm, and we motored down the coast. By mid-afternoon we were at anchor in the Manasquan River.

We had entered the Waterway.

♥♥♥

# RED NUN AND BLACK CAN

The New Jersey section of the Waterway, from Manasquan to Cape May, wanders between low islands, with perhaps a dozen inlets, usually a mere hundred yards or so wide, leading out to the sea. For the most part these are shallow, with a sand bar across them. Some of them are used by local fishermen, but the official Coast Pilot adopts a gloomy view, usually warning against any attempt to use them. Where it does admit of such use, it suggests that you do so only in emergency, in good weather, with a flood tide, and with local knowledge. Where you get this knowledge in a hurry, if you are out there and want in, they don't specify.

The charts are equally morbid, and fail to show the buoys and markers, for the reason, so they say, that they have to keep moving them as the channel shifts after every storm.

The inference seems to be that if you are out there you should leave well enough alone, and stay put. We did, however, discover a useful

25

gimmick later, and that was to hang around outside until one of the local fishermen came along at high tide, and just follow him in. At low tide, of course, not even the crabs attempt it.

For the present, however, we were inside, at Manasquan, and the ugly memory of Shark River was far too recent to permit of any thoughts of going out again.

At high tide, the Waterway here consists of almost unbroken water, though at low tide whole areas dry out, leaving extensive mud flats. Between these the channel, dredged out to 12 feet, twists and turns in a delightful, if bewildering manner. But fortunately it is well-marked. The system is an ingenious one with the different types, shapes and colours each having their own meaning. All the Waterway markers have a yellow band around them, to distinguish them from the ordinary river, bay or offshore markers not constituting part of the Waterway itself. You are thus faced with two separate systems of buoyage, which can get confusing at times.

You have to remember that under the North American system, red buoys and markers (which carry even numbers and are conical or triangular in shape) are always on the right or starboard hand when you are coming in from the sea, while the black ones (odd-numbered and square or rectangular in shape) are kept to port. An easy way to remember it is to say "Red, Right, Returning." (In Europe they do it the other way round, but let's not go into that now.) This system is fine as long as you know which way is up, so to speak. But what happens when you are in Albemarle Sound, or in a canal joining two rivers, or among islands between two inlets? The Waterway is full of such situations, and you never know from one minute to the next whether you are going up or down. And the flow doesn't help, because the tide keeps changing. So do you put a red nun (a conical floating buoy) to port or starboard? With 12 feet of water on one side of it and 6 inches on the other, you'd better get it right the first time.

They have solved this problem with a very neat bit of legislation. The Waterway must always flow north or east; it is illegal for it to flow the other way. It thus follows that if you are going north (or east) you are legally going down-stream, and the red markers should be kept to port and black to starboard.

Now this is dandy, until you are going north, for instance, up Chesapeake Bay, where the normal buoys follow the system of keeping

26

the red buoys to starboard, but where the Waterway buoys, with the yellow band around them, mean the opposite.

Recognizing this as potentially a bit confusing, the Waterway people come along and paint a little black square with a yellow band around it on this red nun (and conversely a red triangle with a yellow band on a black can). In effect, what they are trying to say to you is:

"We realize that this is a red nun, and that you folks on the Waterway, travelling north, keep all red nuns to port, for the obvious reason that Chesapeake Bay, in accordance with federal statute, flows uphill to the north. But this red nun was put here by some other governmental agency that doesn't understand about federal waterways running uphill. So although it may look like a red nun, and in some respects could almost be considered to be a red nun, let's you and us pretend that it is really a black can, in accordance with the little black square which we have painted on it, and then you can, quite legally, keep it to starboard and thus avoid running onto this dirty great sand bar."

So help me, that's the system. The next time you hear about a ship collision in Chesapeake Bay, perhaps you'll be a little more tolerant about the whole thing.

If in doubt, the best advice that I can offer is to keep a close eye on your depth-sounder. And don't worry—the Waterway is mostly mud.

Next morning it rained. And while the Waterway can be an idyllic place in good weather, it can also be a dreary one on a cold, wet Monday in late November.

First the anchor wouldn't come up. We pulled and heaved, with much puffing and grunting and with water running down our necks and our fingers white and numb. Finally we raised it, with most of New Jersey still attached—a thick, glutinous ball of mud with the anchor somewhere inside. We sliced away with a putty knife, while the rain spread it around a bit. It was 10 a.m. before we had the anchor, the line, the deck and ourselves relatively mud-free, and as we got under way Kitty wiped a drop of water from the end of her nose and tucked some bedraggled strands of hair under her plastic hat.

"Tell me again what fun it is, sailing down the Trades to our island paradise. I keep forgetting."

The water, cut by low islets of grass and the occasional clump of bushes, was like glass, perforated by a million raindrops, while behind

27

us our widening wake fell away in smooth curves to send tiny wavelets against the shore. Under low cloud and clinging mist we felt our way from one marker to the next, checking the number on each one against a soggy chart.

By 3 p.m. it was clear that the rain had set in for the day, for the cloud was unbroken and it could only get darker. The motion to drop the hook was passed unanimously, and we eased slowly out of the marked channel, with one eye on the depth-sounder. The bottom came up from 15 feet to 6 feet and steadied at that. A hundred yards from the channel, and safe from any passing barges, we anchored, and were soon warm and dry.

Next morning it was sunny and cool, and after cleaning the plugs we returned to the channel and continued south. At Barnegat Inlet, the first since Manasquan, we could see the lazy Atlantic swell rolling in over the bar. All day we motored on between the islands and finally entered Little Egg Harbour. At Beach Haven, for the sake of some shore power to dry out the boat a little, we splurged on a marina, for Kitty was concerned over the perpetual dampness of the children's bedding due to condensation.

The 24th brought a nice sailing breeze, and over breakfast we kicked around the idea of going outside. Little Egg Inlet was an easy one, especially going out, and while Absecon Inlet, at Atlantic City, was too close, Great Egg was 15 miles away and should be passable in any normal weather. Also, the offshore route would avoid four bridges, which was a selling point. And there was the matter of fuel, which we were burning up at the rate of a gallon every four miles. Offshore we could sail, and this removed any lingering doubts on the matter.

It was pleasant down the coast, a mile or so out, and 3 p.m. found us following the line of buoys into Great Egg Inlet, to tie up inside at Ocean City. Incidentally, Great Egg Harbour is about half the size of Little Egg, which I suppose proves something. It would probably confuse the locals if they changed it; right now it only confuses strangers.

Drunk with the success of our 15-mile ocean passage, we decided to go for broke tomorrow and try for Cape May. Unfortunately, as soon as we got outside, the southerly wind freshened and we had to tack down the coast, which delayed us. By mid-afternoon we were faced with the decision of entering Cape May Inlet in the dark or making for a closer one in daylight. Corson Inlet had a bad reputation, so we decided on Townsend. If it proved a toughie we could still go on to Cape May.

Now Townsend Inlet is wide-open with lots of water, only this is spread rather thin in places. From seaward it looked easy enough, especially as the wind had by now died to zero and there was nothing but a lazy ground swell. The markers, though not shown on the chart, were there all right, a line of starboard ones in a long curve. Trouble was, they seemed to be almost on the south shore, that is to port going in, with a bare 50 yards between them and the beach. I double-checked them—red nuns, with no yellow bands and no little black squares, so, "Red, Right, Returning." Yes, keep them to starboard. We approached slowly.

Two boys on the beach stopped and stared at us, as though not wanting to miss what they knew was coming. Kitty's face was jammed into the depth-sounder.

"Four—three and a half—three and a bit—steady at three!"

"Should be okay," I remarked. "Be over the bar soon. Looks like at least two fathoms all the way."

"Not fathoms," she said. "Feet!"

Our depth-sounder reads in either, at the flick of a switch: fathoms for deep water, feet for shallow. Also, anticipating my propensity for running aground, Gene had installed the transducer not on the keel where it would be damaged, but up the side of the hull, so that there was always a foot less water under us than the dial indicated. We now had 24 inches below us, and this was supposed to be the channel! I stared at the markers again, and kept muttering "Red, Right, Returning" to myself.

A hundred yards beyond were some seagulls, sitting on the water. Then I noticed that they weren't sitting at all—they were wading, up to their knobbly knees. Whatever channel there was, which was darned little, seemed to be on this side.

Kitty's voice rose a good half-octave.

"One and a half!"

Six inches under us!

Then we touched. It wasn't all that hard, but you could feel it all right. We stopped, and then the swell lifted us forward and we were over.

29

"Two—two and a bit—going up—three!"

The two boys were now throwing stones at a seagull, apparently satisfied that there wasn't going to be any fun after all. Most 40-footers draw a lot more than three feet, and I don't imagine that many boats of our size enter Townsend Inlet—not in one piece, that is. Maybe we made local history, I don't know. But an hour later we were having supper, safely at anchor in the Waterway.

Next day the tide was a foot higher, and we got out without touching. Cape May was well within range, and under a beam wind we made good time. Before we knew it we had reached the long stone breakwaters, jutting out into the sea. By noon we had entered the harbour, turned to port past the big Coast Guard base, and anchored at the far end of the narrow bay.

As it turned out we reached Cape May just in time, for the weather turned sour and we were pinned down for several days. We also found ourselves faced with another strategic decision, as there were two possible routes from here to Norfolk, Va.

The official Waterway route goes up the Delaware to a point below Wilmington, through the Chesapeake and Delaware Canal and the Elk River, and then right down the Chesapeake to Norfolk, a trip that could easily take ten days or more. The alternative, for the intrepid ocean sailor, was the offshore route. With winter snapping at our heels, I didn't fancy the long Chesapeake route, although the offshore one, with one or two nights out of sight of land, never did appeal to me in the first place. So I compromised. We would cross the mouth of the Delaware and run into the Indian River, just south of Cape Henlopen. If the weather turned bad, we would go up the Delaware, otherwise we would carry on down the coast for the Chesapeake.

For the next few days I worked on the motors, oiling and greasing everything in sight and cleaning all the plugs. They had been increasingly erratic of late, and frequent attempts to start them had been hard on the batteries. Fortunately, our little Honda generator was working well, and we managed to keep the batteries reasonably well-charged.

It was here, too, that I remembered a fact about hydrocarbon fuels, that when burned in air they produced a lot of moisture vapour. Of course! That was why we hadn't been able to keep the cabin dry at night. The more kerosene we burned, the more water we were adding to the air. Kitty was becoming almost frantic in her effort to keep the

30

children's clothes and bedding dry, and laundromats were not always available. A coal stove, vented outside, would have been perfect, but it would have been heavy, and within another month we hoped that the problem would be behind us forever.

Meanwhile, the answer was obvious. We must avoid burning kerosene at night. We must ventilate to get rid of the warm, moist air and replace it with cold, dry stuff. We must let the cabin go cold, and keep ourselves warm with blankets and hot-water bottles. Unfortunately, it calls for a certain amount of will power, at 10 p.m. to turn off the stove, open the door wide, and let in a blast of icy New Jersey air. And at 3 a.m. hot-water bottles tend to become cold-water bottles.

Tuesday morning was beautiful, and we all rushed around in a frenzy of activity. This was the day. But first we must go over to the fuel dock for gas. And just as I was coming about, to approach the dock starboard side to, old Murphy gave us a quick one-two.

First, the port motor, despite all my loving care in the rain, quietly died. Then, as I tried to counteract the loss of power on the port side by giving her more rudder, the wheel spun free in my hand. No steering! A quick look into the chart-house confirmed things, for the steering cable was hanging dejectedly with frayed ends.

As we drifted helplessly down onto some old pilings, I threw a line over the nearest one and suggested a cup of coffee. It seemed a logical first step. Meanwhile, the gas jockey stood on the quay with a puzzled look on his face and a rather superfluous-looking delivery nozzle in his hand. To heck with him! I'd explain later.

The motor was easy to fix. After coffee I changed the plugs and she ran like a clock. The cable took a little longer, but pretty soon we had that replaced too. Why had it gone?

Later I discovered that the problem was one of sheave, or pulley, size. Ours were far too small for the stainless steel cables, and the repeated bending round the small radius had caused fatigue and consequent fracture. The answer lay in larger sheaves, and since fitting 3½-inch ones we have had no more trouble. But, not being a naval architect, I didn't know this at the time. Such gems of wisdom came later after bitter experience.

It was noon before we finally filled our tanks, and I vaguely wondered what new disasters would befall us. I remembered how, when I was a child, my mother had a theory on such matters. If she ever

31

broke a cup or plate she would immediately take two other items of no value, such as jam or pickle jars, and break them into the garbage pail with a hammer. The idea was that all such catastrophes came in threes. Thus if you broke one item, you must inevitably break two more, and if you didn't want these to be cut-glass goblets that had been in the family for generations, you had better smash two other things, now, that didn't matter a hoot.

At the age of six I used to watch this ritual of demolishing two glass jam jars with a faith in the rightness of adult beliefs that is found only in the very young. At the age of 15 I ridiculed this senseless and pagan superstition with the confidence and derision that only a teen-ager with a grade 10 science education can muster. At age 50, and heading out into the broad Atlantic with two disasters behind me, I had an open mind on the whole subject, but should have welcomed an empty pickle jar, as added insurance.

❦❦❦

# FLIGHT FROM CAPE MAY

With a fair wind we left the New Jersey shore under sail, and soon the outline of Cape Henlopen appeared off the starboard bow. I closed the land a bit, for I didn't want to miss Indian River, a few miles south.

Ah, there it was!

The chart showed a bascule bridge, but as we came to within about a mile we saw that this had been replaced by a fixed bridge of unknown height. From the size of a tractor-trailer crossing it, it looked about 35 feet, obviously not enough for our 51-foot mast, and we hurriedly inspected the chart again. To the south there was nothing that we could reach before dark, and to the north Henlopen was already up-wind and offered dubious shelter in a northerly. In addition, the Delaware route would cost us another ten days or so. There seemed to be little choice but to accept a night offshore. The children listened as we discussed it, accepting the verdict almost with disinterest. What Daddy and Mummy

32

decided was obviously all right. Such is the supreme faith of the very young!

We paralleled the coast, heading almost due south, with just enough easting to clear Chincoteague Inlet, with its offshore reefs and shoals, by about ten miles. As darkness fell the wind freshened, but by running more or less before it we were comfortable enough. Then the clouds thickened, the night grew darker, and the wind higher. The seas began to build up astern, and at times we were logging 9 knots as we surfed down them. It was exhilarating, but very lonely, out at sea for the first time at night.

Bundling the children off to bed early, we sat in the cockpit drinking coffee, keeping each other company, and pretending that the whole thing was just great. As the larger seas came up behind we could hear them hissing angrily, while hundreds of tons of water lifted us bodily and carried us forwards. Looking astern, all we could see was the pale glow of breaking water and the faint sparkle of phosphorescence. Occasionally a big one would snatch at our stern, pulling it around sickeningly. I would spin the wheel and hold my breath, afraid of a broach.

Obviously we ought to reduce sail now, for it might be a lot tougher later, and as we had never used the roller-reefing gear at sea, let alone in the dark, I decided to drop the main entirely. I put on a life jacket, more to satisfy Kitty than anything else, for if I did go overboard she would never find me again in this sea. I switched on the deck floods, which are a blessing at such times. With the motors we brought *Caravel* round into the wind to take the pressure off the sails. Immediately she began to pound in the head seas, and the wind seemed to double in force. Kitty took the wheel and I crept forwards on my hands and knees.

As I took the weight of the boom on the topping lift, it began to swing violently from side to side and was impossible to hold. So I sheeted it in tight, something I should have thought of before, and started to lower the halyard. The sail came down easily enough, flogging and thrashing like a wild animal, and it took a full ten minutes to tame it, clutching at the whipping Dacron with broken nails and trying to get a lashing around it. Gradually I got it furled, grateful to be doing this on deck and under floodlights, and not up on a yard-arm as they did a century ago. When I crawled back to the cockpit Kitty

33

wore a haggard expression, and had obviously not enjoyed things any more than I had.

Back on course again, we found that our speed had dropped hardly at all, but the ride was a lot more comfortable and less frightening. *Caravel* could obviously stand worse than this without too much trouble.

The occasional light would appear on the horizon, and soon we could make out the loom of Chincoteague, with its two flashes every five seconds, to the south. Then the light itself appeared as we came closer, but a rough bearing showed that we were not going to clear it by anything like the ten miles that I had intended, but rather three to four. Had I miscalculated? An on-shore current? I set a new course to take us well out. That evil light, which seemed to be saying "keep clear, keep clear" every five seconds, was far too close for comfort. We bore off and headed for Cape Town.

Once south of Chincoteague, it would have been logical to come back onto our previous course, for the coast now trended to the southwest. But the Maryland shore was desolate and poorly lighted. I was afraid to close it too soon, and we continued on to the southeast.

Not being used to night sailing, and with no stars visible as a frame of reference, it was easy to lose all sense of direction in the black void. A faint light on the starboard bow disappeared, and another appeared astern. Was it the same light, or another one? The compass showed us to be off course, but I had difficulty trusting it instead of my own senses.

Nor could we even gauge our speed. The wind in the rigging, the rushing of the breaking crests, the feel of being picked up and swept forwards, all created the illusion of turnpike speed. It was hard to believe the Sumlog when it showed a mere 5 knots, with the occasional burst to 7. Only the odd fleck of foam, drifting slowly by just beyond the rail as we stared into the blackness, gave any picture of our real speed.

A feeble light, far off, became an old friend, evidence that other humans existed too. If it disappeared we mourned it. But if it came too close it was a threat. On one occasion, coming accidentally up into wind, the sails luffed and flogged, while a light that had been on the starboard quarter suddenly went round to the port bow. I muttered some excuse and glared accusingly at the compass, which I felt had

34

somehow deceived me. Gradually we wallowed back onto course.

Mary and Nora slept as though drugged, as unconcerned as if they had been in their cosy beds at home.

Since 1 a.m. there hadn't been a glimmer in the west, and we must have been far out of sight of the one lonely road leading down to Cape Charles. The weather, while no worse, was certainly no better, and for hours we sailed on into the blackness, our senses numbed by lack of sleep and tensed nerves. I imagined rocks, just ahead of us, and suddenly I was convinced that they were there so I switched on the depth-sounder. No bottom! I gave up looking at my watch, for time seemed to have stopped.

Gradually the night wore on, and at one point I realized that the sky was not quite so black. The moon? No, it was the false dawn.

Then I could make out the outline of the jib against the sky, and finally the thin line of the mast. The nearer seas began to assume a shape, instead of being merely pale crests suspended in the blackness. And there appeared the depressingly leaden grey of an Atlantic December dawn, than which there are few things more depressing.

Now that we could see them, the seas were even less inviting than before. They had grown a lot since last night, and it was frightening to watch those Juggernauts of water, ponderous and irresistible, sweeping in from the north and threatening to trample us underfoot. It seemed that their curling tops must surely crash onto us. But somehow, as they approached, *Caravel* seemed to sense the danger and lift in time, allowing them to pass harmlessly under her. High on the foaming crests, we would teeter for a moment, and then slide down the after-face into the relative shelter of a trough.

We felt so puny, so fragile. How could mere plywood resist these enormous monsters, roaring down on us at 30 knots? We felt that our lives depended not on our own efforts or skill, for we were powerless, but on the knowledge and workmanship of those who had designed and built our flimsy coracle. And we developed a new respect for Art Piver and Gene Bucci.

As daylight brought back the real world, with thin, watery colour and a third dimension, Kitty went below to start breakfast. It was ridiculously early, but it gave us a sense of normalcy again. We let the children sleep, amazed that their faces could be so relaxed.

By this time I was beginning to suspect that if we were going to

35

pile up onto any rocks at all, they were more likely to be in West Africa than in Maryland, and I started to think in terms of discovering the lost continent of North America. What with our frequent changes of course, coming into wind, turning erratically to avoid lights, and the possible effects of wind and current, I wouldn't have offered any odds on our position, although I assumed that we probably had one, of sorts. On the other hand, the U.S.A. almost had to be that way, so we headed west. But how far? A couple of hours?

In point of fact, the next five hours produced only three recognizable items: a freighter heading south, a fishing boat heading southwest, and a Ballantyne beer can, apparently hove-to.

We had a D.F. (Direction Finding) receiver, and at 8 a.m., by which time we were seriously thinking of lunch, I began to twiddle the dial. A voice boomed in enthusiastically, and identified itself as coming from Portsmouth. I hoped he meant Virginia, and not England. He kept telling us the time, which we already knew, the state of the roads in and out of Norfolk (which could still be England), and the weather, on which latter subject he seemed to be singularly ill-informed. Here we were, practically outside his studio door, with the wind howling around our ears and huge seas threatening to engulf us, and how did he describe this holocaust? "Cloudy and cool in Norfolk and vicinity"!

His radio bearing seemed to be roughly southwest, which I accepted as evidence that we had at least not managed to round the Florida Keys during the night and enter the Gulf of Mexico. Like the prairie schooners of another age, we headed west, not a little puzzled over the sudden disappearance of the state of Maryland.

At the mouth of Chesapeake Bay was a lightship, equipped with an automatic radio beacon sending out the letter "P" in Morse, 24 hours a day, to guide ships into the channel. But its range was limited, and it wasn't until noon that we finally picked up the first faint signal.

"Bip—Beep—Beep—Bip. Bip—Beep—Beep—Bip."

Gradually it grew stronger, and the wind began to ease and the seas to die down. At 3:30 p.m. we saw the lightship ahead, and at last had a definite position, 14 miles off Cape Henry, at the southern shore of the Chesapeake. Then we raised the Virginia coast. It had taken us 12 days to cover the New Jersey coastline, yet in just 30 hours we had put Delaware and Maryland behind us and were entering Viriginia. Things were looking up.

36

As we closed the coast the wind died, and we had to motor round and into an anchorage beyond the Cape.

That night we slept like the dead, pleased at having survived our first night offshore, and in bad weather at that. It had been frightening to mere beginners, but not really dangerous.

In the morning we ran up the wide channel to Norfolk and Hampton Roads, where we entered the James River. Just inside, to port, was Willoughby Bay, and at the head of this was a lovely anchorage. We coasted in slowly, feeling the sandy bottom with our depth-sounder, and dropped the hook in six feet, a bare 20 yards offshore. The temperature was 65 and the sky sunny as we put the dinghy into the water and rowed the children ashore to unwind. We also needed a supermarket and a laundromat.

The following day I was back at the ailing motors again, one of which wouldn't even turn over. Sitting on deck surrounded by tools and bits of starter, I found the inside a mass of rust, despite its alleged resistance to salt and corrosion. I cleaned, greased and re-assembled it. It was stiff, but it did work, and we had two motors again.

On the Sunday morning we motored out of Willoughby Bay, round the Navy Yard, and up towards downtown Norfolk and Lee Hudgins' marina. Unfortunately there was a stiff wind from the southwest (on our starboard bow), as well as an adverse current. Under our lone starboard motor, the port having quit as we left the bay, progress was slow.

Progress was also unpredictable, for it proved impossible to turn to starboard with the one motor, against wind and current. In fact it required almost full starboard rudder to maintain even a straight course. Every now and then a gust of wind would push the bow to port, and the only way to get back was to complete the 360° turn to port until we were facing south again. What the Navy brass must have thought as they watched this crazy, three-hulled contraption with a Canadian flag, heading up-river at one knot in a series of left-hand loops, I hate to think.

By mid-afternoon we reached the channel to port, leading both to the marina and also to a low, fixed bridge, a hundred yards or so beyond it, spanning the river in a series of long concrete arches. I made a smart 90° turn to port, which was no trick at all, for I had merely to release the wheel for about two seconds and we were round. I hugged the starboard bank, and at the crucial moment started a 180° turn to port, intending to approach the marina up-wind and starboard side to. But Murphy's Second Law came into play halfway through the turn. The starboard motor lost power and, as I opened the throttle wide, spluttered out entirely. I stabbed at both starters, but knew the result even before I did so.

*Caravel* drifted sideways, and I did nothing, for I know when I'm licked. Seconds later the wind and tide set us against the bridge. We leisurely put out fenders between the buttresses and our topsides, while the main shroud began to saw gently against the concrete arch.

As we lay there, unable to move, several faces appeared at the balustrade above, peering down in silent, cud-chewing curiosity. A small face full of ice cream asked a larger one next to it what we were doing, and I wondered absently if it would be possible to reach it with the long boat-hook, the one with the spike in the end. The larger face asked if we needed help.

Actually we did, in the worst way, but I resisted the temptation to ask whether he happened to have a steam winch handy. It isn't easy, I find, to be affable and polite on such occasions, and at the same time maintain your dignity and keep up the illusion that everything is under control and that this is all part of some master plan. I considered going below, in the hope that the faces would lose interest and go away, but it seemed an unseamanlike approach.

Kitty and I discussed the problem quietly, each feeling that this was a family affair which should not be aired in public. When Mary appeared on deck, asking pointed and tactless questions in a loud voice, I ordered her below with a snarl that I immediately regretted.

Then another voice hailed us, from the local base of the Coast and Geodetic Survey, a few yards away. Two young men were apparently on week-end duty. Would we care for a tow? This was no time for false pride, and I took them up on it. They jumped into a launch, took our line, and soon had us tied up at the marina across the way.

Lee Hudgins was a typical Southern gentleman, and next morning insisted on driving us around town to see the sights, buy supplies, and consult the local Johnson dealer about our problems. Our propellers, said the latter, were too large. He sold us a smaller pair and a set of new plugs. Soon we were purring sweetly again.

We cast off the following morning on the next leg of the long journey south, a strictly inland one through the Dismal Swamp Canal, the Pasquotank River and across Albemarle Sound. To enter the canal, however, we had first to go up the Southern branch of the Elizabeth River, which is far more dismal than the swamp beyond it, and consists of shipyards, railway sidings, naval depots, warehouses and junkyards. The river is several hundred yards wide, and is crossed by two lift bridges some 500 yards apart. The first of these carries the tracks of the N. & P.B.L. Railroad and the second provides a road link between Norfolk and Portsmouth. Beyond them are various swing and bascule bridges.

If you don't happen to be a civil engineer, the difference between these three types is that a bascule is hinged at one end and the roadbed tilts up at about 45° or more to let ships pass. A swing bridge, as the name applies, is balanced in the middle and rotates horizontally out of the way. In the case of a lift bridge, the roadbed stays horizontal, but is raised vertically at both ends, by cables and counterweights set in towers. This type goes up only as far as the operator thinks necessary to clear the ship.

We cleared the first bridge with no problems, and the second started to go up on schedule. But at the halfway point it stopped. The bridge-keeper leaned out of his little hut which goes up with it, and watched us casually.

Now I'm the first to admit that he's probably a first-class bridge-keeper, and has doubtless been raising bridges for nigh on forty years, and never lost a mast yet. But on the other hand, after Shark River, I wasn't taking such qualifications on faith any more. On top of that, it was *my* Ian Proctor masts, all two thousand bucks' worth, that we were discussing, a fact which I felt entitled me to at least a minority opinion.

I gave him three more blasts and slowed down. His whole body seemed to stiffen in disbelief.

When he made no attempt to do anything about it, I stood on the top deck and tried to indicate, with two fingers of my right hand, that he should raise the bridge a little. He seemed to construe this as some sort of rude gesture, and made the same one back. We were too far apart to shout, so I gave up the attempt at arguing in sign language and made a 180° turn to port. I wasn't about to get dismasted to satisfy his silly ego.

This seemed to infuriate him, for he disappeared from the window and the bridge came down. I cruised back to Bridge "A" to think things out, before returning to Bridge "B." This time he reappeared, leaning out of his window and reading a newspaper. I got the impression that he intended to keep this up for a long time. For twenty minutes or so I made a series of anti-clockwise circuits between Bridges A and B, unable to get out either way. I was just wondering whether to drop the anchor, in the interest of fuel economy, when I heard three deep and very authoritative "WHOOOOHS" from downstream. Bridge A went up. A tug came through and signalled for Bridge B, which promptly went up to the three-quarter level, far higher than was necessary for the tug. I took this as a peace feeler and went through on the tug's coat-tails, wallowing in his wake. But I just couldn't bring myself to wave my thanks to the bridge-keeper as we passed.

♥♥♥

## THE FOREST PRIMEVAL

The Great Dismal Swamp was named by somebody who had no eye for beauty. Although described in the chart merely as "Cypress Swamp," it is actually a dense forest of conifers and deciduous trees, almost undefiled by man and teeming with wildlife of every sort, on the land, in the air and on water. The canal which crosses it to join the Elizabeth and Pasquotank rivers is 200 years old, the oldest man-made waterway in the U.S. still in use. It is 30 miles long and stretches endlessly from horizon to horizon, with only one hamlet, South Mills, along its entire length. It has been deepened and widened by the Corps of Engineers, and the undergrowth cut back, so that along the edges are numerous tree stumps, cut off at the waterline.

Delayed by the bridge episode, we were late entering the canal, so we motored slowly until dusk, and then found an open spot on the left bank, slid quietly in and tied up to a tree.

The silence was oppressive, except for the occasional forest sound

40

and the rustling of birds as they settled for the night. The darkness, when it came, was equally heavy, and we seemed alone in the world, tucked away in our tiny cabin and eating by the soft glow of a hurricane lamp. How different from that other night, when we had seemed even more alone, off the wild Maryland coast!

It was cold, but completely still, and we turned in early, for there was no reason to stay up. As a result, dawn found us wide-awake. I took my coffee on deck, and was met by an amazing sight.

The sun was just appearing, and the world was a delicate pink. A touch of hoarfrost covered the deck, and the water was like a huge mirror, so still as to be unreal. A mist hung over it, like a wispy veil in the breathless air, moving almost imperceptibly across the surface. The sun, a huge red ball, rose above the point where the water, bisecting the forest, met the horizon. It threw faint shadows onto the thin, pink mist on the water, shadows from the arms of fallen trees lying half-submerged in the shallows, and from the grotesque shapes of the white branches of dead cypress along the banks. These were etched against a sky that was already yellowing in the east and turning blue overhead.

The forest held its breath as it waited for the day. The occasional dead leaf, hardened to a crispness by the night's frost, fluttered down from a treetop, and the rustle that it made against the lower branches in its long, slow fall could be heard a hundred yards away. A small fish jumped, and the tiny ripples spread out in widening cricles, destroying for a moment the illusion of a mirror.

Out of the corner of my eye I caught a flicker of movement in the undergrowth, and a momentary glimpse of a brown body. A fox? A bobcat? A fawn?

I called Kitty on deck, to share the joy of the experience, and for a little while we just sat there, hardly noticing the morning chill as we stared with misty eyes at the water and at the forest beyond, fondling the warmth of our coffee mugs as we tried to fix the scene in our minds forever. We thought of the folks we knew back in Toronto, at this moment driving downtown, bumper to bumper, or crowding into the Bloor subway. And for what? We knew that we had made the right choice, and that if *Caravel* should never provide another moment of pleasure, it would have been worth it.

As the sun climbed, the shadows hardened, and the mist on the water began to evaporate. An eagle made long, gliding turns high above the trees. The forest was awakening.

I started the motors and we cast off the lines, almost ashamed of our raucous exhausts as they tore away the silence and our screws shattered the surface of the water.

Most of the day we cruised along at a steady 5 knots, leaving a smooth-flowing wake that washed the roots along the banks with water stained the exact colour of Coca-Cola. Both motors were running perfectly, though to save fuel we switched one off. The second doubled our fuel consumption, yet added a mere knot to our speed. The steady drone of the motor was smothered by the denseness of the forest.

Thousands of boats use the Waterway every year, but this was December 8th, and we ran all day without seeing another craft. We had the forest to ourselves, and were seeing it as the early settlers did, though in far greater comfort.

At Lock South Mills, ten miles short of Elizabeth City, the canal ended and joined the beautiful Pasquotank River, although the only difference seemed to be that the latter was wider and no longer straight. The sky was blue and cloudless, and there was a feeling of frost in the air, even in mid-afternoon. As the evening hush settled over river and forest, we looked for a suitable spot for the night, out of the main channel in case the odd boat should come by during the night, although this seemed unlikely.

It was another breathless night, black except for the stars, and without even the loom of a distant city. We rode at anchor, with one line ashore, and there was a faint chuckle of water along the hulls, the only indication that this was a river, not a canal.

The morning run to Elizabeth City was a short one, and by ten we were rounding the last bend in the river and looking for the bascule that was shown on the chart. There it was! I reached for the air horn.

These horns are small but effective. You screw on a pressure can of Freon and press a button. The result would do credit to a bad-tempered battle cruiser. But our can had already lasted from Toronto. The first blast was 100%, the second sounded like a sleepy spaniel, and the third never did get past the stage of a gentle hiss. I reached for the spare can, and rammed it home. There was a loud "psssss" as the pin punctured the seal, but the thread wouldn't start. Kitty took the wheel while I fumbled.

Now Freon is also used in refrigeration, being highly effective when released under pressure, which this was right now. Both horn and fingers became white with frost, and I began to suspect frostbite. Then the hissing subsided and the can was empty. I uttered several words that I hadn't used since my old Air Force days, and Kitty hurriedly motioned the children below.

There was no time for an autopsy right now, for the bridge was still down and I had no way of discussing things with the attendant. So we pulled over to a wharf belonging to a fish-processing plant and asked permission to tie up.

To the casual observer, even with 20/20 vision, which I no longer have, the threads on horn and can seemed identical. But measure them with vernier calipers and you find a difference of no more than a hundredth of an inch—just enough to ensure that the can of one manufacturer doesn't fit the horn of another.

On the theory that it's an ill wind that blows nobody a nice fish supper, we wandered into the plant and managed to buy some fresh fillets. The owner, moreover, on hearing of our horn problems, insisted on driving us to the local marina. They didn't have cans of Freon, but they did have mouth horns, so I bought one. What it lacks in ear-splitting enthusiasm it makes up in reliability.

But when the marina operator heard that we were about to cross Albemarle Sound he was horrified. Nobody, but nobody ever went across at this time of day. Suicide, that's what it was! We must stay overnight and start at first light, before the wind had a chance to whip up the shallows into a frenzy. See what I mean about local knowledge?

Promptly at dawn next day we slipped our lines, motored down the lower Pasquotank, and entered Albemarle Sound. The wind was light at this time in the morning, and we were hard put to to make 2 knots. Shortly after 11 a.m. we saw two crazy fools in a rowboat, far off to starboard, fishing. Were they in for a shock!

By 3 p.m. we were becalmed, and just sat there on the glassy water. I turned on one motor and we crawled across, getting in around 4:30. So much for the horrors of Albemarle Sound!

By dusk we were well into the Alligator River, but had difficulty finding a suitable spot for the night, as the shallows were full of stumps. At last we found a place and edged in slowly, with Kitty at the bow to fend off and myself at the controls, until one of us could get ashore with a line.

"Okay forward?"

43

There was no reply.

"Where are you?"

The reply was thin and feeble.

"Down here—I fell in!"

She had, too. I ran forwards, shouting for the children to come and lend a hand.

"How did you do that?"

I realized as I said it that it was largely a rhetorical question, and that the answer could probably wait. We grabbed each other's wrists.

On dry land and in a bathing suit, Kitty still has a pretty good figure, and her weight is well within acceptable limits. But in the water, under numerous layers of Kuron thermal underwear and sweaters, all of which soak up water like a sponge, it is considerable. As I lifted her from the water she seemed to gain weight rapidly, and I finally had to drop her back in again and give her a life preserver instead, while we considered the next move.

I could, of course, have gone in for a lot of false heroics and jumped in beside her, but I felt that this would only compound the problem. The primary objective was to get her out, not me in. Also, she was a better swimmer than I was, and might end up rescuing me, which could be embarrassing. In addition, she already had a life preserver, so that she was in no immediate danger. Come to think of it, she was really quite safe, except that the water was probably pretty cold, in mid-December, here in the Alligator River.

*Alligators!*

You don't, I suppose, call a place the Alligator River because it is full of bullfrogs. This didn't seem the right time to mention the point, although she admitted later that essentially the same thought had occurred to her, and she was convinced that every slimy root that touched her leg was an alligator.

I finally towed her aft with a boat-hook, and we managed to load her aboard via the outboard bracket. For a while she just lay there on deck, panting for breath in a pool of cold, muddy water and exuding probably less sex appeal than at any time in our entire married life.

We lit the Primus, put water on to boil, and broke out the whisky bottle. Mary, who invariably rises to such occasions with a resourcefulness beyond her years, went off in search of dry towels and fresh underwear. I tied *Caravel* to a tree and we settled down to a hot supper and a post-mortem.

She wasn't sure how it had happened, but thought that the boat-hook with which she was trying to fend off was too long for her, and had got caught in a stump. At any rate, it was an hour before her teeth stopped chattering, and to this day she wouldn't thank you for an alligator skin bag.

During the next few days we went up the Alligator, down the Pungo, through the delightful Goose Creek and Bay rivers, until we reached Morehead City, where our first mail since Toronto awaited us. It is a quaint old city, one of the few places that seem to have been bypassed in the headlong rush to the twenty-first century. Some of the stores along the main street have changed little since the 1890's, and are the better for it.

We collected our mail, stayed overnight, and moved on in the morning, managing four knots under sail in a nice breeze. This was a pleasant change, for the motors were beginning to act up again. The channel was wide and the wind just forward of the beam, our best point of sailing.

Mary and Nora decided that their dolls needed a bath, and were soon dangling them over the side on a string, with squeals of delight. A few minutes later, however, Nora let out a howl of anguish and pulled in an empty piece of string. At this point she still had a lot to learn about knots and splices.

She ran below, flung herself onto the bunk, buried her face into the pillow, which she started to chew, and just bawled her heart out. The doll had been part of her life for as long as she could remember, and we couldn't even get her attention, let alone console her.

"Oh, Penny, Penny, Penny! You've gone! I'll never see you again—never, never!" And she dissolved into deep, gulping sobs that shook her whole body, clenched her little fists, and kicked her toes into the bunk.

Now that sort of thing I defy any father to ignore. The chances of finding the doll, even if it were afloat, seemed quite remote, but I had to try.

At the main mast I let go both halyards, shouting to Kitty to do the same with the mizzen. The sail collapsed on the deck, and as I dropped the anchor *Caravel* came about with a jerk. I got the dinghy into the water, grabbed the oars, jumped in, and started to row back.

There was a light chop, which made it difficult to spot anything so small, and in addition we had travelled a quarter of a mile against the current and across the wind. The doll was a mere 11 inches long, and the

45

Waterway a good 400 yards wide at this point. If it floated high in the water, the wind should carry it to the west bank; if low, it would drift to the north. It might not float at all. In any event, the waves were nearly a foot high.

As I rowed back I wondered how she would react to another identical doll. How does a little girl's mind work on a subject like that? *Caravel* was an almost impossible distance away now, and I was satisfied that I should never find it. Had it not been for the memory of her heaving back as she lay on the bunk, I should have given up. But how could I tell her that I had failed, after raising her hopes like this?

Then I saw it—a white dot on the surface, a good hundred yards further on. How trivial it looked, floating like a plastic bottle.

It was a long row back, and as I turned to get my bearings I saw three figures on the deck, two anxious and drawn and one tear-stained, all looking at me with a mixture of hope and fear, for they had been too far away to see whether I had found it or not. As I climbed on deck and gave the doll to Nora she grabbed it with both hands, hugged it passionately to her breast, and then flung her arms around my waist and buried her face in my stomach.

"Oh, Daddy, Daddy! Thank you, thank you, thank you!"

She reached up and planted a wet, salty kiss on my cheek, while Kitty turned away to hide her own expression.

At Swansboro we splurged on a marina for the night, and then powered on past a number of inlets—Bogue, Bear, Brown's, New River, New Topsail and Old Topsail, before reaching Wrightsville. Progress was steady but unexciting as we entered the Cape Fear River, passed Southport, and reached Lockwood's Folly Inlet. I should have avoided stopping at a place with a name like that, especially on a Friday. But I was still inexperienced in the ways of the sea.

Both motors were sick, so we dropped the hook and I got a new set of plugs from a local service station. This did the trick, and they started, but when I tried to raise the anchor it was fouled on the bottom, with the line caught up in something.

As the tide was coming in and the light fading, we gave up for the night. In the morning the tide was lower, and we could see what the problem was. The line ran under an old engine block, and round a slab of concrete and an old wooden piling. The bottom was an absolute garbage dump. But the trouble was that while we could now see everything

46

clearly, we were firmly aground, and by the time we were afloat again the water would hide the line. And I didn't fancy wading up to my middle in that stuff.

By mid-afternoon we reached the critical point where we could still see the bottom, but there was just enough water to float the dinghy. It all had to be planned with the precision of a moon landing. Poling around in six inches of water, I got the line sorted out and back on board. Then I sluiced the mud off both it and myself. *Caravel* wasn't anywhere near afloat, and by the time she was it would be dark again, and we wouldn't dare lower the anchor for fear of getting back into square one. Lockwood's Folly was right!

At this point a fisherman came in and tied up at his private wharf, so I explained the problem and got permission to raft onto him until morning. I also tried to buy a fish supper, but it seemed he wasn't that sort of a fisherman—his business was shrimps. He pressed some onto me, and refused payment.

Neither Kitty nor I had ever met a shrimp in the pre-cocktail stage, but at Morehead City we had bought a book on seafood recipes, on the theory that if we are going to be sailors we should at least know how to cook all the fish we were going to catch. From this we learned that you behead and skin them. It sounded a tedious job, and it was.

The problem in beheading them was that they didn't seem to have one in the first place, at least nothing that was readily identifiable as such. They had a thick end and a thin one, and as the former had two black dots that could have been the eyes, I assumed that this was the head. With no working blueprints, it was a matter of conjecture how much of the creature was head, so I decided on a one-third, two-third split, snipping off a third from the fat end. The best way to skin them seemed to be to slit them up the front (or maybe it was the back) with a paring knife, and squeeze.

Progress was slow, and the eventual pile of heads almost as big as the pile of torsos. I suspect that I erred on the side of safety. At any rate, the end product didn't seem very much for four people, but fortunately Mary took one look at them and said they looked like snails. This ruined Nora's appetite for them too, and Kitty and I wound up sharing them between us with a clear conscience. They were pretty good, at that!

Soon after this we entered the Waccamaw River, one of the most beautiful sections of the Waterway. It wound in endless curves through

47

an extremely dense forest that pressed in so close that it was impossible even to see the shore, let alone land there. The trees were in full leaf and were quite different from those in the Dismal Swamp.

Near the mouth of the Waccamaw lies Georgetown, S.C., and in a southwest wind you have several hours' notice of the fact that you are approaching the city. It boasts one of the largest pulp mills in the world, and one of the prices you pay for a paper mill is the stench of sulphur and rotting pulpwood. This can be a high price indeed.

We changed plugs, made a hurried call at the local laundromat, and pushed on towards Charleston. It was here, incidentally, that Mary first came across the colour bar as it was then practised in the South. As she helped Kitty tote in our bundles of laundry she noticed a sign over the door, reading "WHITES ONLY."

"Oh, Mummy, look! What are we going to do with all our coloured things?"

ᑡᑡᑡ

# CARAVEL ISLAND

On the 22nd we entered Charleston Harbour, which is really the mouth of three rivers, the Wando, the Cooper and the Ashley. As we crossed the estuary we could see Fort Sumter, of Civil War fame, off to port, and over to starboard the lovely old colonial homes along the Charleston waterfront. Turning up the Ashley River we made for a rather unusual marina just beyond the park.

This comprises three high concrete walls, forming a rectangle with the shore, the entrance being a gap in the wall parallel to the shore itself. Inside were the marina quays, as well-protected by the walls as any we had seen. Outside, there was a strong tidal current.

Entering cautiously, I decided on an empty space at one of the piers, while Kitty waited with the fenders, ready to tie them on to the appropriate side as soon as this could be determined.

"Starboard side to," I shouted.

She and the children rushed to tie them on, while I started a full turn

48

to port, throttling back to dead slow. We leaped at the empty space at a full 6 knots, and if I hadn't completed a snappy turn we should have been climbing the north wall. There was obviously a wicked current in there, and this demanded a change of strategy.

"Port side to!"

She gave me a dirty look.

"You sure? *Port* side to?"

"Yes. Sorry!" Explanations could wait, especially as I didn't have any.

Changing over the fenders took time, so I made a few circuits while they did so, leaping north at dead slow ahead and crawling south at full ahead both. Finally we came slowly alongside, at full throttle, and got lines ashore. I complained bitterly to the dockmaster, who thought the whole thing a great joke.

"Don't let it fool you. Those concrete walls don't go down to the riverbed—too much current for that. They sit on piers. Tide comes through there lickerty-split!"

It sure does!

The marina was also the local Johnson agency, and they diagnosed our troubles as too big propellers, causing too low speed, causing fouled plugs, causing problems. They sold me some smaller ones, and new plugs all round. When I pointed out that I would likely reach Miami with enough propellers to start my own agency, they saw my point and took my entire stock as down payment on the new ones.

In the Stona River, just south of Charleston, we saw a fawn swimming across ahead of us, and just managed to get within range and photograph it before it scrambled up the bank and disappeared.

It is south of here that the Waterway undergoes a dramatic change, as thick forests give way to wide-open savannahs. These are land, rather than water, but only just, being about a foot above water and as flat as a table. Apart from the odd hammock of slightly higher ground, with a cluster of evergreens on it, they support nothing but swamp grass. Creeks and backwaters meander aimlessly through these vast savannahs, some navigable, some far too shallow for boats.

If anything, they are even more remote than the Dismal Swamp, and you can sail for hours and not see a sign of human life. They are home to millions of water birds, and when we anchored for the night we could hear these rustling and twittering in the tall grass, only a few feet away, yet completely hidden. Here they live in complete seclusion and safety, with an apparently endless supply of fish that never seem to learn that it is highly dangerous to swim on the surface, where they can be plucked aloft in the twinkling of an eye.

That afternoon I went ashore and cut down a small pine, bringing it on board amid squeals of delight when the children realized the reason for my strange behaviour. We had little in the way of formal decorations, but it was amazing what they managed to create with bits of coloured paper, cooking foil, and anything else that was bright, interesting and sparkly, and they had a whale of a time doing it. They cut out stars, angels, and other emblems from cardboard, paper and plastic, colouring them with paints, crayons and ball-point pens. And they used the cuttings from the tree to add a touch of greenery around the cabin.

But then we hit a snag, for this was the 24th, and while we had the presents, all gift-wrapped and ready, we had completely forgotten about their stockings, and had nothing for these. Where could we get something out here in the savannahs? It was Kitty who hit on a plan.

Tomorrow, with luck, we should reach Beaufort, S.C., and even on Christmas morning we ought to find at least something open. So we announced that today was the 23rd, and that tomorrow would be Christmas Eve.

On the morning of the real 25th we tied up at Beaufort on schedule, but found that they take Christmas seriously. Downtown was as tight as a drum. Christmas Eve, we explained, was a big holiday down south—didn't they realize that? They shook their heads.

All four of us strolled round town in search of some store that might be open, although to Mary and Nora it was merely a routine exploration of a new town. The white mercantile and residential sections were dead, and we eventually found ourselves in the sprawling coloured section. Here the only sign of life came from a local Gospel hall, where someone inside was working hard on a harmonium while a number of voices sang out a spiritual.

Most of the streets were unpaved, and the single-storey houses were unpainted shacks with a washing machine on the front stoop. In the backyards were weeds, collapsing fences, and old car bodies on concrete blocks. The general air of poverty, disinterest and defeatism was only partly erased by the sight of a little boy running about firing a new six-gun, or by his sister pushing a doll in a glossy new carriage. For all the

50

poverty, Santa had not passed up Beaufort last night, although our own children saw nothing unusual in the new toys on what was supposed to be Christmas Eve.

Down a side street was a small, decrepit building with a Coca-Cola sign over the door. Two black children emerged, their faces wrapped around large suckers. It was no A & P, but Kitty muttered something about a loaf, and turned towards it.

"Let's see what that is," I suggested, pointing in the other direction and giving them no chance to object. We lost Kitty with very little trouble, in fact we lost ourselves too, and were hot, tired and dusty by the time we reached *Caravel*, where Kitty, having got back before us, gave me a faint nod to indicate that she had done what she had set out to do.

Santa did, in fact, come down the mast that night, and he left the most gosh-awful conglomeration of jelly babies, chocolate bars and other candy-coated goodies that you could imagine. But Mary and Nora thought it was wonderful, and never did realize that somewhere in the South Carolina savannahs they gained a day.

On the 26th, after a boisterous 4-mile crossing of Port Royal Sound, in which we lost a couple of fenders through leaving them tied on in the rough seas, we staggered into the shelter of Hilton Head Island on one motor. The other was dead. To make matters worse, Kitty began to feel sick, with the symptoms of the flu, so we put her to bed. We turned out of the main channel into Jarvis Creek for the night, and dropped the anchor.

During the night we swung with the tide, and in the morning *Caravel* had a 30° list to port, her starboard outrigger high and dry on a hammock. There wasn't a drop of water within twenty yards, nor any sign of human life anywhere.

It was embarrassing, but hardly dangerous, for we assumed that the next tide would lift us off again. Meanwhile our chief concern was over the plumbing, being now faced with a difficulty that might not be immediately apparent to the long-time city dweller. To flush your toilet all *you* do is press down that little handle, and an endless supply of water at 60 pounds a square inch pressure does the rest. Furthermore, you are connected through a complicated system of underground pipes to a sewage disposal plant, and I'll bet you don't even know where it is, let alone how it works.

51

In *Caravel* we have no such luxuries. Oh, we have a toilet, which for some inexplicable reason is called a "head," but to flush it you pump about 20 times on a handle. On the *up* stroke water is sucked in from the ocean, while on the *down* stroke the contents of the bowl are pumped out into the same ocean. Please note that the essential ingredient of the whole operation is the ocean. No ocean, no flush! You can pump all right, but all you'll get is a hollow gurgle.

So you can see that when aground you have to make certain adjustments to the schedule of your personal habits. Briefly, what isn't done at high tide waits until the next high tide, some 12½ hours later.

As time went on, we learned to insure against this eventuality, when aground, by laying in a stock of sea water at high tide, in what became known colloquially as the "flush bucket." A couple of quarts poured directly into the bowl may not do a 100% job, but in an emergency it is better than nothing. In English harbours, where tides of 20 feet are common, and where boats thus sit on the mud for hours on end, the flush bucket becomes an essential part of life afloat. But at Jarvis Creek we were new to this problem. One learns fast, though, I assure you.

Apart from this, and the fact that Kitty was feeling grim, life went on much as before, if at a marked angle to the horizontal. Only the children seemed to find any humour in the situation when a cupboard door swung open and hit me in the face, or when I tried to shave in a mirror that was focused on my stomach.

About mid-morning a fishing boat chugged down the channel, coughed in surprise, and turned to inspect us at closer range. We find that a trimaran is often a subject for interested comment by people who are not used to seeing three boats holding hands, and the sight of one perched on top of a hammock like Noah's Ark on the morning after the flood must have given rise to some speculation, to say the least. He examined us from several angles to make sure we weren't some kind of trick of the light, and approached us cautiously.

"You want any help?"

"No thanks!"

What else can you say? The only things we really needed were a bucket of water and a twin-rotor helicopter. So I tried to look nonchalant.

The fishing boat seemed to scratch its head as it turned and thump-a-thump-a-thumped its way downstream.

According to the tide tables, the tide which had dumped us there was 6.5 feet above datum. The corresponding high tide the next night would be 5.7 feet, and you don't need a degree in oceanography to figure out that right there we had a problem. Tides follow the phases of the moon and come in cycles of about a month. Those with the greatest range between high and low water occur just after the new moon and full moon, and are called "spring" tides. Those with the least range come at half-moon and are called "neap" tides.

When *Caravel* discovered to our collective dismay that she was not amphibious, we had just passed the springs (Murphy's First Law). So if we didn't get down into the water pretty soon, we'd be up here for nearly two weeks, until the next springs.

On the other hand, tides don't go in even curves, and the evening one may be higher or lower than the morning one, thus reversing the trend for one tide. The tables quoted the morning tide for the next day, the 28th, as being 6.3 feet above datum, or about two inches lower than the one which had stranded us. It was our last hope.

The main hull and the port outrigger were no problem, for they floated free at every tide. It was the starboard one that had met its Ararat, and at low water I went over the side to make an on-the-spot inspection, which was a terrible mistake. Savannahs are a lot softer and deeper than they look.

If we could lighten the starboard side, by moving things over to port, she might float off at high tide. The children and I spent all afternoon making like stevedores. Kitty was already on the port bunk, so we didn't have to move her. We simply buried her under a mountain of canned food, tools, clothes and bedding, until we could hardly see her. Then we turned the dinghy right way up, on the port deck, and filled it as soon as the tide started to come in. Fuel containers, oars, rope, sails, chain; everything went as far to port as possible.

Sleep didn't come easy that night. Just try tilting your bed at 40°, and you'll see what I mean. I slept on the floor, where I couldn't fall any further.

At 10:30 next morning the children and I were on deck. At 10:50 I started both motors, having given the port one the usual plug transplant. Kitty insisted on getting up too, and took an anchor line. Just before 11 a.m. with all bodies far out to port, I put both motors full astern, and everyone heaved.

She swung a bit, but wouldn't slide free. So I put one motor into forward and the other astern, and then reversed the process, to make her swing, and after several minutes of this she inched back slightly. I put both into full astern and lent my own muscle to the lines. The screws threw muddy water and grass between the hulls and finally, under the combined thrust of 36 h.p. and eight arms, she slid off into deep water.

Kitty's temperature was between 101 and 102, and she had an earache, a combination that I knew to be dangerous. She also had a sore throat. Two days before I had put her on penicillin pills every four hours. We now motored down Old Teakettle Creek, and as she had been on penicillin for three days without noticeable effect, I discontinued it. The next day we reached Brunswick, Ga., and her temperature promptly went down to normal and her condition improved. Whether it was because of my medical skill or despite it, we never learned.

Brunswick was our next mail pick-up point, but it proved no place for yachts, so after a brief stop we powered on to Jekyll Creek for the night.

In a lonely stretch of river the following morning we rounded a bend and came across a heavy-power cruiser, obviously well-aground. The skipper was on deck, disconsolate in his khaki yachting clothes, and I hailed him.

"I don't have enough power to pull you off, but is there anything else I can do?"

"Many thanks! You going on to Fernandina?"

"Yes."

"Would you ask the marina there to send the work-boat to tow me in. Tell them I've lost both screws."

Fernandina was quite a way, and I shuddered at the tow charge.

"What about the Coast Guard," I suggested.

"No, no! Not the Coast Guard! The marina! If they can't come, tell them to forget it. But don't call the Coast Guard on any account."

"Okay, will do!" It was a big, expensive boat. It was his nickel, and he probably had money to burn.

Around 2 p.m. we crossed the St. Mary's River and entered the state of Florida. It wasn't the end of the journey, by any means, for Florida has a long coastline. But we somehow felt that we had reached the South.

At Fernandina we tied up at the marina and were welcomed by an official, mini-skirted reception committee of one, who gave us a smile and a free glass of orange juice. To celebrate the occasion the mercury touched 80°.

When I told the pier-master about the cruiser, he sent off the workboat at once, although we had left before it returned, so didn't see our friend that day. In fact we didn't see him until he passed us two days later, pulling over to wave his thanks as he went by.

"You're welcome! Everything fixed okay?"

"Yes thanks. Bye!"

He opened his throttles and roared ahead. But now the mystery was solved, and I knew why he wanted no part of the Coast Guard. This time he was dressed differently—in the uniform of a full admiral in the U.S. Navy!

In St. Augustine we ran into more motor trouble, which turned out to be a blown gasket. The cylinder head had to be ground down, although this proved to be both fast and inexpensive, and we just had time to see the city. It had recently celebrated its four hundredth anniversary, and was the oldest city in the U.S.A. The good St. Augustinians, however, seemed to consider their corporate antiquity a marketable commodity, to be peddled for all the traffic would bear. Every store (or church or house or gas station) was made to look as old as possible, and claimed to be the oldest store (or church or house or gas station) in the U.S., proudly announcing the fact in multi-coloured neon and Old English spelling. It was all rather phoney.

Back on two motors again, we continued past Flagler Beach and Daytona, into the Indian River country and past Cape Kennedy, where we could see the gantries and the huge building housing the giant Saturn moon rockets. This part of Florida is also the centre of the citrus industry, and when Kitty went ashore for groceries she came back loaded with oranges. It was the first time she had ever bought them by the bushel, instead of the pound.

The Indian River widens here, and provides excellent sailing. As we got further south, not only was the weather improving, but the Waterway was becoming more thickly populated. The banks were now occupied by smart homes with well-kept lawns sweeping down to the river, and with power cruisers and sports fishermen tied up at every private dock. The water was pale green, warm and inviting under the Florida sun.

Beyond Melbourne the Waterway widened still further, to about 2

55

miles, but in places was very shallow. The Corps of Engineers had dredged a channel, dumping the fill to one side to form a series of low islets each about 100 yards long and a mere 2 or 3 feet high. They had sprouted palms and other trees, and were a delight to see and explore.

Edging slowly in to one, we were able to get the bow almost ashore before it touched bottom, and we put a line to a palm tree and a stern anchor out to hold us off. The children explored the little island with shrieks of delight, playing pirates and hunting for treasure and shells. We swam, beachcombed and had a barbecue supper under the moon.

Operation Palm Tree was in full swing.

The islet is shown on the chart, at Latitude 27°-49'-25" north, opposite Sebastian, Fla., but it is not named. As far as we are concerned, it is now called "Caravel Island."

## OF PALMS AND PELICANS

Resisting the temptation to establish squatters' rights, we cast off in the morning and sailed on past Vero Beach and Fort Pierce, tying up at the private dock of some friends at Port Salerno. This town is near Stewart, at the mouth of the St. Lucie River and at the head of the attractive and well-sheltered estuary called the Manatee Pocket, so named after the manatee, or sea cow. This huge marine mammal lives in these waters and the sight of one can come as a bit of a shock when you are out in an 8-foot dinghy. All you see is an enormous black body, like a whale—but apparently harmless.

We stayed at Port Salerno for ten days, unable to tear ourselves away from the easy life under the palms, while the children played ashore and watched the pelicans.

To the northerner, this bird is quite a sight. It seems to be designed all wrong, with a wing loading that is far too high, like a farmyard duck. To fly, it has to really work. And being essentially a fish-eater, it has developed a built-in trawl in its lower jaw. Hence the jingle: "A wonderful bird is the pelican, His beak can hold more than his belican."

56

Cruising at about 40 knots and some 30 feet up, he scans ahead and, when he sees a likely fish, makes like a drunken Kamikaze pilot. Sticking his head down and his tail up, and without reducing his throttle setting, he assumes an approach angle of about 45° and comes in like a concrete block. The splash can be heard hundreds of yards away, and the whole thing looks like a very painful belly flop.

But when the spray subsides, there he is with his wings spread all over the place, gulping and hiccuping like crazy, his enormous face full of catfish or mullet. You may see a tail sticking out, until with a final convulsive jerk he gets that down too. His problem now is to get airborne again, soaking wet and with the added payload. But by sheer horsepower and a lot of positive thinking he eventually makes it; and is then off after his dessert.

When not actually fishing, the pelican spends most of his time digesting. Perched on top of a post or the branch of a mangrove, he looks very doleful with his long, drooping face, and gives the impression of a badly upset stomach.

One morning we all decided to go into town, and to get ashore it was necessary to pull *Caravel* in with her warps, for we had a breast anchor out to hold her off the quay. I could pull her in all right, but couldn't hold her there, so that it was necessary to time the short jump ashore. Kitty had gone first, and Nora was outside the rail, waiting for the psychological moment.

"Now," I shouted, but she seemed to hesitate. Kitty pulled her hand, and I slapped her bottom to encourage her. She jumped, but her heart wasn't in it. And if you are jumping from ship to shore the last thing you need is a defeatist attitude before you start.

She squeaked in protest, and went in with a splash, hanging onto Kitty's hand like grim death and pulling her in too, with an even larger splash. It wasn't deep—four feet or so—but it was muddy and, from subsequent accounts, cold.

The score was now: Kitty—2; Mary—1; Nora—1; Fred—0.

They were all itching for me to join the club, and Nora, describing her only ducking to date, still says I pushed her. I *didn't* push her. I was just trying to help her overcome her nervousness.

South of Port Salerno lies Hobe Sound, the fabulously wealthy and magnificent winter home of America's top 400. On the island between the Waterway and the ocean, is rolling country, thickly wooded and truly beautiful, with private roads wandering through carefully manicured forest, well-tended golf courses, and large homes that show only the tops of their roofs discreetly above the trees. It is said that if you wish to live there, you make application and wait until, after due investigation, you are advised whether you are considered to be suitable as a neighbour.

Just beyond it is Palm Beach, winter home of the second-rate millionaires who didn't quite make Hobe Sound. The concentration of wealth along the banks was impressive, and the homes, sweeping lawns and luxury cruisers had to be seen to be believed.

Then we went down Lake Worth, where the wide expanse of water made it possible to sail once more, and on past Boynton Beach and Delray Beach. By this time the banks were solidly built-up, and it was difficult to find a place to anchor or tie up. But south of Delray we came to a perfect lagoon, and I hailed a man having fun in a "Sailfish." Could we anchor for the night?

"Sure, but why not tie up over there, at the wall?"

We did so, and within minutes he had introduced himself as Arlie Buck and asked us over for a drink. He and his wife, Martha, had recently retired, and we soon became good friends. They were interested in trimarans and accepted our invitation to come down to Miami with us, for a sail.

We went inside as far as Fort Lauderdale, the Venice of America and a paradise for the yachtsmen who live there. Many parts of the city had been reclaimed from the swamp. The homes faced onto the road but backed onto a canal, so that you could tie your boat up at the foot of your garden. The city had an excellent inlet, several rivers, and hundreds of canals.

This was our last stop before Miami, and while we could have continued inside, we decided to go out. For one thing there was a fixed bridge that we could clear, but only just, and I wasn't keen on taking any chances. I also wanted Arlie to sail a trimaran in open water. Keeping close inshore to avoid the north-flowing Gulf Stream, and with a stiff east wind, we heeled over to our maximum of about 11°, lifted the port hull clear of the surface, and "creamed" our way down the coast at 9 knots. The water was a lovely shade of green, showing about 3 fathoms, and *Caravel* lifted easily to the incoming seas, knifing through with her narrow hulls and leaving three separate wakes astern.

The Bucks were so enthralled with this delightful and exhilarating

58

sail that their retirement plans underwent a sudden switch. Arlie took a job for just long enough to earn the money to buy materials, and then retired a second time, to build his own trimaran, *Whisper*.

Miami Beach slid by, with its long string of magnificent, if slightly gaudy hotels, and then came Government Cut, the channel leading into the City of Miami itself. At 5:47 p.m. on Saturday, February 5th, three months and a day out of Bronte, we tied up at the City Yacht Basin.

The long journey south was over.

The City Yacht Basin is not the most unpleasant place in Miami. There is, for instance, the jail and the city dump. But in an onshore wind, from the east, it takes a lot of beating. (In all fairness, it should be stated that in 1970 a new yacht basin was under construction, and promised to be a big improvement.)

For the first week, the wind blew strongly and steadily onshore, and we were berthed in the extreme western corner, smack up against Biscayne Boulevard, which is about as far west as you can get without obstructing a bus route. This situation created two problems.

Firstly, it permitted the tourists, of whom there are a considerable number in Miami in January, to pause in their stroll and look down into *Caravel's* cabin to see what we were having for lunch. Secondly, there was the problem, arising directly from the wind, of the fact that the waters within a 100-foot radius became the focal point of all the floating garbage from Biscayne Bay, all 250 square miles of it. I suspect that the present anti-pollution scare started when someone got a good look at the City Yacht Basin in an east wind.

I never did take a written inventory, but memory lingers on. The main items were one very dead dog, two dead cats (one somewhat bloated), a number of dead fish or heads thereof, a great many items of domestic garbage, at least one empty plastic bottle for every known brand of liquid detergent, quantities of human and other waste, plastic bags, and a Portuguese man-of-war population that ran into thousands. If you don't know these creatures, they are a beautiful type of jellyfish that floats on the water, looks like a tiny blue or mauve plastic bag of air, and trails tentacles many yards long. Touch one of these latter, and you suffer excruciating pain and paralysis for hours, with death a distinct possibility. The thought of falling among them while stepping ashore from a heaving boat was not a pleasant one.

Then there were the logs: enormous things that hid under the pilings all day and came out at night to thump against the hull until dawn. I would go out in my pyjamas, ignoring the cabin-gazers, and push the darned things away with an oar, but they'd only drift back again, and were far too heavy to lift out of the water.

For several days there was also a dead pelican, but I don't really count that, for it became over-bloated, burst and sank.

One must not, however, judge Miami by the City Yacht Basin, nor should one confuse Miami with Miami Beach, the former being on the mainland and the latter on an island across the Waterway. The Beach consists of hotels, stores, night clubs and bars—nothing else! Miami, on the other hand, is a sprawling city, colourful and interesting, with a climate that is hot and humid in the summer but delightful in winter. It is roughly one-third Anglo-Saxon, one-third Negro, and one-third Cuban, with the Negro section growing the most rapidly of the three.

At first, we disliked Miami, and found it squalid and tawdry. But it grew on us, and we found that it had a lot to offer: climate, good transportation, some pleasant suburbs, good parks and beaches, entertainment to suit every taste, and sport. The stores are good, you can buy just about anything there, and at a discount if you know where to look. The Cubans, too, we found interesting. Most of them had fled from Castro, and were now intent on learning English and starting a business, be it a grocery store, a laundromat, a barber shop or a gas station. There was even the odd family cigar factory.

As soon as the wind permitted we crossed Biscayne Bay and found a perfect anchorage in an almost land-locked lagoon called No-Name Cove, surrounded by a forest of pines and coconut palms and without a building in sight. The state of Florida has since taken it over as a park, and a little to the north is President Nixon's Florida White House.

For a while we relaxed, before crossing to Dinner Key, where the Boat Show was to be held. I wanted to buy a ship-to-shore radio telephone. While there, we ran into Ray and Gloria Colot, who had recently bought Arthur Piver's own trimaran, *Bird*. They made a suggestion.

"If you're staying in Miami, why not come up to Hardie's, where we berth? It's a lovely spot, and cheaper than Dinner Key."

Three days later we followed *Bird* 2½ miles up the Miami River to Hardie's Yacht Basin, and knew at once that we had found a home. No-Name Cove had been beautiful, but was too isolated for a long stay.

Hardie's was operated by Bill Hardie and his nephew Dan, and both were pleasant and friendly.

Bill's father had been Sheriff Dan Hardie of Dade County, in which Miami is located, and a tough, gun-slinging lawman in the Tombstone tradition, who did much to clean up Miami in the early days. His methods were simple and effective, even if he wasn't too fussy about civil rights and the Fifth Amendment. If a man was even suspected of a crime (and Dan had a nasty, suspicious mind), he would be hauled down to the railroad depot at the point of a six-gun, put on the next train north— passenger or freight didn't much matter—and told that if he ever appeared in Dade County again he would be shot on sight. Dan's reasoning was that it was a whole lot better to ship a criminal over into Broward County and points north than to waste time and money on a long trial, and then have to feed him in jail as well.

His theories on crime prevention, however, found little favour with the northern sheriffs, or in Tallahassee, where the state governor got so fed up with Dan that he had him impeached and thrown out of office. Dan put up for re-election, but found that there weren't enough voters willing to risk the governor's ire by re-electing him.

But Henry Flagler, the railroad baron after whom the main street in Miami is still named, happened to be extending his Florida East Coast Railroad south at the time and was, like Hardie, a staunch Irish Catholic and no friend of the governor. He also had a rail gang of several hundred Boston Irish labourers on his payroll and they were, of course, also good Catholics and behind Hardie to a man. Flagler had them registered as voting residents, and Dan was back in office.

His last-known act was in 1932, at the attempted assassination of Franklin Roosevelt, who was making an open-air speech in the park. The killer, using a rifle from a hotel window, missed F.D.R. but killed the mayor of Chicago at his side.

The strongly Democratic crowd went after the assassin, but Dan reached him first and bundled him off to jail under a load of garbage.

Life at Hardie's was pleasant indeed. Situated in a residential part of Miami near North-West 17th Avenue, it was peaceful and sheltered. Indeed, the main hazard was dock-fever, of which the chief symptom is a fear of casting off lines. Some skippers at Hardie's hadn't been to sea in years. They had water piped on board, and electricity for air conditioning and TV. They strolled across the lawns under the palms for a shower or to collect their mail, and generally had a relaxing time. If they grew overly restless, they might go down to Biscayne Bay for an afternoon's fishing, although this meant untying a lot of lines and disconnecting pipes and wires and getting the engine to start.

Another thing that made you think twice about it was the river itself, which is something of a 2½-mile obstacle course, being narrow and winding, with no fewer than ten bridges below Hardie's. Through downtown Miami the banks are littered with boat repair yards, marinas and fish-dealers, though further up, near Hardie's, it becomes residential, with lawns, gardens, trees and a city park.

On the second trip up-stream, and still a bit touchy on the subject of bridges, I was approaching one in a narrow section of the river with a sharp bend to starboard. It was a bascule, so I gave it three blasts and was agreeably surprised when it promptly went up. In a burst of gratitude I went into full ahead both, doing about 7 knots, so as not to keep him waiting.

But just short of the bridge I got a shock, for round the bend came the stubby bow of the *Eva*, a tug well-known on the river. To make matters infinitely worse, there appeared behind her, like an elephant guided by a small boy with a rope, a bow that dwarfed the *Eva* and most of the buildings around.

This second bow, subsequently identified as belonging to the Panamanian freighter *Johnny Express*, was obviously going to monopolize most of that bridge, and if I pressed the point I was liable to go in a trimaran and come out a monohull. The bridge itself occupied only about half of the river, there being a corner at each end where a small boat could, if attacked, sneak in and hide. I aimed for the port one, and slammed everything into reverse. The bank, solid though it was, looked a whole lot more inviting than did the bow of the *Johnny Express*. *Caravel* shuddered protestingly and started to yaw. For a while I thought she was going to climb up into South River Drive, but she finally came to a grudging stop with her pulpit buried into the trees on the bank. Now I knew why the bridge had opened so conveniently.

I later discovered a little gimmick of my own for negotiating these bridges, especially when going down-stream on an ebb tide, which tends to give me heartburn anyway. I would wait for a freighter to come down

62

and then slip in under his stern. For it is a fact of river life that while a bridge-keeper may be a bit casual with a 16-foot sloop, he is always on the bit when a freighter approaches. After all, with 14,000 tons of solid steel coming down even at 6 knots, it is going through either way, so you either open up with a smile, or you buy yourself a new bridge. And while it is open, along comes little *Caravel*, tooting like crazy in case anyone fails to notice her and starts to lower away too soon. It works!

I have also discovered that tugs, fishing boats, auxiliaries, cabin cruisers, even the sheriff's patrol boat, all yield the right of way to *Caravel* promptly and without question—if we happen to have an 8,000-ton freighter in front of us.

At Hardie's it was a joy to fit out *Caravel* and to work on her in the Florida sunshine. Within walking distance were hardware and marine stores, war surplus stores and supermarkets, laundromats, fabric stores and a lumber yard. I bought a refrigerator, an extra sail, a Seagull outboard for the dinghy, and many other items, while Kitty ran up curtains for the cabin windows.

Until now it had been difficult to keep the children at their correspondence course lessons, but now we put on the pressure, and made sure that they did a fixed number of lessons a day, seven days a week. We would give them a day off if we were going somewhere special, but this was not necessarily Saturday or Sunday. For recreation they played around the marina, visited other boats, romped in the local park, or swam in the nearby open-air municipal pool. I don't think any of us were feeling much pain at the thought of the folks up north shovelling snow.

## INEZ AND DOLORES

With the approach of summer, we decided that we really ought to make plans if we were to avoid dock fever and being stuck at Hardie's for the rest of our lives. The logical thing, of course, was to cruise the Bahamas, which were less than fifty miles away. But there were two snags.

Firstly, we had to do something about the motors, for I was now convinced that it was only a matter of time, if we continued to use them, before they would let us down badly, and disaster would result. They had been bad enough in the Waterway, but among the coral reefs of the Bahamas, and in the open sea—never! Even when running they were unsuitable for use offshore, for they cavitated, producing a lot of bubbles but little thrust. What we needed was an inboard diesel, with good, solid thrust and low fuel consumption. And I couldn't think of a better place to have one installed than right here in Miami.

Secondly, there was the little matter of the hurricane season, which was now coming up, and Hardie's seemed as safe a place as we could find.

So we decided to stay, to install a diesel in the fall, and be ready to sail out for the Bahamas in November with a spanking new engine and eight hurricane-free months ahead of us. This strategy was also a good excuse for doing nothing all summer.

Finally we started to shop around for a diesel, getting bids from several yards. It all took time, and I had other jobs too, such as painting, wiring extra lights, putting up shelves, and so on. By the time we were ready for the engine it was late September, and the Miami River Boat Yard was all set to start work.

Unfortunately, we were delayed by Inez.

Born a thousand miles east of the Virgins a week before, she had travelled rapidly westward, growing from a mere tropical disturbance, through tropical storm, to hurricane! As she came closer the advisory notices became warnings, and it was considered possible that she would hit the mainland.

On October 1st she was over Cuba, creating a ruckus, and then she paused, as though wondering where to go next, before turning N.N.E., towards the Bahamas. The diesel would have to wait.

Miamians were putting up shutters and bringing in everything portable. Storekeepers, with large areas of glass, produced heavy steel shutters, designed to interlock and clamp to the wall, protecting the glass from flying objects and people from flying glass. City trucks cruised the streets, cutting down coconuts from the thousands of palms before the storm brought them down on someone's head. Awnings and deck chairs and sidewalk displays disappeared. The city braced itself for what might, or might not, come. It was exciting for us, but to Miami it was routine, and the people had been through this many times before.

Up the river came boats, all seeking the shelter of the upper reaches: boats from exposed moorings on Biscayne Bay, and Dinner Key, and the City Yacht Basin, and over at the Beach, and at waterfront berths for miles around. Suddenly the river was the *in* place to be, every marina filled to capacity, every inch of bank rented out. Yet still they came, in the hundreds. The phone at Hardie's rang incessantly. "Sorry, no room!" The bridges no longer opened on request, but waited until they could pass 15 or 20 boats at a time, and every so often a group of them would surge through, big and small, inboards and outboards, fishing skiffs and million-dollar cruisers, sailing auxiliaries, house boats and racing sloops. They came through the bridge at 17th Avenue, past Hardie's, and on through the 22nd Avenue bridge, searching the bank for enough space to tie up and ride out the coming holocaust—if there was going to be one! This was the crazy part of the whole drama. Inez might never come within 500 miles. But then again, she might!

We did the same as everyone else at Hardie's, securing ourselves, bow and stern, to both the quay and to heavy pilings, with ½-inch diameter nylon line, with a breaking strain of over 3 tons. We took lines across to the next quay, and we used chain. Where chafe was likely we threaded the line through lengths of vinyl hose, or tied rags around it.

The dinghy was light and vulnerable, so we weighted it, paid out enough line, and sank it to the bottom. That should keep it quiet for a while!

The sails we took off the booms lest they be torn away, and the booms themselves we lashed down. Oars, boat-hooks, cushions, life preservers, jerry cans and other portable items we stowed in the out-riggers, and we hung fenders and old tires over the side to protect us from the next boat and him from us. Dan Hardie inspected us, and suggested only that we slacken off our warps a little, to allow for the abnormally high tide that Inez would produce.

When we could think of nothing further to do, we wandered round the quays, where people were chatting and joking to cover up their nervousness, and inviting each other to come out for a day's fishing in the Gulf Stream. It was hot and muggy, but this wasn't unusual. It was clouding up, but it certainly didn't look like a hurricane. Even the palms were relaxed.

Down below, I turned on the radio, and thought how lucky we were to have it. Not many years ago, boats might even now be setting out for

65

Bimini or Gun Cay, across the Stream, unaware of what lay in store. I switched from WGBS to WFUN to WKAT to WINZ to WOCN, hoping that one of them might have some scrap of information before the others. Each described itself as "Your Hurricane Station," as though it had personally sponsored this spectacular for our entertainment and had an exclusive on the gruesome details.

By October 2nd Inez, moving towards the Bahamas and Florida, had slowed down again.

By the 3rd she was on the 78th meridian, which runs north-south about 100 miles east of the mainland. She had changed course slightly, and the Hurricane Centre at Miami was now predicting her path as a little to the west of Nassau and across Andros Island. This would put her 120 miles from Miami, in which event we should probably be on the outer fringe of the hurricane-force winds. As the normal track tends to turn to the right, she could easily miss us by more than this.*

Late on the 3rd we started to get winds from the northeast, and then they began to back a little to the north as the eye advanced. There was little or no rain, just a solid mass of cloud scurrying overhead. The palms would sway a little, and then settle down again.

By about 8 p.m. they were reporting the eye as being east of Miami, and still moving slowly north. By 9 p.m. it was over Grand Bahama Island, northeast of Miami, and we went to bed a little easier in our minds.

During the night the wind increased, but it wasn't as bad as we had feared, and we slept intermittently. At 6 a.m. I turned on the radio.

It was still over Grand Bahama—and had stopped!

When a hurricane stops it is because something, such as a high pressure cell, has interrupted her normal path, which in this part of the world would be a swing to the right, towards Bermuda. The forecasters seemed hesitant, for Inez could do anything.

By now the hourly broadcasts had been abandoned in favour of continuous coverage, and the radio stations were having a ball. It had been a dull day in Vietnam.

About noon on the 4th she seemed to be making up her nasty little mind. Slowly, very slowly, she began to move again—to the southwest!

We plotted her position and apparent course, and didn't like the

---

*The chart on page 89 shows the actual track of the hurricane.

66

Kitty and I, with Nora (left) and Mary (right),
on deck at Fareham (near Portsmouth), England

Kitty in the galley.
Note portable oven on stove.

Mary and Nora on their fo'c'sle bunk, in January 1966

◄ Myself in the chart-house,
where *Journey with Caravel* was written

At Bronte, Ontario in late 1965
*Far left: Caravel* is launched, by crane.
*Centre:* Loading up on the day of departure
*Right:* Leaving Bronte Harbour under full sail
and wondering what the future held for us

A plumber's nightmare: filtering
rain water (in the cockpit)

Highlight of the day: plotting the noon position

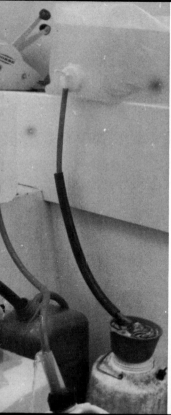

*Caravel* Public School, ▶
with Grade 3 on the left
and Grade 4 on the right

◄
Arriving by helicopter
at Mount Sinai Hospital,
Miami Beach, after
the accident at Gun Cay

Far left: Caravel under power in the Florida section of the Intra-Coastal waterway
Far centre: Tied up at Hardie's, in Miami, and preparing for the Atlantic crossing
Left: Weather ship Echo (U.S.S. Androscoggin). She paid us a welcome call in mid-Atlantic.
Centre: 1,000 down, 3,500 to go! The crew looks pretty happy on reaching St. George, Bermuda safely, after a Force 11 storm.

► by R.A.F. recon-
ance aircraft,
iles off Land's
Mary waves the
dian flag
ntification.

*Top left:* My mother was on the quay to greet us as we entered the inner harbour at Padstow after the crossing from Miami.

*Bottom left:* Getting to school at Padstow was sometimes a problem, especially at low tide.

*Top:* Our crewman George holds up a press placard announcing *Caravel's* arrival at Padstow.

*Above:* Tied up at the Sussex Yacht Club. Shoreham-by-Sea, England

*Top:* At Tangier, Morocco. Kitty and the children hunt for bargains as they explore the famous *kasbah.*
*Left:* The children examine the intricate Moorish relief design on the walls of the Alhambra at Granada, Spain.
*Below:* Scraping and painting *Caravel's* bottom on the beach at Agadir

—*Star photo by Reg I*

A DREAM COME TRUE for former Scarborough insurance man Frederick Carlisle is his three-hulled Caravel II. He bought it 5 years ago for $25,000 and has cruised more than 20,000 miles with his daughters Nora. 11 (left) and Mary, 13, (right) and his wife. During the five-year getaway on the world's oceans the girls managed to pick up six years' credits on correspondence courses. The Carlisles are thinkin crossing the Atlantic Ocean a second time next y

# 5 years at sea--home looks good

**By LIONEL GOULD**
**Star staff writer**

Five years ago Scarborough insurance man Frederick Carlisle decided that at the age of 55 it was time to see the world instead of spending the rest of his life trying to make more money.

He spent $25,000 of his savings for a 40-foot trimaran sailboat, $12 more for a plastic sextant, arranged Ontario Department of Education correspondence courses for his two young children. and sailed away from the Toronto rat race.

Scarborough family has since cruised 20,000 miles aboard the three-hulled Caravel Ii. And the youngsters, Mary, 13, and Nora, 11, returned from their five-year voyage with six 'years' credits in their correspondence courses.

But their voyage halfway around the globe was not all sunshine and soft breezes, Carlisle said last night back at his Cliffcrest Dr. home.

Near Miami, Carlisle lost the tip of his thumb on the anchor chain: the hull of Caravel II splinters minor coll'

ish in the Atlantic, 1,000 miles from land.

They also weathered a hurricane, but were nearly rammed by a 10,000-ton freighter.

Caravel II left Toronto Nov. 4, 1965, under overcast skies. The Carlisles sailed across Lake Ontario to the Erie Canal, through the Five Finger Lakes country and then down the Hudson River to New York. From there they skirted to Miami.

Mrs. C'

hauling up the anchor in a heavy sea and the tips of both were severed.

A U.S. Coast Guard helicopter rushed him to Miami where surgeons grafted his finger tip on again but they couldn't save the thumb.

They reached Bermuda in 1967 and set sail for the Azores Islands, 2,000 miles way, with George Biggs to help as crew.

It took 26 days to reach Azores. another 16 days England's Co'
'hey w'

## THOUSANDS TO MARCH IN LABOR DAY PARADE

Thirty bands and thousands of union members march in the annual Labor Day parade sponsored b Labor Council of Metropolitan Toronto.

Beginning at 9.30 a.m., Monday the parade w'' down Spadina Ave., from just above Queen St., ti along Queen to Dufferin St. and then south to the National Exhibition.

The parade has two themes this year with 127 flags of different countries, will sa Nations. A second section will honor 25 immigration to Canada.

### Beaten unconscious

After 20,000 miles and 22 countries, *Caravel* is tied up at the foot of Bay Street, Toronto. We sit on the foredeck and live again some of the high points of the last five years.

result one little bit. This would bring the eye down west of Bimini, and within 30 miles of Miami. We should be well within the circle of maximum winds, almost in the eye itself.

And to make matters worse, we were now in the wrong semicircle. As a hurricane moves forward at, for instance, 20 knots and with winds of 100 knots, the air travels anti-clockwise. Thus if you are in the right-hand semicircle, facing the way the storm is moving, the actual wind speed is 100 plus 20, or 120 knots. In the left-hand semicircle it is 100 minus 20, or 80 knots, a big difference. While Inez had been travelling north we had been in the so-called "navigable" semicircle. But now she was travelling the other way, and we were in the "dangerous" semicircle (a far more realistic term).

We considered going ashore, while there was still time, to shelter in one of Hardie's concrete buildings. But our food, clothes, bedding and equipment were all on board, and for all we knew the thing could last for days. We decided to stay. The children were surprisingly casual about the whole affair, treating it more as a game than anything else. Anything unusual—even a hurricane—appealed to their sense of adventure.

The water itself was quite calm. There were small waves, and the surface was white with flying spume. But the far bank was a mere 100 yards away, and there just wasn't room for real seas to build up.

Now the wind was rising, and the palms plunged more violently. Newspapers, rags, cardboard boxes, bits of plywood flew about. A palm frond, breaking loose, travelled quite a way before crashing to the ground. Beyond the marina office an overhead power cable swung madly, touching something that was grounded. Each time it did so a shower of sparks would fall. The street and the quays were deserted.

The rain, still intermittent, came in great gusts that lashed the side of the boat furiously, while clouds pressed lower and flew past at abnormal speed. It was still hot, and the wind had no cooling effect at all. It rose to a crescendo and fell away again, and the masts leaned over in unison as the boats heeled before it. Running rigging slapped rhythmically with different sounds and tempos, as steel or Dacron or plastic hit metal or wooden masts. Dock warps grunted, groaned and threw off spray as they brought a heaving hull up short. Stays and shrouds moaned and whined above the shriek of the wind itself. It was a strange symphony that added to the visual scene.

Now I realized why ordinary roofs are forbidden, for a roof that would be normal up north would be lethal here. Tiles, slates, shingles, roof-boards, sheets of corrugated steel would become missiles, hurled by 120-knot winds, to decapitate a person, slice through a car or smash a window shutter. Roofs in Miami are solid, of poured concrete, with tiles embedded in cement.

With the eye now close and the barometer so low, the tide rose higher than we had ever known it, literally sucked up by the partial vacuum. The quay and part of the lawn were under a foot of water, and lines that had been slack were now taut.

At 4 p.m. the radio put the centre at 26 north, 79½ west, which was northwest of Bimini and 50 miles northeast of Miami.

By 5 p.m. it was only 30 miles away, between Cat Cay and Miami, and we were on the edge of the eye itself. Inside it, winds drop to zero and reverse themselves. We didn't experience this phenomenon, but they did at Key Biscayne, five miles away. We were grateful for our sheltered berth, and didn't envy the spotters in the old 4-engined Constellations who flew into the eye to take readings and make observations. The wind was now screaming like a banshee, with little relief between gusts. The rain, too, was heavier, though still not continuous. For five in the after- noon it was remarkably dark.

I crawled out on deck on hands and knees, to avoid being carried away, and checked the lines for chafe as I worked my way along the starboard side. Every time *Caravel* was slammed by the wind it seemed as though they must part, but nylon is very elastic, and fantasti- cally strong. None seemed in danger of sawing itself through, and no knots had worked loose. Coming back down the port side, I saw a piece of wood that looked like the lid of a packing crate. It hurtled overhead, end over end, and knifed into the water a few yards away.

Only the children got much sleep, for even if the movement of the boat, thrashing about like a wild animal in a net, had permitted it, we were both too tense to relax. I shall never understand how a little girl of seven can sleep through a raging hurricane in a small boat, and yet scream in panic at the sight of a moth or spider above her bunk.

I lay there, listening to the frenzied howling of the wind in the rig- ging, the groaning and shuddering of the lines, the angry slapping of waves between the hulls, the rattling hiss of rain on the deck-head, and other noises impossible to identify. I wondered whether Inez would come any closer, and whether it would make any difference if she did. I thought of the strain of 10 tons of boat snapping at the warps.

I slept.

At 7 a.m. the sky seemed a little lighter, although the wind was as strong as ever. The rain had stopped, and it seemed cooler. There was no sign that we had suffered any serious damage, and as Kitty lit the stove for coffee I turned on the radio.

During the night Inez had started to move a little faster, travelling southwest between Cat Cay and Miami. The eye was now over Marathon, fifty miles south!

She had gone! She had passed us! We felt unashamedly glad that she was now threatening someone else and not us. The wind would soon ease off and the worst was over. We had lived through a hurricane, and we were safe! What do you want, bacon and eggs?

By 9 a.m. I was starting to untie some of the extra lines across to the next quay, for Inez was centred near Key West.

Then she stopped again!

Damn!

We just couldn't win. How often was she going to seesaw back and forth like this, clobbering Miami each time?

There was nothing else to do so we drank coffee and listened to eye-witness accounts of the damage, especially down in the Keys, where mobile homes and tractor-trailers had been rolled over, roofs blown away, and the smaller Keys inundated. Some places were cut off except by radio, and people were warned to boil all drinking water. Schools, churches, shops and offices were closed, and motorists were asked to stay off the streets. All activities except rescue and essential services ground to a halt, and I was reminded of Liverpool, England, in 1941 and 1942, on the morning after a bad air raid.

At about 2 p.m. Inez started to move again, slowly and erratically. By 4 p.m. a westward pattern seemed to be developing, and by 6 p.m. she was definitely heading into the Gulf of Mexico. Miami heaved a corporate sigh, and a few of the shutters came down. For a while the radio stations tried to squeeze the last bit of mileage out of Inez by estimating the damage and casualties and by comparing her with the famous hurricanes of the past. But most people were too busy cleaning up the junk.

The stations along the Gulf Coast, from New Orleans to Brownsville, could get excited and preempt their regular programs, for she was

now their problem. I have a vague idea that Inez hit the coast somewhere south of Corpus Christi, Texas, but I'm not sure. The Miami
stations report news, not history.

And Inez was history.

It was now time to take *Caravel* down-river for the diesel, and as
though to prove that the whole thing was a complete waste of time and
money, both outboards started at a touch of the button and purred
sweetly all the way. But we weren't being fooled by that sort of thing
any more.

At the yard they hauled her out onto the slip, where she sat sedately,
her decks 10 feet above the quay. Carpenters swarmed all over her and
started to hack out great holes.

On the slip we ran into much the same problem that we had at
Jarvis Creek—the plumbing ceased to work. Only this time there was
no high tide in a few hours, for the estimate of the completion date was
nearly two weeks. I discussed the matter with the yard foreman.

The Miami River Boat Yard, in a gesture of paternalism, did provide
certain facilities for its work gang. As owner of a visiting yacht I was an
ex officio member of that gang, and thus entitled to use these facilities
24 hours a day. Indeed, I had it made. But as they didn't employ girls
in the work gang, they saw little point in installing duplicate female
facilities. Moreover, the M.R.B.Y.'s sense of *noblesse oblige* did not
extend to the provision of such fancy and unnecessary gadgets as locks
on the door, or even a latch. If you wanted in you kicked it, and if it
swung open you walked in. If it stopped halfway you hung around outside for a spell.

So if Kitty or the children should need to go in between 8 a.m.
and 5 p.m., Monday through Friday, they had a problem. They could
either watch the door from a distance for 20 minutes and, if nobody came
out, take a chance. Or they could, if I happened to be around, get me to
investigate first.

But even inside, their problems were far from over, for there was
always a good chance that some husky rigger's mate would kick the
door open and barge in unannounced. Kitty found it all rather embarrassing.

They finally overcame this by stationing a guard outside, which
wasn't foolproof, for half of the gang were Cubans who spoke no English.

70

It was Nora who was first faced with the difficulty of explaining to a Cuban, in sign language, that Mummy was in there, and could he wait? By the end of the first week most of them seemed to have got the idea, and if they saw Mary or Nora standing at attention outside the door they would simply wander off behind the paint store instead.

Even so, Kitty was less than enthusiastic over the whole set up, for she felt that the standard of fastidiousness left much to be desired. The lack of a seat, for instance, seemed to bother her, as did the instructions for the correct use of the equipment and the exhortations to achieve accuracy, all written on the wall in highly colourful and descriptive iambic pentameter. She failed to see any humour in these verses, and feared for the effect on the minds of Mary and Nora.

By and large, I don't think Kitty was sorry to leave the Miami River Boat Yard.

With such preliminaries as engine bed, skeg, strut, stuffing box, shaft and propeller all completed, *Caravel* was returned to the water for the installation of the engine itself, an operation which turned out to be quite something.

To begin with, space under the cockpit was at a premium, and a 450-lb. diesel, with transmission, takes a bit of wiggling to get down through a tiny hatch, on end, and then turn it level and lower it to the exact spot on the engine bed. One false move, and the thing would have gone through that ½-inch plywood skin like an anchor through wet paper, to end up in the mud at the bottom of the Miami River.

You have to remember, too, that the M.R.B.Y.'s work gang consisted of 50% white Cubans, who spoke no English except "Sonofabeech" and "Godam," and 50% Negro Americans who spoke even less Spanish. The foreman or superintendent or whatever his rank was (he wore a white shirt as a badge of office), was a W.A.S.P. who spoke excellent English, no Spanish at all, and only passable sign language for use with his Cuban contingent. The whole situation tended to produce, in moments of crisis, something of a communication gap.

"White Shirt" soon realized his limitations, and retired to his office at the back. If they dropped that engine through the hull he wanted to be able to ask why they hadn't called him before touching it. That man would go far.

The way I saw it, if they were to drop it, and this seemed a distinct possibility, there was going to be a very nasty action for civil damages,

*Carlisle vs. M.R.B.Y. et al.*, with the only defence being that of contributory negligence. In other words, some smart lawyer would claim that I, simply by being present, had assumed control and was thus the author of my own misfortune. So I backed into the cabin, closed the door, and put the tape-recorder microphone to the ventilation grill. This would not only prove that I hadn't said a word, but should also have a certain entertainment value. That tape provides 25 minutes of grunts, bangs, thuds, groans, clangs and growls, all interspersed with a great many urgent requests, in Spanish patois, for increased caution, as well as an almost equal number of expressions and exhortations in what might loosely be described as basic English.

When it was all over I opened the door. There, sitting right where she was supposed to be, and resplendent in her bright yellow paint, was "Dolores the Diesel." In the shed a dozen glistening bodies were standing around the Coke machine, still panting as they pulled at their drinks, and explaining to each other how the whole operation could so easily have been improved.

A few days later we took *Caravel* down-river on a test run. She fired first time at a flick of the key. And oh, the sheer joy of an engine that continued to run, hour after hour, and that pushed us along, in rough water and smooth, with a solid, driving thrust!

We returned to Hardie's a happier crew, and Mary christened the engine Dolores, adding the words, "And may she always start when we need her!"

♥♥♥

## TROUBLE AT GUN CAY

It was now November, and the first phase of Operation Palm Tree was over. We had our boat and we had, after a fashion, learned to sail her. We had survived our first year afloat, and had covered nearly 2,000 miles. Now what?

The idea of an Atlantic crossing was an intriguing, if rather frightening, one. At no time had I suggested to anyone that we might try it, in case it fell through, and even with Kitty I had been vague on the subject. But what an achievement, if we could bring it off!

My mother was a widow in her 80's, living alone in the little Cornish village of St. Merryn, near Padstow, 30 miles along the north coast from Land's End. I hadn't seen her for several years and didn't know how long she would be with us. I put the matter to Kitty.

As a mere sailing adventure, she was against it. But as a means of letting my mother see the children and myself again, she thought it had merit. If I thought that we could make it in reasonable safety, she would cooperate willingly.

Could we? Who could tell? I had crossed the Atlantic several times before, but never in a small boat and never, in fact, as a seaman. From what I recalled of the northern route, during the war, it was a pretty bleak and stormy region. On the other hand, small craft had crossed it safely, and *Caravel* was supposed to be safer than most. Perhaps if we chose the longer, more southerly route, close to the Azores High, and away from the normal storm track along the westerlies. . . .

We bought a set of pilot charts for the North Atlantic, which are printed one for each month of the year. They show the winds, currents, percentage of gales and calms, temperatures and barometric pressures, ice limits, normal hurricane tracks, lines of magnetic variation, and even the major shipping lanes, plus a lot of other data essential to the navigator. They are based on thousands of observations by ships over many years, for each 5-degree section of ocean. It is thus possible to know, for any part of the ocean, not what the weather will be, of course, but at least what it has been, on average, over the years. With these charts one can plan more intelligently.

Our best route seemed to be from Miami, through the Northern Bahamas, and northeast to Bermuda, about 700 miles. The next 2,000 miles would be due east to the Azores Islands, and on this leg we could expect good weather and following winds along the northern edge of the Azores High. Then we would turn north until we found the westerlies, before turning in for England.

Of equal importance was the timing of the whole operation. The spring gales between Bermuda and the mainland were notorious, and we mustn't cross this "Dangerous Triangle," as it is called, too early. On the other hand, we must be well-clear of the hurricane track, east of Bermuda, before July. And we should approach the English Channel well before the autumn gales set in. It all boiled down to leaving in

73

April, and if we started soon we should be able to see the Bahamas on the way.

So it was decided. The children were told, but sworn to secrecy. At Hardie's we spoke only of a trip to the "islands," without specifying which ones. We bought a genoa sail for light airs and jerry cans for extra fuel. We coved the upper deck around the edge and drained the corners through plastic hose to form a water catchment system. We bought charts and a cheap, plastic sextant, a nautical almanac and some sight reduction tables. I studied Bowditch on how to use them. We made snap-on harnesses for use on deck, and swung the compass to check the deviation after installing the diesel. We drew up a list of supplies and food for 180 days. As far as possible, we felt that we were ready.

The closest of the Bahamas to Miami are Gun Cay and Cat Cay, twin islands about 45 miles across the Gulf Stream. But the trip across is not to be taken lightly. The Stream sweeps northward at up to 4½ knots, and you have to allow for considerable drift. You can aim south of your target point, and cross crabwise, or you can go south first and then aim straight across. We decided on the latter.

On November 26th we sailed south down Biscayne Bay in lovely weather, and anchored in the lee of Pumpkin Key, a small island.

I was too excited to sleep much, and at 2 a.m. the alarm rang. By 2:30 we were motoring out of Angelfish Creek, between the mangroves, and my mind went back to Black Caesar. This negro slave had escaped near here and built up his own, highly successful pirate gang, hiding out only a few hundred yards away in Caesar's Creek, until he was finally caught and strung up.

Suddenly the mangroves ended, and we were in open water. The full moon was just starting to sink behind us and hardly a breath of air disturbed the water as we motored on. I turned on the D.F. radio and the Bimini beacon came in by Morse, loud and clear (B-Z-Z).

The bearing was 065°, and as long as it stayed that way we were on course. If it increased to 070°, we were being set too far to the north by the current, and must turn to starboard.

Dawn appeared, and the sun rose ahead in a cloudless sky that soon turned blue. I tuned in Miami for the weather. "Wind southeasterly, five to ten knots, becoming variable later. Visibility unlimited." If only this could last to Padstow!

We trailed a line with a yellow feather, and soon had a 32½-inch

74

dolphin—not the mammal normally called a porpoise, but the fish of the same name. Within minutes he was on board, and was cleaned and ready for the pan.

At 11:40 a.m. we sighted the palms of Cat Cay, just south of Gun Cay, but not the land itself. These Bahamian cays are usually so low that by the time you see them you are within about five miles. Then we saw the red and white lighthouse on Gun Cay, and knew that our landfall was about right.

All the way across, the water had been deep, up to 3,000 feet, as clear as crystal and blue-black in colour. Suddenly, within a few hundred yards of the shore, the colour changed to a deep green, indicating only a few fathoms. The bottom had come up like the wall of a house. Then the green became lighter, and we could see the bottom in detail at five fathoms—30 feet—rocks, sand, coral, grass, even a can shimmering like a mirror.

At 1 p.m. we slid into Honeymoon Bay, the shallow bay on the west side of Gun Cay, and dropped the anchor 2 fathoms down into a patch of sand 100 yards across. We backed off to snub it in hard, and switched off the engine.

We were safely at anchor, swinging gently a mere 100 yards from a palm-studded shore, ringed with coral. We had reached our first Bahamian island, the first short step on the long passage across the ocean, and could relax before an early dinner. Plenty of time tomorrow to go through the narrow channel between Gun Cay and Cat Cay and enter customs at the little harbour on the east side of Cat Cay. Meanwhile, the light breeze was from the southeast, so this would be the sheltered side.

The evening weather from Miami spoke of the wind veering to the west, but remaining light. Good! It would help us along to Chub Cay, two days across the Great Bahama Bank to the east. After being up since 2 a.m., we turned in early and slept well.

At 4 a.m. I was awakened by *Caravel* plunging about rather a lot, and the wind moaning softly in the rigging. On deck it was light under the setting moon, but the wind had gone round to the northwest, and had increased to 20 knots. Being close to shore, even closer now that we had swung round on our anchor in the veering wind, the seas were building up rather badly. They probably didn't amount to much further out, but in the shoaling water they were beginning to break. The sooner

75

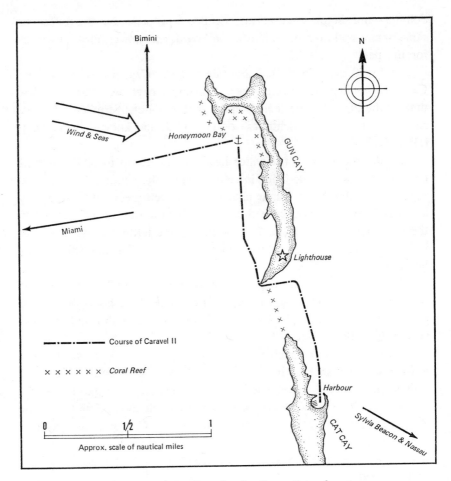

*Gun Cay and Cat Cay, showing* Caravel's *anchorage*

we got out of there, the better, for if we started to drag anchor we should be on that coral reef, now a mere 75 yards away and dead downwind.

On the other hand, the wind was already worse than forecast, so probably wouldn't rise any more. And I didn't fancy running that channel between the cays in the dark. There was a strong current through the narrow gap, and it was tricky enough in daylight. You had to aim at the southern tip of Gun Cay and then, when almost on the rocks, turn hard to starboard and round them only a few feet away. The water between the cays looked wide enough, but only the northern edge had

76

any depth. Once through the gap, you could swing to starboard and run down the eastern side of Cat Cay to the harbour. All in all, with daylight only 2 hours away, it made sense to wait.

But by 6 a.m. both wind and seas had risen considerably, and *Caravel* was in the middle of a solid mass of high, breaking surf. The combers were rolling in from the Gulf Stream, hitting the shallows, and building up into seas that, under other circumstances, would have been majestic. In the cold morning light, and on a lee shore, they were merely terrifying. They picked *Caravel* up and slammed her back against her single half-inch nylon line. This brought her to a shuddering stop and pulled her bow down into the next wave, which broke over her deck. We were thrown about unmercifully, the rudder hammering from side to side.

I was convinced that we were either going to drag anchor or snap the line, it being just a matter of which happened first. Either way, we should be flung against the reef in seconds, with its knife-edge of extremely hard, jagged coral which would tear us to shreds the moment we hit. *Caravel* was going to be wrecked, and we ourselves, the children, Kitty and I, should stand little or no chance of getting ashore alive, either in her or separated from her.

Then I was violently seasick!

I took a Dramamine pill and lay down, hoping to recover enough to think rationally and take some logical action. Kitty, who was not sick, then said that the steering cable in the chart-house had parted. If only I had lashed it earlier!

There could be no question of getting away without any steering, so I'd just have to hope that both anchor and line would hold until I could repair it. Staggering to the bosun's cupboard for tools, and to the port outrigger for cable, I set about repairing it.

It took me almost an hour to do a job which should have taken a quarter of that time, and every few minutes I had to climb the steps, lean over the side and vomit. The ship's movement, bad enough any-where, was exaggerated so far aft, and it was hot and stuffy. But eventually the work was done.

We confined the children to their bunks for they couldn't help any-way, and would be safer there in their life jackets. Kitty stood by and fetched tools or lent a hand, her face drawn and haggard.

Then we discussed strategy. I would start the engine and stay at the controls, ready to fight our way out the moment the anchor was free, for every second would then count. This meant that Kitty would have to raise the anchor. We arranged hand signals.

At 1,500 r.p.m. *Caravel* crept forward with power to spare, but the seas threw her off wildly and it was impossible to maintain a heading without full power, which caused us to override the anchor. So we did it a bit at a time, Kitty hauling in the slack and cleating it, pausing only to signal to me whether the line was running out to port or starboard. Then it was almost straight up and down, and she was pulling hard. She shook her head, indicating that it wouldn't break out, which was strange with the angle so steep and the bow jerking up and down. Puzzled, I left the wheel and went forward to help.

It was hopeless! So we fell back to the original position, and found that in the short time that I had been away from the wheel it had swung so violently to the end of its travel that another cable had parted. God, would I never learn? I started to vomit again, and set about the second repair.

Then I had a most unpleasant feeling.

For the moment, I knew what I had to do, and I had the strength to do it. I had to replace this damned cable, as fast as my aching fingers, broken nails and heaving stomach would allow. I had to get the thing fixed before we broke loose entirely and hit that bloody reef.

But quite suddenly, in a boat that was being flung about helplessly in the surf, with steering that kept failing, with an anchor that refused to come out, weak from overstrain and lack of sleep and violent seasickness, I lost confidence in my ability to take the steps necessary for the survival of us all. The pressure of outside events was becoming too great. If one more thing happened, just one more stupid, God-damned crisis to prevent me from following through with this simple plan ot action here in front of my eyes, I couldn't cope with it. My capacity for rational thought, for constructive ideas, had gone. I hadn't lost the will to survive—that was stronger than ever—but I had lost the capacity to do so. I was like a man, or animal for that matter, who sees death uncomfortably close and, as in a nightmare, lacks the strength to run or fight. I no longer had any reserves of physical or mental endurance, no resourcefulness. Death could very easily be just around the corner, and I was afraid that I might, if one more crisis occurred, lose my will to fight. I tried to shake off the feeling, to force myself to assume a dominance over events around me.

The job of replacing the cable seemed endless, but it was eventually finished. I lashed the wheel while we planned the next move.

If anything, the seas were now worse. They were running to 10 and 12 feet from trough to rolling crest, and while this may not sound too high, for wave-height figures tend to be unconsciously exaggerated, it must be remembered that these were not deep-water waves, several hundred feet long, but breaking surf, with a steep, leading face and tumbling crest. I couldn't imagine how that thin strand of nylon could stand the strain.

This time I would go forward myself, leaving Kitty at the controls. If the anchor broke free I would raise one hand in a circling motion, and she would at once go to maximum power and head straight out to sea, taking each wave head-on to reduce the yaw until I could secure the anchor and get aft to take over.

At 2,000 r.p.m. we forged ahead, but overrode the anchor, and I had to signal for a cut in power as I cleated in the slack. Gradually, a few feet at a time, I got the line in until it was almost straight up and down again, the angle at which no anchor should hold the bottom. I expected to feel the slack at any moment, and hoped that Kitty would be able to bring the bow up in time, before we fell back onto the reef.

But it still refused to break out. The bow was heaving 6 to 10 feet with every sea, and I had to kneel astride the jib boom and hold the forestay as the seas threw me upwards and sideways and the line jerked the boat to a stop.

Then came a brief lull, and I heaved in more line with all my strength. It *had* to come out, damn it! It was only a lousy 22-pound Danforth. I got in another 6 inches and cleated it as the bow fell off into a trough. Now the line was holding the bow down, not letting it rise fully. The seas were breaking on board, soaking me and forcing me to hold on grimly. I ceased to care whether the line held or not. If it parted, so much the better! I'd just signal Kitty to take her away.

Down went the bow, and I got in another few inches. Up again—POW! Down again! Up again! More slack. Cleat it! Up! POW! Down again into a deeper trough! I held the line with my left hand and tried to cleat it with my right, but before I could get it off the cleat the bow

79

jerked up again, higher than before. The line whipped taut, like a steel cable, not through the chock, for it had jumped out, but over the side of the bow and straight down into the boiling surf, *pinning my left thumb and third finger to the edge of the deck!*

Time stood still. Everything happened in slow motion. There was no pain. I didn't try to move them or pull them out, for it was obviously impossible. I just stared at them, fascinated. Then the tips of both thumb and fingers swelled up to twice their normal size, like overripe grapes, and simply burst wide open.

The bow went down again, and the line went slack. With my right hand I picked it up and put it into the chock. Then I picked up my left hand with my right, as though it were an inanimate object.

Both tips were hanging down by shreds of skin.

There was still no pain, not even shock. A sickening sort of horror, perhaps, and unbelievable surprise. Then the thought came to me that, although severed, they still belonged to me, were still a part of my own body. I mustn't drop them overboard. With my right hand I placed them carefully in my left palm and folded the hand over them in a primitive, animal desire to protect my body from further violation.

Then I remembered how it had happened, and why. The anchor, the boat, the reef — they were still with me. This hadn't solved anything, hadn't wiped anything out. It had simply made things far worse. It was the added crisis that I had dreaded.

Strangely enough, I began to think more rationally, with a detachment that I hadn't known before. All right, if the anchor was as firmly embedded as all that, let it stay there! Where was the problem?

The other anchor, a 25-pound CQR Plow, was already on deck, with 4 fathoms of chain and 100 feet of nylon line attached. Better get it down now, as extra insurance.

These thoughts went through my mind in far less time than it takes to tell them. My hand was bleeding, but not much, and to reduce the flow I held it shoulder-high and rose to my feet, my right hand holding a forestay for support. As I did so, another sea hit us, and I was thrown hard to starboard, round in an arc, backwards, until the pulpit rail hit the back of my thighs. My arm was twisted backwards, but I managed to keep a grip on the quarter-inch steel cable, while my feet groped blindly for something solid.

There was nothing, for I was over the water. But even as I decided

80

that I was going into the sea, the bow lurched back again, flinging my body round the way it had come, and I landed in a heap with my shins crashing down onto the metal jib boom and my right hand now groping for a hold on the hard, wet folds of the furled Dacron jib.

In the cockpit, Kitty knew nothing of my fingers, for it had all happened below her line of vision. But she did see me grab the forestay, stand up, and be thrown overboard. She was convinced that I had gone completely, and knew that my chances of survival were zero, it being only a question of whether I should drown or last long enough to be smashed to pieces and cut to ribbons on the coral. Then she saw me thrown back onto the deck, like a sack of potatoes.

She was even more mystified, a few seconds later, when I got my breath back and the pain in my shins had subsided a little, to see me on hands and knees on the starboard bow, heaving the CQR over with one hand and giving what looked like a left-handed communist salute with the other. I crawled back, slowly and carefully, and she realized, from my ghost-like expression, that something was very wrong.

As she came out to help me below, I told her that I had just lost a finger and thumb.

Nora, her head framed in the galley door, heard me and simply broke into uncontrollable sobs. Mary, older and more determined, turned pale and bit her lip, but she didn't cry. I dropped onto a seat in the cabin. Kitty looked ten years older, but tried to stay very calm. We had to decide what to do next.

Nora clung to me, buried her face against me, and sobbed.

♛♛♛

## CHOPPER TO MOUNT SINAI

As far as *Caravel* was concerned, we decided that no action was either necessary or possible. The danger of dragging had probably never been great in the first place, and when Kitty checked the weather she reported that the wind seemed to be veering fractionally, that is moving clockwise. This is normal in the Bahamas, for when the wind does leave the usual trade-wind direction of southeast, it almost invariably goes right round the clock through south, west and north, dying out in the east again. She also thought that we were getting a slight lee from another reef running west from the northern tip of the island. This would tend to reduce the seas somewhat, and it was these, rather than the wind itself, that were the real danger.

Fortunately I was no longer seasick, and was able to think more rationally and in medical terms.

Tetanus! Not much danger there. I had had shots recently.

Infection! That could be bad, especially with bones involved. Penicillin! I still didn't have the injectable kind, but pills were better than nothing. A million units? Make it one and a half. Mary got the bottle and I took four tablets.

Antiseptic? Better do something, after all the filth I'd been handling. Dettol? That was an English brand that seemed suitable. Kitty made up a solution and I dipped in the entire hand. There was still no pain, and very little bleeding. No shock, either, as far as I could judge.

For some reason, probably nervous reaction, I began to joke about it all. I looked under the table and asked if anyone had seen any fingers around. I didn't feel funny — far from it! And I didn't feel brave or tough or anything else, except maybe sick down inside, from the sheer horror of it all. I didn't get any laughs, either, and they looked at me with drawn faces. Nora was chewing her lip to hold back the sobs, and I told them to look away while I bathed the fingers. They did so, and I wished that I could have done the same.

I bound the tips back in place, as though I expected them to grow back where they belonged. Somehow it seemed the right place for them. Then I bound the fist, with Kitty helping. Mary made coffee on a stove that was still bouncing around alarmingly, and Nora was staring up at me with her big, tear-stained eyes and an expression that I shall remember for a very long time.

That was the limit of my surgical skill. What I needed now was a doctor — medical advice.

The radio! I remembered that they had stand-by medical advice facilities on the marine band. I switched to 2,182 kHz.

"Miami Coast Guard — Canadian yacht *Caravel II*, Victor Charlie 5723. Come in, please."

"*Caravel II* — Coast Guard Radio Miami. Go ahead."

I explained the situation and asked for advice. They reached a doctor by phone and relayed the information that there was nothing more I could do, but I should see a doctor within 12 hours. I asked where the nearest one was. There were doctors at Bimini, Nassau and Miami.

Bimini was the nearest, but it was up-wind and had a difficult entrance, especially in bad weather and with one hand. The others were too far away. They said they would try to trace a nearer one, if there was one, and to stand by on this frequency.

It was beginning to look as though we should have to rely on our own meagre resources, and I knew just enough about gangrene to be scared. I wondered about sewing them on. The chances of saving them seemed almost nil, but there was nothing to lose. I asked Kitty if she thought she could do it. She obviously dreaded the prospect, but braced herself.

"I guess so, if necessary. What about an anaesthetic?"

That thought had already occurred to me.

"We don't have much — no local or anything I'm afraid. We have Demerol and a syringe. That should reduce the general pain level, and there isn't much feeling in them yet anyway. You can always stop if it gets too bad."

For the rest, we were reasonably well-equipped. We had dressings, a tube of neomycin antibiotic, antiseptics, a sterile strip pack of surgical needles and thread, alcohol — everything except Xylocaine for a local. Well, in Nelson's day they got you good and sloshed on rum before an operation. Demerol should at least be better than that.

Mary boiled some water while Nora collected bowls, towels and lots of Kleenex. We laid things out on the cabin table, and rehearsed the whole thing verbally. The children were to stand by, but were to avoid watching if possible. Kitty started to wash her hands vigorously, while I read up on Demerol in a pamphlet that contained a long list of contra-indications, which I took to be "Don'ts." These seemed to relate to people who shouldn't get it and places it shouldn't go, most of which were in Latin. I had to assume that I wasn't on the short list of ineligibles, and that the upper arm was okay to inject. I began to wish it was tomorrow, or better still, yesterday. For someone who is scared of the dentist, the next hour wasn't going to be fun.

"*Caravel II* — Coast Guard Radio Miami!"

I grabbed the microphone, glad of a reprieve.

"There are no doctors closer than Bimini. We have a helicopter out now, and are diverting it to your position. The pilot will call you on this frequency. Please stand by."

A HELICOPTER! They were sending a helicopter! We just couldn't believe it. We were going to get help, a doctor. We all laughed with sheer joy and relief, the four of us chattering at once. We cleared the table, glad to get the stuff out of sight and forget about the Ben Casey bit.

If we all went, *Caravel* would be left unattended, and heaven only knew when we could get back to her. Yet if only I went, Kitty and the children would be left here alone, which was unthinkable.

"Look," I said. "We can't just abandon *Caravel* here, and we can't leave you three on board alone. We'll have to cut loose and get round to Cat Cay. You'll be safe there, tied up in the harbour. And they can land the chopper, too, which will be a lot easier than airlifting me from the deck here in a sling."

It made sense.

Then we heard the rattling throb of the helicopter overhead. Kitty took one look at it and burst into tears. The realization that human help was at hand, that the entire resources of the United States Coast Guard were now available to us, was just too much for her.

I discussed the plan with the pilot, who agreed to land at Cat Cay and wait for us. He made a climbing turn and was away.

We started the diesel and were in the process of buoying both anchors to let them go when we discovered that the Danforth was free, and Kitty hauled it on deck with no trouble at all. We cast off the CQR and I gunned the engine to 2,000 r.p.m. *Caravel* yawed badly as a sea hit her, but recovered under full power, and soon we were beyond the breakers and in deeper water. The wind had definitely eased in the past hour or so.

When I saw the Danforth on deck, the mystery was solved. The thing hadn't been buried at all, but jammed under coral. One fluke was twisted like a pretzel, and the steel had torn like cardboard. No wonder my fingers had gone, if the pressure had been enough to tear steel like that. Apparently since I had put down the CQR the Danforth had broken free without warning, and we had ridden to the Plow. We could easily have gone onto the reef after all, and just when I had decided that we were relatively safe!

84

Kitty was now conning from the bow as we approached the narrow channel between the cays. We skirted the rocks close in, as directed in the Cruising Guide to the Bahamas, and felt the backwash tugging at us as we entered the gap. I increased power, for better steerage, and we went through easily enough, even with one hand. Down the lee side of Cat Cay the water was strangely calm after the tumult on the western side, and we were soon entering the little harbour.

Inside the breakwater I turned for the old wooden pier, badly damaged in a recent hurricane, and saw a group of figures on it. Willing hands took our lines and John Saunders, the customs officer, helped me ashore. Mary had already packed an overnight bag for me, with pyjamas, toothbrush, shaving kit, and a bar of chocolate, the most eloquent "Get Well Quick" gift that she could think of.

Helicopter 1375 was only a few yards away, and after perhaps 30 seconds on shore, which must surely go down in the books as the shortest Bahamian cruise on record, I stepped inside. The motor started, the rotor began to turn, and we were airborne. A crewman closed the sliding door.

"Have you any preference for hospitals?"

I couldn't have cared less.

"Okay, we'll make it Mount Sinai. They've got a heliport there, and we can put you down at the door."

As they radioed ahead, I looked out the port window. There was Caravel at the quay, with three rather forlorn figures near her, all holding hands and staring up at the helicopter as it wheeled around to the west. They fell rapidly astern, and grew smaller.

Forty minutes later we landed on the lawn outside the emergency entrance to Mount Sinai, where a small crowd had already gathered. It included several nurses, two reporters, a photographer, a few spectators, and Dr. Lamphier, a hand surgeon.

Sixty seconds later I was on an operating table, with the surgeon carefully undoing the bandages.

The events that followed can be covered briefly for, like every other stay in hospital, it was a matter of deep concern to Kitty, the girls and myself, but of far less interest to others. It is enough to say that both tips were stitched in place, and that the finger grafted successfully. For the thumb, however, there seemed to be insufficient blood flow, and it

85

eventually shrivelled and died. It turned gangrenous, and had to be removed, or "revised," as they so delicately put it, about 2 months later.

Kitty, of course, was marooned at Cat Cay, with no money. She had travellers' cheques, but they were in my name and not endorsed. So she used her head.

First she radioed the Coast Guard and learned where they had taken me. Then she put through a radio telephone call to me in the hospital, learned that I should be there for at least a week, and asked what I thought of her bringing *Caravel* back, provided she could get a local Bahamian as crew. I was dubious, but felt that the decision should be hers. If the weather was all right, she might as well come, where she would be back at Hardie's among friends.

A Bahamian agreed to come across with her for a fee of $15 plus another $15 for his air fare back, and before dawn on December 1st they set out. She wanted to pick up the buoyed CQR on the way, but he said he would collect it later with his dinghy and keep it for her.

They were hardly out of sight of land before he said the $15 fee wasn't high enough. He wanted $45 plus his air fare. No reason. He just wanted three times the agreed price.

A man would probably have invited him to swim back if he had changed his mind, but Kitty, with the children in mind, was scared of him and realized that he was a crook if not worse. If he turned nasty, *Caravel* could disappear into the Everglades or to some uninhabited cay, with nobody any the wiser. So she agreed to his new price and went below, leaving him at the wheel. With the cabin door closed and the diesel only inches below his feet, he could hear little. She turned on the radio, called Miami Coast Guard, and gave them her time of departure, course, speed, and E.T.A. at Miami. If *Caravel* didn't arrive at Government Cut by the E.T.A., would they look for her? They would!

Then she opened the cabin door and announced what she had done. He glowered at her, asked why she had thought that necessary, and said not another word all the way across. Every few minutes she checked the compass from the corner of her eye, but it never left 225°. The Miami Beach skyline appeared on schedule, and as they tied up alongside she called the Coast Guard again to confirm *Caravel*'s safe arrival. The crewman took his $60 and she never saw him again.

When she heard nothing about the anchor she wrote to John Saunders, the customs officer, who knew the crewman and questioned

86

him for her. It wasn't there when he returned, the Bahamian reported—must have been those Cuban fishermen who sometimes take shelter in the bay!

We bought a new anchor and chain, but the thumb was irreplaceable. And plans for an Atlantic crossing had to be postponed for a while.

When the first shock of the accident had worn off, I tried to decide what, if anything, we could learn from the event. Had it been due to negligence, or lack of experience, or bad luck, or a bit of all three? Certainly if I had gone to Cat Cay on the afternoon of the 27th, instead of anchoring in Honeymoon Bay, nothing would have happened, and I wished that I had done so. But Honeymoon Bay is a recognized and widely used anchorage, recommended as such in the Cruising Guide. Also, on the afternoon of the 27th it was on the sheltered side of the islands. It was not until 7:15 p.m., after dark, that there was any mention of a wind shift, and even then the forecast had been merely for "light winds, becoming westerly." Certainly this did not seem to justify trying to run the channel in the dark, with the risk of hitting the rocks.

Was I wrong to try so desperately the next morning to raise the anchor and move out? We did not, in fact, drag anchor. But then there seemed to be a good chance that we might, without warning, and the sight of that coral, right under our lee, was just too much to contemplate. I felt that the decision to move out was a sound one.

Why, then, had I not simply cut the anchor loose, buoying it for recovery later or even just letting it go? This decision isn't so easy to justify, in retrospect, but at the time it had seemed logical enough. The anchor was the only thing holding us off the reef, and I wasn't at all sure that I could hold the ship's head up to sea if we cut loose. Had I failed to do so, and been swept back those few yards onto the coral, it would have been tantamount to suicide and manslaughter. I just couldn't bring myself to cut that life line, even though I was trying frantically to raise the anchor, which amounted almost to the same thing.

There seems little doubt but that a combination of many factors, lack of sleep, long hours of tension, fear, frustration over the steering cables, violent and prolonged seasickness and a general breakdown of moral fibre, all contributed to preventing me from thinking as objectively and clinically as I should. Immediately before the accident my entire attention had been focused on one thing—the anchor! It had developed

87

into a life and death struggle between that piece of steel and myself, and I could see no further than that. I had to pull it out of the sea bed by sheer, brute strength — the lives of four people depended on my doing just that. My mind was insanely concentrated on this one thing, and had ceased to look for other more rational alternatives.

An experienced skipper, reading this account now, can doubtless suggest errors that I made. For instance, I had become embayed — cardinal sin of the sea. Over the centuries this has led to the loss of hundreds of ships and thousands of lives. If a sailing captain lost his vessel in this way, unable to fight his way out of a bay against headwind and breaking seas, he would probably never get another command even if he himself survived. I had made this mistake and we had all come out of it alive, at the cost of only a thumb.

But it must never happen again.

Where did we go from here? Was this a warning that I was attempting too much? We decided that it was not, and that we should try again, but should also profit from the experience. *Caravel* was still a well-designed and well-built boat. She was also well-equipped, and no corners had been cut in fitting her out for such a voyage. We were not, as was the case with so many would-be ocean travellers, doing it on a shoestring and in a vessel that was inadequately found. If attention to detail and a conservative approach meant anything, we should be safe. And there was still plenty of time, even after a delay of several months in Miami. By the spring I felt capable of handling *Caravel* once more, and we planned our second departure.

We revictualled, did some additional fitting out as new ideas occurred to us, replaced the 25-pound CQR with a 35-pound one, for increased holding power, and by spring we were ready again.

On April 3rd we crossed Biscayne Bay and anchored in No-Name Cove. Why I decided to leave from here, instead of from Angelfish Creek again, I don't know, unless it was due to a psychological fear of taking the same route that we had in November. We made one other change, too, and while we still joke about it, who can say that we weren't half-serious? In November we had sailed on a Friday; this time it was on a Monday.

This attitude, of course, is just silly superstition. Any sane, rational, clear-thinking landsman will tell you that.

At 6 a.m. next day we were under way, passing through Biscayne Channel, between groups of those incredible houses on stilts in the

88

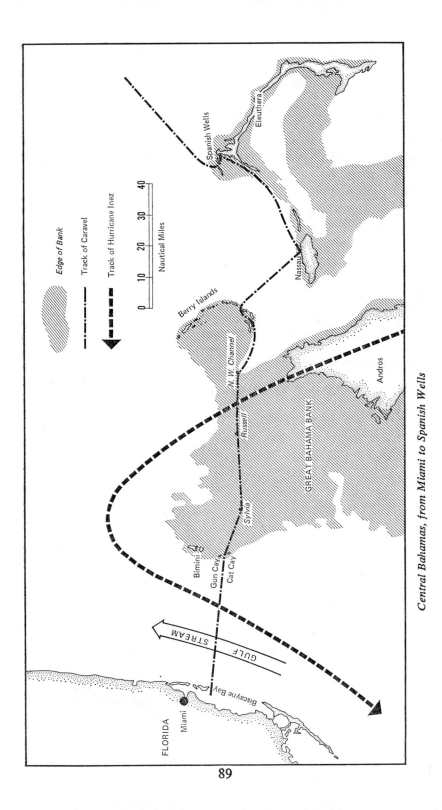

*Central Bahamas, from Miami to Spanish Wells*

shallow waters of the reef, a mile or so from land. How they survive hurricanes, and whether anyone stays out there during one, I don't know. At 8 a.m. we took our departure from Fowey Light in a gentle south-easter.

We raised the Gun Cay Lighthouse, not without a faint shudder of distaste, at 4:10 p.m., and by the time we reached it daylight was fading, but we went through anyway. I'd have done so in a pea-soup fog before facing another night in Honeymoon Bay. It was almost pitch dark as we slid into the little harbour at Cat Cay and dropped the hook.

John Saunders cleared us next morning, and asked about events since "Black Monday." I told him of our plans, and he sent us on our way with a warm handshake, heading southeast for Sylvia Beacon, the first navigational point on the journey across the Great Bahama Bank.

# WESTWARD BOUND

## ⱱⱱⱱ

## OF CONCHS AND COVES AND CORAL REEFS

The trip across the bank is some 60 miles, a slow one for an auxiliary yacht. The base course is E.S.E., which is smack into the prevailing wind, so you either tack or power. Either way you find yourself fighting the short, steep seas that build up in anything over a light breeze. Fortunately, although there are no cays or islands on the way across, land is never very far away—7 feet, in fact, straight down! The Great Bahama Bank, rising sheer from the ocean bed several miles below, tries hard to become an island, but just fails to make it except at a few points round the edge, such as Cat Cay, Gun Cay and Bimini in the west, the Berry Islands to the east, and the big island of Andros to the south. So you don't have to stay up all night when crossing the bank. When you feel sleepy, you lower your hook and simply turn in.

At 9 a.m. we raised Russell Beacon, and shortly afterwards the engine temperature shot up and we had to switch off in a hurry. The raw-water pump drive shaft had sheared, and we plodded on under sail in a light breeze. By 6 p.m., Russell was still visible astern. We got discouraged and decided to anchor for the night.

In the morning there was still no wind, and I seemed to be left with little alternative but to get my hands dirty. With a hand-operated bilge pump I managed to feed sea water through the heat exchanger and keep the temperature down to normal, provided we didn't exceed 1,500 r.p.m. With our badly-fouled bottom this gave us a mere 3 knots, but this was better than standing still, even if it did mean taking turns on the bilge pump.

Northwest Channel Beacon went by slowly, and it was 2 p.m. before we could see the round ball of the water tower at the Crown Colony Club at Chub Cay, at the southern end of the Berry Group. Soon we were at anchor in the 200-yard wide channel between Chub Cay and Rhoda Cay, in about 6 feet over sand. It was a well-sheltered and delightful spot, with several sandbanks that dried out at low tide — a perfect place to beach *Caravel* and to scrape and paint her bottom, between tides. We had the copper paint on board for just such an opportunity.

93

Exploring by dinghy and by wading, we found a suitable spot, and cleared it of conch shells, which abounded on the bottom and which are big enough, hard enough and knobbly enough to do a ½-inch plywood skin no good if we sat on them on a falling tide. We jammed stakes into the sand to act as range markers, so that we could bring *Caravel* to the identical spot at high tide.

In the morning it was a bit windy for the operation, so I worked on the water pump instead, repairing the coupling with a filed-down bolt, and securing it with epoxy resin. We had power again.

On the 10th the weather was perfect, and we eased *Caravel* carefully into position. When she touched bottom we carried out anchors to hold her there. Within minutes she began to settle in the falling tide, and with all personnel in swim suits and armed with scrapers we attacked the barnacles viciously. Long before low water the scraping was complete, and the water around our feet thick with barnacles. Tiny fish swam fearlessly between our ankles, gorging themselves on the free meal.

Then we started to slap on the thick copper paint with 4-inch brushes. It is made to go on between tides, and can be immersed the moment it is on. We did the keel area first, and then came up in a series of spirals in a race against the tide. By high water *Caravel* had a clean and painted bottom, even if the water line was a bit wiggly in places, and the net result was an extra knot under way.

Kitty has always objected to the expression "Cleaning Her Bottom," and wanted to know if there wasn't some other phrase that would convey the same idea and yet sound less biological in mixed company. There isn't. The term is as old as sailing, and if you studiously put it another way you only make things worse.

As a matter of fact, there is another expression which bothers her even more, and which she flatly refuses to use. We have a refrigerator on board which works on Propane. Unfortunately, some countries don't have Propane and use Butane instead. It seems to be similar, but is stored in tanks with fittings of a different type. This can be a problem if, as we did, you travel through various countries and want to fill your tanks. To overcome it, I decided to have an adaptor made up in brass, so that I could always fill our Propane tanks with Butane. I made up a drawing of the necessary item and, as Kitty was going ashore for groceries anyway, asked her to drop it off at the machine shop down the road and have them make it up for us. She took the drawing, pleased at having been entrusted with such a highly technical mission.

"Just ask them to make it up as it shows here, with the female thread at this end and the male one at the other, so that. . . ."

"With the *what* sort of thread?"

"The female one! The male is at the other end, to convert. . . ."

A horrible thought seemed to strike her.

"And what exactly is the difference between a male thread and a female one?"

"Well, you see, the male one has the thread on the outside, like a machine screw, and fits into the female thread."

She nodded. Obviously I had confirmed her worst suspicions.

"Do you seriously expect me to go up to some strange man in a machine shop and ask him for a disgusting thing like that? I suppose this is one of your nasty Air Force expressions, is it?"

"Of course not," I protested. "Well, I suppose it is, really, only not the way you think. It's a perfectly normal engineering expression — old as the hills. Look, I'll show you in the fitters' manual."

But I couldn't convince her—never have! She would give the man my message, and would give him the drawing. But she would not discuss sex with some grinning machinist's mate.

In the shop the burly mechanic took a look at the drawing, sucked his teeth, and nodded.

"This end," explained Kitty, selecting her words with great care and precision, "is to be threaded to fit a Butane regulator, and the other end has to fit a Propane tank."

"Sure, lady, I got it okay. This end is for Propane, with a male thread, and this is for Butane, with a female, right?"

She gulped, blushed, nodded and hurried into the street, convinced that all men were alike.


Nassau was only 35 miles away, but we decided to take in a few of the Berry Islands on the way, for they should be worth the short detour. They form a long, curving chain running east from Chub Cay, then turning northeast, and finally through north to northwest. If we cut across from Chub Cay, roughly northeast, we should hit the middle of the chain, and could then run southeast to Nassau.

The difficulty is that this crescent-shaped chain forms the eastern edge of the Great Bank. Westward of the islands, that is on the bank itself, the water averages 3 feet in depth, while on the outside, east of the islands, it drops off to 3 miles. The inside route is shorter, more

95

sheltered, and infinitely more beautiful. But if you are sailing in anything much deeper than an 8-inch pie plate you are going to run into difficulties. The official guide indicates a dog-leg route across the bank, and allegedly affords 4 feet or more all the way. I suggest that in their next edition they amend this to read 2½ feet. We draw 3, and that proved too much.

We followed the prescribed route religiously, taking bearings exactly as instructed. As we cleared Frazer's Cay the water was a pale, watery green, indicating about 5 feet. In places it was flat calm, and it was literally impossible to see the water at all. A floating leaf seemed to be hanging mid-air, its own shadow sharply defined on the bottom. The sky was blue, with just the odd puff of summer cumulus, like cotton batting, here and there. The air was hot and still, but not at all humid. Away on the horizon, to the north and west, were some low-lying cays, sometimes a mere smudge on the water, sometimes a cluster of palms. This was Bahamian sailing at its best.

Several times we touched bottom as the water shoaled, the keel hissing gently over the sand. Once we stopped altogether, our sails drooping. This, I thought, was a good chance to photograph *Caravel* under full sail, something you can't often do with your own boat. So we put out the dinghy and, with the camera round my neck, I rowed a few yards away and got the shot I wanted. Then Mary shouted in consternation.

"Daddy, Daddy! We're moving—hurry up!"

They were, too. *Caravel*'s sails had filled in a puff of wind, and she was already off on a close reach under jib, main and mizzen. I pulled hard, while the children danced around and advised increased speed. Only Kitty was doing something constructive, like reaching out with a boat-hook, which I managed to grab before I ran out of steam. Someone took the painter, and I clambered on deck.

Shortly afterwards we slid into a bay on Bond's Cay, which was uninhabited, and waded ashore to explore. It was a beautiful beach, of virgin coral sand, and backed by semi-tropical growth beyond.

Within the hour we were away again, and by late afternoon had rounded the northern tip of Alder Cay, to enter a lagoon roughly circular and about 400 yards across. It was almost landlocked, and the shore was partly fine, powdery sand, lapped by ripples of water, and partly coral, with fantastically hard, needle-sharp edges. Wading or swimming along the shore, with face mask and snorkel, we could see conchs and other shells on the bottom, and hundreds of small, gaily-coloured fish.

The children had a wonderful time, beachcombing and collecting shells, while I wandered off to explore the island. It was a bare 20 feet or so high, and covered with coarse grass, cactus, creeper and a few palms. It was a breeding ground for noddies and terns, who took a poor view of my intrusion near their nests. Circling above me and shrieking in protest, they dived at me in a threatening manner, always from behind. They never actually touched me, but always seemed on the point of doing so.

Strolling back towards the others, I saw the unmistakable outline of a shark, 30 feet out, and about 8 to 10 feet long. It was moving towards the children with a slow, almost disinterested grace, and was about 75 yards away when I shouted a warning.

"You folks want to see this? There's a shark coming towards you."

On previous occasions, when we have called them in from swimming to supper, the elapsed time between the original order and their reaching dry land ranged from 45 to 90 minutes. Today, however, as close as I could judge without the stopwatch, they made it in about 1.4 seconds.

The shark, apparently much alarmed at the sudden commotion, made off for deeper water.

That was the end of swimming for the day. But unfortunately they had already collected a dozen or so live conchs, of which they wanted to keep the shells as gifts for people back home.

Possibly you have seen a conch, if only as a shelf ornament or adorning a front lawn. It is a huge shellfish, 8 inches or more across, and shaped like an old-fashioned bell-tent with an opening down the side, but closed across the bottom. The fellow can actually propel himself along by doing push-ups and then toppling forward an inch or so. As a means of transportation it leaves much to be desired, for his cruising speed seems to be only a few inches an hour.

The Bahamians consider the large Queen Conch a delicacy, but to extract the meat they have to knock a hole in the end at just the right spot, insert a knife, and cut loose the muscle by which the creature firmly attaches itself to his shell. Then out he falls. However, I was expected by Mary and Nora to remove the meat without defacing the shell. Well, I'm no marine biologist, but before I was through I could have written a treatise on the conch, believe me!

The only part of his body that you can see looks like a piece of rubbery tongue. It comes out, but the instant you touch it, it backs in again. Grab a piece, with a pair of long-nosed electrician's pliers, and he simply cuts his losses by retreating, leaving you with the tiniest bit of meat. He seems to be a slow learner, and within ten seconds is out again, asking for more trouble.

Even at that it isn't easy to get a piece of him, for his reaction time is amazing. What you don't grab in the first split fraction of a second just isn't there any more.

After 20 minutes or so it was apparent that I was getting nowhere. Ninety percent of conch number one was unscathed, and I hadn't even slowed him down. There must be lots of him in there that I'd never reach anyway.

Okay, let's starve him out! When he died, I'd get at him with some bent wire, at my leisure. I put them all on the top deck, until morning.

Well, it didn't work out that way, for conchs are determined creatures. During the night they started to march towards the water and home. Between the 12 of them, weighing upwards of a pound, they set up quite a racket on the plywood deckhead, as each one raised itself a couple of inches and then collapsed. After a two-minute rest he was off again. That adds up to 2,880 kerplunks in an 8-hour shift.

By morning they were scattered far and wide over the upper deck, although none had the necessary cruising range to reach the water. I put them back amidships, and waited. It took them about 48 hours to die, but when the last one stopped marching I thought I had won. But conchs, I found, don't give up when they die—far from it! They were still firmly attached inside, and no amount of prodding with bits of coat-hanger wire did any good. It's like trying to pull a cabbage out of the ground by tugging at the edge of one leaf with a pair of eyebrow tweezers. I slept on the problem.

Next day they changed their tactics and went onto the offensive, using C.B.W. (Chemical and Biological Warfare). By noon you could hardly get close to them. The stench of a two-day old conch, after lying in state on the top deck in the Bahamian sun, is something that is neither easily described nor soon forgotten.

Kitty was all for dumping the lot overboard, and the children were rapidly coming round to the same point of view. But after all this I hated to admit defeat. Holding my nose, I bundled them up in some old netting and dangled them overboard. The marine micro-organisms would soon do what I couldn't.

98

Next morning, trailing a bundle of dead conchs, we set sail for Nassau. It was an uneventful trip, and by mid-afternoon we were anchored at East Bay, near to Potter's Cay.

To judge from the number of cruise ships which arrive at Nassau, disgorging hundreds of pink-skinned tourists with jingling pockets into Bay Street, with its Straw Market and its night clubs, its gift shops and its allegedly duty-free liquor stores (they are not duty-free at all), the city must be a very popular tourist spot—if you happen to like popular tourist spots. We don't. They all, from Antibes to Waikiki, try to squeeze every last dollar from the tourist before he goes back home. Nassau is at least as bad as most in this respect.

But it does have one redeeming feature of interest to the cruising yachtsman. It is a good place to victual up, at least for certain items. We had done most of our buying in Miami, but had left certain things for Nassau because we thought that the British import would be cheaper or better. Some items should definitely be bought from a British source, rather than from an American, and these include:

*Full Cream* Powdered Milk, Nestlé's Nespray or Nido (Instant)

Biscuits (Sweet or plain, including crackers)

Jams and Preserves, as well as sauces and sandwich spreads

Canned Meat (Better quality, more variety, and cheaper than the American)

Flour (Canadian Bread Flour or All-Purpose makes much better bread than does either the U.S. or British.)

Freeze-Dried Vegetables (The British make excellent peas, beans and carrots in this form. They are cheap, light and keep well. The Irish make good freeze-dried cabbage, too. "Vesta" freeze-dried dishes such as curried dinners are very good to have on board.)

Canned Fruits, such as gooseberries, plums and other soft fruits are good and inexpensive.

Generally speaking, we find that in the Bahamas, as in other British Islands, British products are a better buy than American, possibly due to a preferential tariff. Butter from Holland and West Germany, obviously subsidized for export, is usually ridiculously cheap outside of Continental North America, where we are apparently not allowed to see it. Bahamian bread is out of this world, but unfortunately doesn't keep well.

Not wanting to leave Nassau with the conchs still trailing astern, I hauled them in and discovered that apparently the micro-organisms

99

didn't like the smell any more than we did. However, I did discover that several bits of meat, if you could still describe it as such, had begun to fall away. With a bit more shaking and poking I got the rest out. And finally, although the shells still stank, they were at least empty. An overnight soaking in chlorine bleach helped, and after being sprayed with deodorant and left on the fantail for a couple of days, it was possible to wrap them in old sacking and stow them in the port outrigger, up in the bow behind the things we hardly ever used.

We took jerry cans ashore to top up our diesel and water supply at a service station. The Negro attendant asked if we were going on a trip, and I nodded.

"To Bermuda."

He stared at *Caravel* for a few seconds.

"In that?"

There's nothing like a few words of encouragement when you are beset with your own private fears, is there?

On April 22nd we sailed E.N.E. along the line of cays, and two days later were at anchor in the snug little harbour at Spanish Wells. It was from here that we were to leave for Bermuda.

Spanish Wells is about as much like Nassau as Dry Gulch, Wyoming is like New York City. There is one filling station (but very few cars to fill) and several stores. Most of these are private homes with the stock laid out on a table in the front room. The bank opens two days a week, and there is no public transportation because there is no place to go. There is no airport either, although the mailboat does come in from Nassau. The power station consists of a diesel generator in a wooden shed, and one night, when the fuel filter got clogged, Spanish Wells went to bed early, and in the dark.

The place got its name from the fact that the Spaniards used to call in for water on their way home, and it is a warm, friendly and delightful place to relax. There is no Negro population, which is strange for the Bahamas, and most of the locals seem to be called Pinder, which gets rather confusing.

A mile or two north of the island is a coral reef, and inside this the water was calm, a beautiful shade of emerald green, and about 6 feet deep. Beyond it, the bottom drops off vertically to nearly 3 miles.

Far to the north, off the New England coast, a spring gale lashed the sea into a fury, and while the winds did not reach this far south, the

100

residual swell did. Measuring hundreds of yards from crest to crest, this was harmless in open water, for although each swell moved at about 30 knots and contained tens of thousands of horsepower, the vertical movement was slow. Even a dinghy would hardly notice it.

But when such a swell approaches a coast, it starts to rise. And when that coast is a solid wall, several miles high and with its coral top awash, the result is simply terrifying. The leading face of the swell rises and steepens until it becomes a vertical wall of water, hurtling forward with unbelievable force. When it reaches a certain point it can no longer support its own gargantuan weight, and collapses like an avalanche, spending its incredible energy in one final roar that can be heard several miles away. Huge rocks are picked up and tossed into the air like tennis balls, and the ground itself shudders under the impact. Not even the largest ship could survive.

In the Bahamas such conditions are known as a "rage," and from a vantage point atop an old wooden tower we watched this one, through binoculars. Even from several miles away the rollers seemed gigantic, and we stared in horrified fascination for minutes on end, without speaking, unable to understand how the island itself could long survive such a pounding. We were very subdued as we came down from the tower and bumped into Aziel Pinder, a local fisherman. He warned us not to leave Spanish Wells till he gave the okay. I promised.

That night, over the radio, we heard that a large power cruiser had tried to enter Nassau that afternoon during the "rage." It was flipped end over end, and they were still looking for the bodies.

It was May 2nd before Aziel Pinder told us that it was safe to go out through the reef, and we decided to move out the next morning, in order to be well clear of the land by nightfall.

That last night I didn't sleep very much, but lay staring at the deck-head and thinking. Mary and Nora were sleeping peacefully now, with all the faith and innocence of small children. But suppose something happened, out there in the vast reaches of the North Atlantic! Suppose I survived, while one or more of the others did not. Could I take that?

But boats had crossed in safety. Why not us? *Caravel* was safer than most. Yes, but many of those boats had been manned by experienced skippers, with a skilled crew, young and strong. I had myself, pathetically short on experience, Kitty with even less, and two little girls, aged 8 and 9, whose knowledge of the ocean was what I had told them. And that

101

had been a one-sided description at best, designed mainly to allay fears. They had had no say in any of the decisions, and didn't even know enough to be scared. They had been told that they were going to sail across to see Grandma, and thought it would be fun. I hadn't stressed the fact that it would entail crossing 4,500 miles of the North Atlantic, one of the worst bodies of water in the world, in a plywood box.

My God!

## TEXAS TOWER

The met forecast spoke of a high to the north, which ought to bring us a few days' settled weather. At 10:40 a.m. Kitty photographed me raising the anchor for the last time, and we sailed out in a light swell. The children were quite unimpressed by the significance of the occasion, and seemed more interested in their dolls than in the receding land. Perhaps it was just as well.

By mid-afternoon we were on our base course of 050°, close-hauled in a freshening wind and with the sails carefully trimmed so that it wasn't necessary to steer manually. Even a model sailboat, of course, will do this, provided the wind is not blowing from astern or nearly so, and *Caravel* can be made to steer herself at least 50% of the time and sometimes up to 80%. However, a nasty slop soon developed, with confused seas, and while neither of us was actually seasick, we both felt tired, lethargic and off our food. We had lost our sea legs at Hardie's, and were probably victims of nervous tension too.

As darkness fell we kept each other company in the cockpit, drinking numerous cups of coffee to stay awake. Ship sightings averaged one every 4 hours, for we were in a V between two shipping lanes and didn't dare leave *Caravel* unattended. But we did sail without lights, to conserve batteries, on the theory that when we saw a ship we could switch on our own lights.

But it was obvious that we couldn't keep this up for 2 weeks, so we took to sleeping in turns. Unfortunately, I couldn't sleep at all during daylight, yet at night I couldn't keep my eyes open. The first few days of a passage are, we find, tough, until we settle down to a routine.

Dawn was bleak and typical of the North Atlantic, with the seas producing moderate pounding as we headed into them, causing them to hit the underside of the wings. By noon we had travelled 75 miles, and clearly were not going to establish any records. To make matters worse, the wind had backed a little, forcing us onto 030°, which was north of our desired track.

In the morning the seas eased somewhat, the wind went back into the southeast and our spirits rose. Then the sun came out, and at 9:45 a.m. I took my first sunsight, more to see whether the system really worked than anything else, for I already had a fair idea of our position from dead reckoning. At noon I took another one, for each sight gives you only a line of position and you need two of them, taken a few hours apart, to obtain an actual position. After a considerable amount of pencil-sucking, figuring, refiguring, referring to tables, crossing out, checking, plotting and muttering to myself, I came up with a rough, approximate estimated position of about 28 north, 74 west—give or take a bit. This proved to be in the western north Atlantic, which I thought encouraging.

At 7 p.m. a dark, threatening cloud appeared up-wind. A squall! I decided on evasive action and changed course. It came closer, so I turned on the diesel and ran at full power across the wind. But it grew bigger and more ominous by the minute, and in a desperate bid for survival I dropped all sails. Better meet it under bare poles.

By now it was right overhead, and we cringed. There were 7 or 8 large drops of rain, widely spaced, and the wind dropped to zero. Fifteen minutes later we were still becalmed, and the cloud was well down-wind, as harmless as a kitten.

Well, what do you know?

That night we got some sleep, though not much, and on the morning of the 4th day *Caravel* was self-steering again. I got a pair of acceptable sights, which put us at Latitude 28°-45′ north, Longitude 73° west, at noon. This was close enough to the dead-reckoning position to suggest that we were not entirely lost, and it also indicated reasonable, though hardly spectacular progress. We made only half-hearted attempts to keep the children at their lessons, feeling that if we could get them across the ocean alive, it would be something, even if they couldn't spell when they got there. So we left them largely to their own devices and were happy to find that for hours on end they would play with their dolls, creating an imaginary world that kept them fully occupied.

Meals were less of a problem than we expected, largely because nobody seemed interested in food. Toast, sandwiches, a can of beans or a bowl of soup was about all we could face. It wasn't until much later that Kitty was able to develop her skill as a sea cook.

Weather forecasts were still reaching us from station WOM at Fort Lauderdale, although they indicated little to bother us. But lows are a feature of this area in the spring, and the pilot charts suggested that we could expect an average of about one a week to go roaring up the coast past Cape Hatteras, trailing their troughs and frontal systems far to the south and producing south-westerly gales between Bermuda and the mainland. As we had left Spanish Wells on the tail end of the one which had given rise to the rage, we could reasonably expect another and possibly two before Bermuda. Happy thought!

That night we both stayed up until after midnight, by which time we hadn't seen a ship for over 12 hours. So we took a calculated risk, turned on the mast-head light, and both slept at once. After all, lone sailors did this every night, even in congested waters.

We went out like a light, until at about 2:30 a.m. Kitty's frantic scream woke me up.

"A *ship*! It's going to hit us."

There may be even less humane ways to wake anyone from a sound sleep, but offhand I can't think of one. In actual fact it didn't hit us—quite! I clambered on deck and stared in horror as the huge bulk slid by, its deck-lights frighteningly close and its propellers throbbing violently. There was no sign that anyone had even seen us as it swept by in the blackness, leaving us to wallow in its wake.

We were badly shaken by the incident, by the suddenness and closeness of it all. One moment we were fast asleep and the next we were almost being trampled underfoot by 20,000 tons of steel, forging along at nearly 20 miles an hour. Even now, several miles away, we could hear the thrump-thrump-thrump-thrump of the screws, through the water, and it was probably this sound that had wakened Kitty. After that we went onto a 2-on and 2-off schedule, day and night, sleeping as and when we could.

On the afternoon of the 5th day the wind freshened and went into the south, which was fine for sailing, but suggested a possible front. There was a heavy overcast, and *Caravel* would no longer steer herself, no matter how I juggled with the sails. By 4 p.m. the wind had veered further, and was now too far aft for the mizzen sail to do anything but try to turn us around, so I dropped it and we ran under the jib alone.

By 5 p.m. it was obvious that we were in for something bad, and I had to decide on a course of action. Should I run before it, or use the mizzen to hold us head to sea, or back the jib and heave-to, or put out the sea anchor, or drop everything and lie a-hull under bare poles? I had pondered this question many times, but always on shore. This was for real! Of the various methods I rather favoured the last. It involved only dropping the sails and lashing the helm, with no further action being required of me if things got a lot worse. The less I had to do, the less the chance of making any mistakes and doing the wrong thing. Also, I didn't fancy the idea of having to fight with sails or sea anchors later, under survival conditions.

By this time the wind was really strong, although I didn't check the actual force on the Beaufort Scale by the portable anemometer, possibly because I didn't really want to know the worst. I never have been one of those "Tell me the truth doctor, I can take it" types. So I put on the safety harness and, with the diesel holding us into wind, crawled forward to drop the jib. The expression "Drop the jib" is something of an over-simplification, for it took both time and considerable persuasive power, and I couldn't afford any mistakes. But eventually it was furled along its boom, looking like an untidy bundle of wet laundry. I put on an extra lashing, for safety, and crawled below. Now, at least, *Caravel* was as safe as her design and construction could make her. I just hoped that Piver and Bucci knew what they were doing, that was all.

Then I tuned in WOM at 6 p.m., to see what their opinion of all this was. If they spoke of "light and variable," I'd sue them, so help me! But apparently the news had leaked out, for they admitted the existence of an "intense low" near Bermuda. Now they tell us!

As the night wore on the wind grew stronger and the seas became not only higher but also steeper, for they had not yet had time to lengthen.

When allowed to drift, *Caravel*, like most vessels, lies beam to the seas. As each one rolled up from the south, that is from our starboard side, the weather outrigger rose to it without much effort and paused

105

for a moment on the crest, to plunge sickeningly down the after-face and into the trough. As she fell off like this she might pull out smoothly, like an aircraft coming out of a steep dive, or she might, if the angle happened to be beyond a certain critical point, dig in her starboard hull and send up a solid mass of water, partly over the topsides and partly onto the underside of the wing.

The sound of this pounding under the wing was particularly frightening, and I felt sure that the resounding BOOM would be accompanied by the splintering of plywood. The whole ship shuddered violently and, as I lay on my bunk over the starboard wing I was thrown up clear of it each time, and soon developed a headache from the incessant pounding.

Why she didn't break up I couldn't tell, for it seemed more than mere plywood and 1 x 2 stringers could stand. Every time she poised for a plunge I would try to lift my body by sheer will power, to ease the weight and the impact. As we teetered on the top of a sea there was no way of knowing whether this was going to be a smooth pull-out or a thunderous boomer! It was like waiting for a dentist's drill to hit a nerve.

This was no time to discuss our personal fears, and I tried to appear casual about the whole thing, especially in front of the children, who seemed unconcerned as long as we ourselves showed no fear. But I have since asked Kitty how she felt at the time. Her answer was brief.

"Scared sick!"

I guess that made two of us.

As there was nothing constructive to do, we turned in early. Shipping was the least of our worries now—it might even have been nice to know that there was someone else out in this lousy ocean too.

It was a rough night, with the seas running to 15 feet and the occasional one higher. There were a lot of what they laughingly call "Granddaddy Greybeards," huge, tumbling ones with a foaming face, usually the result of one sea being superimposed on another. Sometimes there was a correspondingly deep trough, and we quite literally fell into a hole in the ocean, hitting the bottom with a frightening, bone-shaking jolt. And yet strangely enough, through it all, we managed to get some sleep.

In the morning there was no point in getting up at all, for there was nothing we could do about anything, and the longer we slept the sooner it would be over. So we lay on the cabin seats, where the motion was less than on the bunks, munched toast and tried to concentrate on a

106

whodunit. All day we lay a-hull, with conditions much the same as during the night, except that now we could see it all. The whole world seemed to be rolling around like something in a nightmare, and it was impossible to sit upright, let alone stand, without bracing against something. There were no sea gulls around, no sign of life anywhere. It was a dead, primeval planet, with nothing on it but the howling wind and the raging, rolling tumultuous sea. The only living creatures were here in this silly little floating matchbox, a man, a woman and two little girls— alone in space, like something out of H. G. Wells.

I counted the ratio of seas that produced a boomer to those which didn't. Two out of five! Last night it had been one in four. The storm must be getting worse, the seas higher.

There was no question of sunsights, of course, for we could see neither sun nor horizon, but only ocean and cloud and a mass of spume and spray and mist between. But the storm was at least pushing us to the north, and we were forereaching a little to the east, so that we should be approaching Bermuda at about 1 knot.

Feeling that I ought to have a wind-speed figure for the log, I took the little hand-held anemometer on deck. It bobbed around between 40 and 50 knots, briefly touching 60 at one point, so I suppose 45 would be a fair sustained average. On the Beaufort Scale the windspeed is supposed to be read at a height of 33 feet, where it is said to be 25% greater than at sea level. I wasn't about to climb any masts to check the truth of this little gem of information, so merely added the 25% and let it go at that. This produced 56 knots, bordering on Force 11 (storm), which was at least comforting in one sense. For I didn't want to stagger into Bermuda with harrowing tales of our brush with death, only to have some joker who had also just arrived look up casually and remark, "Oh, really. What wind?"

This, I supposed, would really be something to tell the children about in years to come—except that the children were right here in the thick of it all, on the port bunk, and were vitally concerned with some complicated game which involved a birthday party for Kathy, one of the dolls. They complained bitterly because the guests, sitting around a meal laid out on a cardboard box for a table, kept falling over sideways as *Caravel* tried to stand on her ear.

With evening, the wind seemed even stronger, but I didn't check it in case it really was. On the other hand, the skies seemed to be clearing a little, suggesting a possible cold front. We tried to convince each other, and thus ourselves, that the worst was over.

By morning the wind had definitely started to veer, and the temperature dropped—a good sign! By noon it was out of the northwest, and the screaming in the rigging eased off noticeably. The seas were as high as ever, possibly higher, but they seemed to be lengthening. I counted the boomers. One in five! We spent most of the morning tapping the barometer. If it flickered upwards, we said the storm was over. If it dipped, we blamed the diurnal low.

This was the 7th day, and although the GCIA* was dead, we did manage to get Bermuda on both 965 and 1390 kHz on the D.F. set. Navigationally this meant little, but it was a great morale-booster. By evening the boomers had ceased altogether, and we slopped around in what was left of the decaying and lengthening seas. But the wind was still too strong for us to carry any sail.

The improvement continued during the night, and in the morning we took one look at the sky and gleefully raised all sails. An hour later they were down again as we sat becalmed, wallowing around in the swell like a drunken sow. Wouldn't you know it?

So I got to work on the GCIA, for we needed the time pips to navigate. A $15 Timex is all very well, but you have to check the error once a day. I'm no radio mechanic, although I do have my methods. If a set doesn't work, I open it up and stare at the innards disapprovingly. If this doesn't help—and sometimes it doesn't—I poke around with a pencil until something sparks, crackles or gives off smoke. Sometimes this doesn't help either, but this was my lucky day, for when I touched a certain blob of solder the Voice of America came booming in on 25 metres. A touch of heat with the soldering gun, and we were back in business.

A pair of shaky sunsights at 11 a.m. and 2 p.m. put us about 250 miles from Bermuda, and an hour later, when the wind came to life, I set a new course, for we were now well to the north of the original Great Circle route.

Next morning, the 9th day, the wind was back in the southwest again at a healthy 20 knots, and we roared along with the jib boomed out one way and the main the other, surfing at 9 knots and over. By

---

*The shortwave radio receiver.

108

noon we had 130 miles to go and that night, feeling that we both needed sleep for the final approach, we turned in. There were squalls about, with lightning, so I shackled a chain to the mast and threw the end overboard.

The 10th day dawned clear and sunny, with a 15-knot breeze out of the north. At 9:45 a.m. I turned on the radio and switched to 2182 kHz.

"Bermuda Radio—Canadian yacht *Caravel II*. Victor Charlie 5723. Come in."

Even as I released the "talk" button, a voice came back.

"Good morning *Caravel II*. Bermuda Radio. Over."

For a moment I didn't know what to say. How do you tell a perfect stranger that you just wanted to hear his voice? So I gave him our E.T.A. and asked the exact position of the Texas Tower. It was supposed to be about 26 miles southwest of Bermuda, and we hoped to make it our landfall. He gave us the position, and the fact that it carried two red flashing lights, one over the other.

There was great excitement, of course. We had actually spoken to Bermuda. The place really existed. It was good to be alive!

I took more sights, and decided that we ought to raise the tower at about ten that night. But at 10 o'clock, with the children asleep and Kitty below, there was no sign of any flashing reds.

At 10:15 I saw a faint white light, far ahead—a fishing boat maybe, or a low star. Eleven o'clock came and went, but still no reds, flashing or otherwise. By midnight I was wondering what was wrong. Two hours, of course, was only 8 miles, which wasn't too big an error. And then, maybe the horizon was misty.

There was another white, far off to port. A second ship? But still no reds.

But the first white looked rather bright for a mast-head. Big, too. Almost like several lights close together. I got the glasses on it. Yes, it was a cluster of them, like a ball park. Floodlights! And high above the water, too.

*THE TEXAS TOWER!*

I called Kitty and we both stared at it.

"I think they really are floodlights. How long have they been there?"

"Two solid hours."

At 3 miles, through the glasses, there was no doubt at all. We could

109

see the platform, a heliport probably. It was the tower all right, but without any red lights. After 10½ days at sea it was right on course and only 15 minutes late!

We laughed with glee and, having promised to do so when we sighted it, we woke the children. They scampered into the cockpit in their nighties, staring eagerly ahead.

After celebrating with a tot of rum, and giving way to a much diluted one for the crew, we hove-to for the night. At dawn we were under way again, and by 7:30 a.m. the tower was abeam, a high, yellow structure with the words "Argus Island" painted on the side.

We expected to sight Gibbs Hill, at the southern end of Bermuda, about mid-morning, but before we did so Mary drew me to one side and pointed out that as this was Mother's Day it was only fit and proper for Kitty to sight Bermuda first. I agreed.

At 10:30 a.m. I was alone at the wheel when the faint outline of Gibbs Hill climbed slowly out of the morning haze, on the port bow. I asked Kitty to take the wheel for awhile, and as I went below I whispered to her that as a Mother's Day present she was to sight land first. It was there, on the port bow, and she should "discover" it after a reasonable interval. She nodded as she took the wheel with a smile.

Two minutes later she gave a shout.

"Land ho!"

There was an excited exodus onto the deck, with the children leading the way.

"Where Mummy, where?"

"There," shouted Kitty, "on the port bow." And with a dramatic gesture she directed everyone's attention to a large cumulus cloud, low on the horizon, on the starboard bow!

Nora's eyes were a lot younger than Kitty's, and she knew a cumulus when she saw one.

"Oh, Mummy, that's a cloud!" She glanced around and pointed to port. "There's Bermuda, over there."

The whole thing fell rather flat, and Mary looked at me and shook her head sadly.

"Nice try Dad."

Kitty never did know her left from her right!

At 2 p.m. I radioed our revised E.T.A. for that afternoon, Sunday, and 3:15 found us with our lines ashore, 11½ days out of Spanish Wells.

110

Our first long ocean passage was over and we had survived our first real Atlantic storm. We had found the Texas Tower and, best of all, we were in good health and very happy.

After the customs officer, the first person to greet us was Susan Hiscock, wife of Eric Hiscock, the round-the-world sailor whose *Wanderer III* was tied up a few yards away.

"Do come aboard for a cup of tea," she invited.

We almost giggled as we stepped ashore, to feel solid ground under our feet and to stare at the green fields of Bermuda and the pink houses of St. George.

Suddenly it was all very worth it.

\*\*\*

## *ECHO* AND PICO GORDA

The final decision on the Atlantic crossing was to have been made at Bermuda, although from the moment we sighted the Texas Tower there was never any serious doubt on the matter. And the storm had merely confirmed Arthur Piver's prediction—that *Caravel* could take it if we could.

I did, however, take the dinghy between the hulls to inspect the corners of the wings carefully, for it was here that any structural failure would first appear. There wasn't a paint crack.

Okay, we'd carry on for the Azores—gulp!

Bermuda is on the traditional sailing route for Europe, and May is the favourite time for it, when the spring gales are over and the hurricanes haven't begun. That's the theory, anyway. But other boats were still limping into St. George after an obviously bad pasting. *Georgiana* set out for the mainland but had to turn back. *Gytha*'s sails were blown out and her engine flooded. She sent out a Mayday on her failing batteries, and was escorted in by the Coast Guard. Another boat was presumed lost on the way from New York—she had no radio. It seemed that the spring gales were far from over.

111

The Hiscocks left for the Azores shortly after we arrived, as did Frank Caspar in *Elsie*, another round-the-world sailor. But Cliff Hunt in *Romany* and ourselves decided to wait until the met office at Kindley Field, the big U.S. air base on Bermuda, could promise us a few days' peace after we left. For although Bermuda attracts spring gales like a magnet, the frequency about 3 days east of there drops considerably.

The locals, too, urged us not to leave until after May 24th, although we discovered that this was based not so much on meteorological grounds as on the fact that that is the date of the Fitted Dinghy Races, an event which is in Bermuda what the World Series is in the U.S.A.

These boats are, as I recall, about 14 feet long and have a draft of about 10 feet. This enormous keel is made necessary by an even more enormous rig. The latter looks as though it has been borrowed for the day from a 12-metre.

With a crew of 6 there isn't a lot of freeboard, so 5 of them hike out to weather while the sixth bales like fury with a bucket. If he slows down, they sink, and to take care of the above-average casualty rate a committee boat follows astern to pick up survivors.

On the final, down-wind leg they don't need such a large crew—they only slow things down. So on the last turn the skipper gives the signal and over they go, to be picked up by the committee boat. The skipper romps home alone like a scalded cat under full main and spinnaker. It's not the sort of spectacle you will see at Newport or Cowes, but it's a lot more fun than the Americas Cup, and is followed at night by a wingding that would make a race riot look like a church social.

The harbour master, who had survived many a race night at St. George, suggested that we might feel safer and more relaxed if we left the quay and anchored a little further away until morning. He suggested Fiji! We moved into the bay, but underestimated the time it takes them to sober up after these events, and came back too soon. A large cabin cruiser was trying to anchor near us, but the crewman who threw out (literally) the anchor forgot to let go, and by the time they had fished him out the cruiser had drifted into *Caravel*'s bow. I was mildly annoyed, but there was no sign of any damage.

Next day a young American, George Biggs, stopped by to ask if he could crew with us to the Caribbean. I said that we were bound, hopefully, for England, and he shrugged his shoulders. Could he crew to England? We talked it over, liked the idea of the extra muscle and someone to share the night watches, and agreed. He didn't know the sharp end from the blunt end, but insisted that he knew his left from his right and would recognize a light if he saw one.

*Romany* was to leave with us, but would take a more northerly route, so our tracks would diverge. As long as we were within radio range, however, we agreed to hold hands, electronically, and compare disasters twice a day. Cliff was also a first-timer, and liked the idea of company as much as we did.

On May 27th we were refuelled and fully stocked with food, water and paperbacks, but Kindley Field spoiled the whole thing by reporting a low to the north. On the 28th it was still around, so we started in on the paperbacks.

By the 29th it was out of the way and the next one was over Kansas. This seemed about as far from a low as we could reasonably expect to get, so we moved out, and noon found both *Romany* and ourselves leaving the harbour and heading east. Our own course was 080° true, and the Azores were nearly 2,000 miles away as the crow flies, which is not, unfortunately, the way *Caravel* sails. What with our usual zigging and zagging, we could figure on about 2,200.

The wind was astern, and in a trimaran this produces a very comfortable ride but rather unstable steering, for a moment's inattention can result in jibing booms, backed sails, and other unpleasant things. It usually happens at 3 a.m., when you have been staring cross-eyed at the compass for hours, trying to stay awake, and are far from your best. Suddenly the compass goes way off and won't come back. First thing you know you are facing Bermuda again, and making 1 knot backwards towards the Azores. It's embarrassing.

You now have two choices. If the noise of flogging sails has already woken people up and given the game away, you may as well turn on the diesel to bring her back on course, taking good care to haul in the Walker Log rotor first or you'll lose it around the propeller. They cost $30 and are not available in mid-ocean. The trouble with this method is that it publicizes the fact that the skipper has gone into irons, which makes it difficult to admonish others for doing so later.

The other method is to uncleat the fore-guys (lines holding the

113

booms forward), sheet all sails in tight, back the jib if necessary to sail her round onto course, lash the helm, sneak forward to reset the fore-guys, and finally nip smartly back and grab the wheel before she goes into irons again. This is slow, and there is always the chance that some-one is lying awake, listening to you struggling and clomping around over-head, and waiting until you've finished, at which point he will ask, "Get her back on course okay?"

With George available, we could follow a definite watch schedule. I took the 6 p.m. to 10 p.m., so that I could be up at dawn for a longi-tude sight. Then George came on until 2 a.m., when Kitty took over. Thus everyone got 8 hours' sleep.

On the 2nd day out, with the wind still light and astern, I decided to put up the spinnaker, that great balloon-like sail you see in the brochures of Hawaii. Technically ours isn't a spinnaker, but a mast-head genoa cut in an isosceles triangle so that by attaching the bottom corners, or clews, to the outrigger bows, it can be used as such. So we call it a "genaker." (The idea is Arthur Piver's, the name my own.)

It so happened that this was the first time we had used it as a spinnaker, and we ran into teething problems. I turned the wheel over to George, shackled the top to the halyard and fed it carefully from its bag as Kitty wound up on the winch. It got to the halfway point and whammo! The whole thing took off, bag and all, streaming from the mast-head like a mad thing.

"Let go the winch," I yelled, as I managed to snag the sail with a boat-hook, grabbed one of the sheets, and began to haul everything in, still with the bag attached.

Now that spinnaker contains nearly 700 square feet of sail, which is a lot to tame with only two arms. If you've ever tried to reconstitute a dismembered week-end edition of the *Miami Herald* in a high wind, you'll know what I mean. I did get some of it down, but Kitty had taken my original order rather too literally, and had released the winch pawl, with the result that the sail was coming down a lot faster than I could hope to retrieve it. Next thing, some of it was over the bow and into the drink. With *Caravel* doing about 3 knots or so, it was soon under the hulls and getting fouled up in the fins, propeller, rudder and other projections. Obviously it wasn't going to come up the way it had gone down, over the bow, so I secured one sheet to the stern bitt.

George, by this time, was bleating about the ship pulling to port and not answering her helm. With the port outrigger all gift-wrapped

114

in spinnaker, this wasn't altogether surprising. We unshackled the halyard and after a lot of prodding and poking with oars and boat-hooks we finally got it free, so that it now streamed astern like a trawl. Then we started to haul it in, a foot at a time, which wasn't too easy, for it was now water-logged and no longer resembled the silken gossamer that had so recently fluttered bravely from the mast-head like a huge battle ensign. In fact it was far too soggy and heavy either to put up or stow away, so we set about drying it out on the top deck a bit at a time. When it rained we brought it into the cockpit, and for weeks we lived with that thing under our feet. It seemed that it would never dry out.

Next morning, the 3rd day, we found a flying fish on deck, just like they do in stories of the Spanish Main. What they don't tell you, though, is that the average flying fish weighs about the same as a sardine. Ours was around 6 inches overall, and was delicious fried in butter, but he didn't go very far amongst five of us.

The 4th day was clear, and provided some excellent sunsights. We were south of our desired track but with the wind on the bow *Caravel* steered herself nicely. *Romany* reported good beam winds, and was making better course and speed than we were, so that we got further apart. But at 150 miles we were still well within radio range.

From time to time we would see porpoises, and the children never tired of watching them as they surfaced, dived, rolled and shot under our bows, often missing us by inches. To Mary and Nora, each one was Flipper, of TV fame, and they wanted to feed them sardines.

Then we ran into poorer weather—no actual gales, but a nasty slop. And we had minor rigging failures, too. Lines would chafe and sail snaps would pop out. One night the halyard winch let go at 1:30 a.m., letting the mainsail come clattering down, so that I had to go out in my pyjamas to sort things out.

On the 9th day the wind went into the northeast at Force 6, which is officially a "stiff breeze." It may seem that way in a battleship, but in a 40-footer it appears somewhat stronger. We grew tired of bashing into it and hove-to for the night.

By morning it had eased, but was raining. We also found some pulled seams in the jib, and Kitty climbed into her foul-weather gear and got to work with needle and palm. When we did finally get under way it was slowly and not on a good course. To make the day complete I discovered that the main battery was almost flat. We had another, which I reserved for starting purposes only, but as they were both the same

115

age I started to worry a little, just in case!

The 11th day dawned sunny, and our spirits rose, until I remembered the battery. Also, Kitty and I were both developing headaches, possibly due to lack of exercise. The wind died and we drifted, roughly in the direction of Dakar, West Africa. I took sights, but all they proved was that we were getting nowhere fast.

On the 12th day, which was beautiful but breathless, we started the diesel, partly to get moving and partly to charge up the ailing battery. I raised *Echo*, the U.S.-manned weather ship permanently located at 35° north, 48° west, about 200 miles east of us, and they gave us a weather forecast—settled conditions for several days.

So we put the genaker out to dry on the top deck and opened the hatches to air the place. Then I found 7 gallons of sea water in the engine bilge. Now where on earth had that come from? There is nothing more discomforting, 1,000 miles from land, than to discover salt water, or any water for that matter, where there isn't supposed to be any. If this was from the stuffing box, then a half turn on the nut would fix it. But then it might be from something that wouldn't respond to a mere half-turn, such as a hole in the boat for instance. I bailed it out and hoped that that would be the end of the matter, although I didn't really expect that it would be. (Murphy's 2nd Law!)

On the 13th day we discovered that there was another ship in the North Atlantic too, the Greek freighter *Athenai*. She came over to inspect us and sailed by with a polite "toot."

The 15th day dawned clear and sunny, with a nice sailing breeze at last. At 8 a.m. I saw another ship 3 miles to the southeast, but heading straight at us as though intent on ramming us. It was a destroyer and seemed in a hurry. I got the glasses on her, and fingered the starter key, but gave up the idea of trying to outrun her.

Then I saw the red, diagonal stripe down the bow. The U.S. Coast Guard! Was it *Echo*? I yelled for someone to take the wheel while I got on the radio.

"Weather ship *Echo*! Canadian Yacht *Caravel II*. Come in please."

"*Caravel II. Echo.* Go ahead."

"We have a large Coast Guard cutter approaching our starboard bow, steering about 315°. Is that you?"

"Affirmative. We are coming over to check on you. Is everything okay? Do you need anything?"

For a moment I couldn't answer him. Everyone was laughing and shouting at once. I was excited and slap-happy, and I started to crack jokes, which was a mistake. The U.S. Coast Guard has many fine qualities, but a sense of humour isn't one of them.

"Thank you, no! We are just fine. As a matter of fact we have just baked some fresh bread—would you like some?"

It was an empty gesture, I suppose, for our two small loaves wouldn't have gone far among 100 or so sailors. And it went over like a lead balloon.

"Understand you need some fresh bread. How many loaves?"

"Negative! I said *we* had just baked some, and would you like some. I was just sort of. . . ."

"Sorry, *Caravel II*. Your transmission is a bit garbled. We will come alongside and talk to you over the loud hailer."

They made a snappy turn to starboard and pulled up on our beam, their rail jammed with seamen. There was a great deal of waving, shouting and shutter-clicking on both sides, and the skipper appeared on the wing of the bridge with a hailer. His voice boomed over to us, asking our last port, how many days out, our destination and E.T.A., and whether all on board were well. I answered through our megaphone and after a few pleasantries they turned off for their station. I heard a very strong radio signal in Morse, and while I couldn't read it I could imagine the gist of it. "It's okay. That radar contact wasn't a Russian submarine after all—just some silly little sailboat. Sorry for the false alarm."

Three minutes later they turned again, and once more came streaking after us, stopping this time on our port beam. Puzzled, we dropped the sails and watched them lower a boat, which powered across to us. We threw them a line and a petty officer spoke.

"Just got word from the radio operator. Seems you want some fresh bread." And they heaved a cardboard box onto our deck.

What do you say at a time like that? Tell him you don't want his bread? For a moment I thought Kitty was going to jump down and kiss them all. The idea that a United States destroyer would chase us around the ocean like that, because they thought we needed some bread, was just too much for her. They asked us if we needed anything else, and I mentioned a weather forecast. Out came a walkie-talkie, and within seconds we learned that the high was still with us, but that in a couple of days we could expect a blow of about 25 knots.

When we opened the box we found two big loaves, a huge blueberry pie, some fresh fruit, and a large photograph of the *U.S.S. Androscoggin*, compliments of the skipper.

Next day the breeze was out of the S.S.E., and we made a nice speed in the right direction. I also discovered the reason for the flat battery: a partial short in one of the radios, which produced a 2-amp drain even when switched off. This was soon corrected, but then I discovered a more serious fault.

We had two water tanks, each holding 50 gallons. Since Nassau we had been feeding from the after one, which seemed to be getting more and more brackish. As we approached the bottom of the tank it became undrinkable. But the forward tank contained Miami water, which we assumed would be fine. It wasn't. When we changed over to it it was worse than the after one. We still had 1,000 miles to go, and had 60 gallons of salt water in the tanks.

With no shipping lanes for the next 900 miles, I thought of going back to *Echo*, but was too ashamed to have to ask them for water at this point. We still had 10 gallons in the after tank that would at least keep us alive, as well as a little distilled for the batteries and some canned fruit juice.

On the morning of the 17th day the wind went round to the southwest and freshened to 25 knots, as *Echo* had predicted, so it was now almost impossible to go back anyway.

In Miami I had coved the edges of the upper deck, draining the four corners through plastic pipe so that we could collect rain water from 400 square feet of deck. We hoped for rain. Meanwhile, I had accounted for the contamination. Under the wings two thin copper pipes acted as bleed and overflow pipes from the tanks, and the heavy seas under the wings had forced sea water back into them. As we used up the fresh water it was being replaced by salt. I would have to seal off these pipes and vent them inside when reaching land.

The wind gusted to 35 knots, but it was still on the starboard quarter and we ran before it like a scared rabbit. At one point we logged 15 knots, the fastest speed that *Caravel* has ever achieved, though she would undoubtedly do a lot better in lighter trim and with stronger nerves than mine at the helm. For the full 24 hours we covered 171 nautical miles, our best daily run before or since.

Then it rained! Hallelujah!

We filled every container on board, including teapot, thermos flasks,

118

hot-water bottles and empty soup cans. We filled the 5-gallon plastic jugs, putting the first ones, brackish from the salt on the sails, aside, to be discarded if, and only if, all others were filled. By dusk we had water in everything that would hold any, and even then we couldn't bring ourselves to pump out the main tanks—just in case! Water was suddenly like blood.

That night you couldn't put your foot down without stepping on a container of water, all graded according to salinity.

The wind eased a bit on the 18th day, though it still seemed strong enough. The sail snaps on the jib all started to pop, as the pistons were pulling out of them. We changed to the storm jib while I replaced them, and still made 5 knots. At 2 a.m. the usual night squall got me out of bed, and the wind veered to the northwest. Ha, a cold front! Now things should improve.

They did, too. The wind eased, and the seas moderated from the 12 feet of a few hours before. But as one problem disappeared, another took its place—which suggests a possible Murphy's 4th Law! The salt water in the engine bilge wasn't coming from the stuffing box, but from a fractured plastic elbow behind the heat-exchanger. I was afraid of damaging it further, so didn't try to tighten it, but merely slapped some Polyester Resin round it. It wasn't entirely successful, but it did reduce the flow to an acceptable level.

Another problem concerned my watch, a $15 Timex that was adequate for navigation, provided I noted the error each day from the time pips. The trouble was that the face showed only the 5-minute gradations, not the minute ones, and even these were not too accurately spaced. So while I could always get the time to within a second or so, I was never 100% certain of the minutes. I guess the Timex people didn't figure on their low-priced line being used for celestial navigation.

Fortunately, Mary's watch, though not too accurate, did show minutes, so I used hers for the minutes and mine for the seconds.

One day now followed another with monotonous regularity, and it was a measure of our pattern of living that when we sighted a small, floating object, way off to starboard, we circled and picked it up. It was an aluminum float from a lobster pot, and had acquired quite a colony of goose barnacles, tiny crabs, and other creatures infesting a mass of seaweed. We duly entered the event in the log. An exciting day!

Then we started to get European radio stations, and heard fishermen

119

jabbering away on the marine band in Portuguese. We must be making progress.

The glass was high, 31.43″, the sky clear and the winds light. The noon sight, a good one, put us 372 miles W.S.W. of Horta, on the island of Faial.

The nights out here were perfect, with the moon making them as bright as day, the stars big and low, and the water like velvet. Steering by a star, rather than by the compass, it was a joy to sit there and drink in the beauty. The water would lap and gurgle along the hull, and occasionally we would hear the whoosh of a porpoise or a whale as it breathed on the surface, sometimes only yards away. On such nights the ocean was benign, with the moon making a bright path to the horizon and the odd cumulus hanging low, moon-lit from the rear and white against the black sky. *Caravel* slid along easily, her gently filling sails silently wiping out the stars as the masts drew lazy circles on the sky. It seemed a shame that people in Toronto, Des Moines and Manchester were even now dying without ever having experienced such nights at sea.

And then there were the sounds. . . .

I suppose every cruising boat has them, and it is easy to understand how a lone sailor can lose touch with reality. After 6 months of absolute solitude at sea, the miracle to me is that any human could stay sane. We were five, yet we felt stir-crazy at times, and each wondered if he really did hear those sounds at night. It was a relief to learn that the others heard them too, at one time or another.

The typewriter was kept in the chart-house, aft. Often at night I would hear someone using it in the dark. Once I opened the hatch and shone a light down. There was the machine, in its case and securely stowed. The typing stopped.

And the dog! That little mutt would bark for hours on end, far off in the darkness—but never in daylight.

And the man shouting for help! It was in a strange language, but there was no mistaking the note of urgency. We all heard him, but never two of us at the same time.

Kitty used to hear the Westminster Boys' Choir, but nobody else ever did, so we told her it must have been her imagination.

On the 24th day the glass went up to 31.45″, with a light, south-westerly breeze. We were able to fall off to the southeast, having been pushed too far to the north recently, away from our desired track. Before

120

leaving Bermuda, I had drawn up a strategic plotting chart, showing the proposed track across, and every day, after reducing our sights, I would plot our position with a little green "X," joining these up to show our actual track. This was invariably the high point of the day and when I got our fix all chatter and play would cease. Everyone would crowd around the table, jogging my arm and breathing down my neck.

"Where are we, Daddy? Mary, I can't see—your head's in the way."

If the day's run was small, which it often was, we'd shrug our shoulders and blame the lack of wind. If it was larger than expected, there would be "oooohs" of delight.

Gradually the green line inched erratically towards Faial. From Bermuda it had gone east for a while, and then southeast. After that it shot northeast, until we were well north of track, and were now edging back again. We had 232 miles to go.

On the morning of the 25th day the wind went up to Force 7, and we reduced to jib alone. By noon we had 150 miles left, and I was taking one sight after another, for I now wanted an exact position at all times.

By noon the next day we had 85 miles to go, and by 4 p.m. this was down to 70, with the wind still strong out of the north. It eased off somewhat at night, but we pounded in the residual seas.

Faial is volcanic, and dominated by Pico Gorda, the Fat Peak, over 3,000 feet high. Just east of Faial is the island of Pico, crowned with a 7,600-foot peak of the same name, Pico. With reasonable visibility one should see Pico Gorda about 12 miles off, which would mean about dawn the next day. To avoid a night landfall we slowed down a little, and I left word for George to wake me if he saw any lights at all on his watch.

The next thing I knew it was daylight—5:30 a.m. Kitty was standing over me, shaking me gently but not saying a word. There was a grin on her face from ear to ear, and with her two hands she silently outlined the shape of a mountain in front of her face.

I scrambled into the cockpit, and we both stared at the eastern horizon, pale, cold and sombre. And there, very fine on the port bow and looming up from the low clouds and morning mist was the biggest darned chunk of rock that I had seen this side of Colorado.

*PICO GORDA!*

We hugged each other and I mussed her hair and we laughed like children. Faial! It was right there where it was supposed to be, after

121

26 long days and 26 long nights of nothing but empty sea and sky. It was a miracle. I don't think I have ever experienced anything quite like the feeling of seeing that huge solid mass of volcano for the first time. Kitty tells me that she did, in fact, have a similar experience before—when she first saw Mary in the delivery room!

"Pico Gorda was there all the time," she laughed. "I just didn't recognize it. It looked like a great big cumulus, low on the horizon, and suddenly I noticed that the edge was too hard for a cloud. And it turned into a mountain, as clear as anything."

We were in European waters!

♥♥♥♥

# DOOM BAR

Horta is on the east side of Faial, on the mile-wide channel between it and Pico, and by 7:30 a.m. we were south of the island and being examined by a Portuguese fishing boat, the *Terra Brava*. We hoisted our Canadian flag and they raised their Portuguese one, waved a greeting and pointed the way into Horta.

A bare mile offshore, and now in calmer water, I realized that *Caravel* had a list to port, something I hadn't noticed before in the ocean swell. Puzzled, I opened one of the port outrigger hatches and got a shock. It was half-full of water!

My God! Were we sinking! What had happened?

Shouting the alarm, I started to bail frantically with a bucket, which was faster than a bilge pump, while George took the wheel and headed for the harbour. Everything was flooded, including the Honda generator, and things that would float were slopping around—clothes, pieces of plywood, cartons of food, empty diesel and kerosene containers. The place was a shambles, and the water 2 feet deep.

But the level was going down, which meant that the leak was a slow one and we were not actually sinking. By the time we rounded the breakwater it was below the sole, and as the hull was shaped like a V, the actual gallonage was now small.

122

A launch came out, and we were boarded by a man in an immaculate white uniform, in marked contrast to my own scruffy clothes, bare feet, wet trouser legs and 12-week old beard. He turned out to be the pilot, customs officer, immigration and police, all rolled into one, and smiled politely as he directed us to an anchorage. We filled in a big green card, and that was that.

As he stepped on board his launch, saluted, and headed for shore, I stared around at Horta, with its palm-fringed waterfront and its clean, painted houses, all set against the green slopes of Pico Gorda, while off to the east was the even more impressive Pico, its mile and a half high peak sliced across the middle by a thin layer of cloud and looking for all the world like a Japanese print. I couldn't take it all in. It was all too new and strange after our world of sea, and sky, and more sea, and more sky, and still more sea.

"This," I announced, "seems to call for a tot of rum all round. Anyone want to argue the point?"

Nobody did.

But before going ashore I had to find that leak. It now seemed to have stopped, which suggested that it was probably above the waterline. I examined the hull from the dinghy, but at first I couldn't find a thing. Then I found it—a 6-inch hairline crack just above the waterline on the outboard side of the port outrigger bow. I didn't notice it from above, for the top overhung the bottom, but I could feel it with my fingers. And I remembered—that drunken cruiser at Bermuda. *Caravel* had been tied up to the stone quay, unable to yield to the blow, and the plywood had cracked along the keel member.

With every sea, another ounce of water had come in, filling first one section and then flowing over to the next so that no water appeared above the sole until all sections were full. Then the weight had lowered the hole below the waterline, and the outrigger had filled quickly. But when it reached about 2 feet, the outrigger couldn't sink any further without lifting the starboard one, so that the list had been limited to about 5 degrees. Arthur Piver had always insisted that a trimaran, even if holed in all 3 hulls, would merely settle a little lower and continue to float. Now I believed him. *Caravel* had proved the inherent safety of a well-built trimaran, had shown that even with one hull holed and with 2 tons of water in her, she could still cross 2,000 miles of North Atlantic in heavy cruising trim, and in safety.

123

Repairs were started at once, with a tiny triangular frame to support a backing piece. Then we dried out the wood with bags of sand heated on the galley stove, and applied epoxy resin. On the outside we waited for a dead calm day, sanded down the surface, and put on a patch of glass cloth and resin. It doesn't have Gene Bucci's mirror finish, but is now stronger than the original.

The contents of the outrigger were another matter. We dried out the Honda and got it going, but it has never been the same since. George's clothes took quite a beating. The case of Kellogg's was a write-off, as was much of the other dried food. The genaker, well, wouldn't you know it? We had to start all over again. The carton of 48 rolls of toilet paper could, I felt, be salvaged.

You'd be surprised at the amount of sea water a roll of that stuff can absorb. Multiply that by 48, and you'll understand the list to port. We squeezed out as much as we could by hand, and then stood on each roll separately to get out more, before putting them on deck to dry. In actual fact we never did get them completely dry. A roll might seem that way, and be put into service. But a dozen layers down it would prove to be still wet, and there's nothing worse than soggy toilet paper. So we'd put it back on deck and replace it with one that had just been outside. It was months before we enjoyed the luxury of dry toilet paper again.

Meanwhile, one of the first people to greet us was Frank Caspar in *Elsie*. He had seen us arrive, realized that this was Saturday and that Monday was a fiesta of some sort, and figured that we might appreciate fresh food before Tuesday. So over he came with bread, tomatoes, lettuce, and some local cheese. Such kindness and thoughtfulness among cruising people around the world make them unforgettable.

Long before we reached Horta we had heard about Peter and the Café Sport, and there it was, right on the waterfront. As we rowed across and landed, Peter smiled and greeted us in English.

"You are from the *Caravel II*, no? Welcome to Horta."

I admitted it, and he gave me a chart, rolled up and addressed in my mother's hand. I had ordered it to be sent to me, General Delivery, Horta.

"But how did it reach you? It is addressed to the post office."

"Oh," he smiled, "they send all mail for the yachts down to me. They know that I shall see you before they do."

Horta is that sort of town, and Peter is that sort of man. His real name is José Ozevedo, and with his father Henrique he runs the Café Sport which isn't really a café at all, for no food is sold. It's a happy little bistro, and Peter is one of the few people in Horta who speak English. He also loves boats and boating people, and can tell you where, in town, you can get welding done, or your clothes cleaned, or a camera repaired, or buy some paint thinner, or some rubber cement or darning wool. You name it, and Peter will take you to buy it and act as interpreter. He also changes money and is a mine of information.

In return, you are expected to sign his visitors' book and, if possible, give him a photograph of your boat. This book dates back a very long way, and is his pride and joy. As you sit at one of the little tables, sipping your wine, you find yourself thumbing through the past. You come across the names of sailors from many lands, some alive today and still making headlines, some now a legend. You see the names and pictures of the well-known boats of today and yesteryear. There are few that have not crossed the Atlantic at least once, and of these most have called at Horta, to lie at anchor while their owners and crews enjoyed good wine and good company at the Café Sport. There a foreign language is no barrier to enjoyable conversation, but rather a sauce to add spice to it, a challenge that makes it remembered long after mere idle chatter in one's own tongue would be forgotten.

If you lose touch with a cruising yachtsman, write him at the Café Sport. Sooner or later he will call there on his way to New York or Cape Town, Gibraltar or Panama.

What with the price of wine at Horta (in your own container it costs from 70¢ to $1.25 a gallon), Peter will never grow rich. But this doesn't bother him, for money seems to matter little. And I have yet to see him without a cheery smile.

Nestling between Pico Gorda and the sea, Horta is a delightful town, a mass of small, clean houses with their upper floors decorated with wrought-iron balconies and ornate friezes. There are lots of stores, but most are small, with neither storefront nor sign. After all, if the whole town knows that Manuel sells shoes, why put up a big, ugly sign?

In the bakery, where a charming girl behind the counter spoke no English, we asked for *pan*, hoping that the Spanish word would be close enough. It wasn't, so Kitty pointed at some loaves.

"Paõ," smiled the girl, and we made a mental note for next time.

125

Kitty held up two fingers and said, "*Dos*," but the girl shook her head and started in on something that sounded like the Gettysburg address in Portuguese. Kitty's jaw dropped, and she turned to me. I shrugged my shoulders and the girl stopped, thought for a minute, and pointed first to her watch and then to the calendar on the wall. She started to recite again, this time, it seemed, from the Koran, but again stopped when she saw on our faces that unmistakable look that we all get when drowned in a foreign language. She took a pencil and circled the 4th day on the calendar, pointing to the loaves behind her.

"This is the 5th," cried Kitty. "She's trying to tell us that these are yesterday's loaves."

We all smiled, and the girl took off her wrist watch, turned the hands to read 3 o'clock, and showed it to us. Then she circled the 5th day on the calendar. On the dot of 3 p.m. we were back, and she proudly presented us with two loaves, soft and still hot. That sort of salesmanship I like, and as long as we were in Horta you couldn't have got us into any other bakery in chains.

About a mile or so out of town, and strategically located down-wind and beyond a high hill, is the whaling factory. We first saw it from the top of this hill, and were amazed to realize that what that tug was actually towing across the bay was a solid mass of whale meat, and that all that red stuff staining the sea for hundreds of yards around was, in fact, blood.

Now I've already made some pretty snide remarks about George-town, S.C., and its smelly paper mill. But fully to appreciate the deeper significance of the superlative form, *stench*, you have to spend a few seconds—2 are usually enough—down-wind from a whaling factory. I'm still not sure whether I'd bet on a whale or a conch, after due allowance for the difference in size.

The Azores lie some 900 miles out in the Atlantic, which is fortunate for all of Europe west of the Oder-Neisse line. And the Horta city fathers showed great wisdom in locating their whaling factory out on a promontory, so that no matter what the wind, the smell tends to drift out to sea.

Before we left Horta, George and I took the dinghy over to the fishermen's quay for diesel oil, water and kerosene.

Water was no problem at all, for *agua* seems to work well in most Latin countries. But "diesel" produced only the blank stare that I

126

recognized at once as meaning that I'd have to try another approach, such as schoolboy French, or Indian sign language, or pictures on the back of an envelope. I looked at the pumps. One said *Gasolina*, which seemed pretty obvious, while another read *Gasóleo,* which could have meant anything from bottled gas to polyunsaturated margarine. I sniffed a sample, and it smelled like diesel. George claimed to be a graduate chemist, but seemed reluctant to make a snap analysis on the quay. We were assured that the fishing boats used it, as though that was supposed to prove something or other.

Okay, fill her up! George, down in the dinghy, put the nozzle into the first jerry can.

After a gallon and a bit, the pump quit. They kicked it, twisted knobs, replaced fuses, and talked to it quietly in Portuguese, but to no avail. George reported nothing but a gurgling sound at his end. They gave him another nozzle from an unmarked pump, and this started before he could get it into the can, catching him full in the face as he was examining it. He gave us a quick chemical analysis on that one—water!

"Stop, *cesa, nada mas . . . es agua!"*

The boy stared indignantly, first at me and then at the pump, as though undecided as to which of us was trying to confuse him. Then he went off to consult a higher authority, while George dumped the oil and water mixture into the harbour.

When the boy returned, he handed George yet a third nozzle, this one connected to a rotary hand pump on a 50-gallon drum very plainly marked *"Gasolina."*

"Hey, wait a minute," I objected. *"No quiero gasolina. Quiero gasóleo*—I think."

He shook his head and went into a long address in colloquial Portuguese. As far as I could judge, which wasn't very far, his main theme seemed to be that you can't believe everything you read in print. George and I went into another huddle, and finally agreed that it was, in fact, diesel fuel. We filled the cans.

Now all we needed was kerosene, a word which obviously left him cold.

"Paraffin," I tried, remembering that this was what the English called it, and then, in a stab in the dark, *"Parafina?"*

Okay, forget it. We'll try Peter. Should have brought him along in the first place.

127

*"Cuanto cuesta?"* I followed him into his little office where he phoned the higher authority again and established a price in escudos per litre. This was going to be good.

*Cuantos litros?* Well, let's see; four plastic jugs at 5 U.S. gallons each, plus four cans at 4½ each, plus the two smaller ones at 2 imperial gallons each (at .83 and a bit to the U.S. gallon). Convert the lot to litres at 4 point something to one. Then convert the escudos to U.S. cents and add 8% for Canadian. How close we were will never be known, and the boy didn't even count the bills I gave him.

Peter sent me to a little shop down a side street for the kerosene, but I forgot to ask what the word was in Portuguese. I tried *"kerosina"* and *"parafina"* and even, as a literal Spanish translation for coal oil, *"óleo de carbón,"* but the stare was the blankest yet.

*"Oleo,"* I shouted, on the theory that most foreigners understand their own language better if you raise the volume a few decibels. He produced a quart of SAE 30 motor oil, which I waved aside.

*"Oleo,"* I insisted, *"no para motór . . . para lámpara."*

His face lit up. We had, quite literally, hit oil.

*"Ah, para lámpara, si! Petróleo!"*

I was about to protest that this was diesel, but remembered that that was *"gasóleo,"* and not *petróleo."* Okay, let's smell it!

He showed me a drum, and I sniffed. It smelled like kerosene all right, except that by this time I don't think I'd have recognized it with any degree of certainty if they'd given it to me in a rum punch. Anyway, I took it, and it worked fine in the Primus and hurricane lamps, without blowing up, so maybe it was kerosene at that.

That afternoon David Lewis, with his wife Fiona and their two small daughters, came to Horta in their catamaran *Rehu Moana*, arriving from Sierra Leone on the last leg of their circumnavigation. We had a meal and a chat with them before we left next morning.

The rest of the evening we spent in the Café Sport, saying *au revoir* to Peter and a group of friends. It was late when we rowed back to *Caravel*, feeling very mellow and sentimental, partly due to the warmth of the send-off, and partly to the excellent white wine which Peter serves.

Horta will always be a pleasant memory, for there are so few places like it left. You feel you have stepped back into the relaxed and courteous atmosphere of the 1890's, with the people happy and at peace with themselves. They live on an island far removed from

Madison Avenue, with a pleasant climate and a lush landscape. Food is cheap and the living is easy.

They can get radio programs from Saõ Miguel or the mainland, but there is no TV. Neither are there any railroads, airports, streetcars or freeways. There are few paved roads, but the sidewalks are things of beauty, laid out in black and white mosaic with no two streets having the same pattern. Perhaps it is indicative of their philosophy that they spend so much effort on their sidewalks, where people stroll, and so little on their roads, where cars travel.

By 6:30 the following morning we were motoring out of the harbour in a light breeze, and by 4:30 p.m. the next island to the north, Graciosa (the gracious one), was abeam, and we came onto our base course of 049° true. The strategy was to make plenty of northing before we turned east, for if we turned off too soon we might be caught by the Portuguese trades, which blow to the south nearer the mainland.

By 7 a.m. on the 2nd day we could still see Terceira faintly, for these are high islands. We also saw several whales and a large basking shark, as well as a number of ships, for we were close to the junction of several shipping lanes.

By the morning we were almost becalmed, but were at least getting good sights, and at noon found ourselves just about 1,000 miles from Bishop Rock. This is some 30 miles off Land's End and is considered to be the trans-Atlantic landfall for ships entering the Channel.

I was getting a bit weather-conscious as we approached England, but while the B.B.C. puts out a good marine forecast on 1,500 metres (200 kHz), we weren't able to receive it. On the 5th day we ran into a strong nor'wester, with seas to 15 feet.

On the morning of the 7th day it was still fairly strong, and we made 6 knots under the jib alone, riding well in the following seas, except where the odd big one tried to kick the stern around.

At 1:30 p.m. we were 660 miles from Bishop Rock, and close to Weather Ship *Kilo*, operated by the French. I tried to raise them on 2182 kHz, but could not. Although all ships are supposed to listen on this international calling and distress frequency, we learned later that the French weather ship, which also serves as a rescue vessel, does not even listen on this frequency. Possibly they keep a sharp lookout for messages in bottles!

I still couldn't get the B.B.C. on 200 kHz, and discovered later that this was due to a poor connection in our receiver. I was, however, able to get an aircraft weather forecast in a delightful Irish brogue, from Shannon Air Radio on about 5.6 MHz. This was better than nothing, even if we weren't too interested in the visibility and cloud ceiling at Rome and Copenhagen.

In the morning the wind was still at about 30 knots, and the seas quite high, so we hove-to all day and tried to sleep. Towards evening things began to improve, and by morning we were under way again, with Bishop Rock 550 miles away. Ten minutes later a huge log, about 10 feet long and 2 feet thick, drifted by within feet of the starboard hull. A nice thing to meet at night under full sail!

By noon on the 10th day we had only 450 miles to go, and were seeing a lot of ships, mainly tankers. Then we picked up a B.B.C. weather forecast—for the north of Scotland of all places.

At 10:30 a.m. on the 13th day, motor-sailing in light airs and under a clear sky, I saw a large, 4-engined aircraft heading for us at a bare 100 feet. A Shackleton! The R.A.F.! They must have spotted us on their radar. I yelled for Mary to wave the Canadian flag while I grabbed the camera, photographing the huge plane as it roared low over our masts. At the same moment they photographed us, and weeks later I was able to get a copy of this aerial shot of *Caravel*, 320 miles off Land's End.

At 4:45 p.m. we made radio contact with Land's End, and again there was a lot of excitement. Mary said it ought to count as a landfall and qualify for a tot of rum to all hands, but I had to veto that one. I gave them our E.T.A., although this was still pretty vague, and asked them to notify the harbour master at Padstow. He would, I knew, let my mother know at once when he got word of us.

Just on dusk a large tanker came up on the port quarter, heading straight for us. It wasn't really dark enough for our mast-head light to show up well, and he obviously hadn't seen us. At 600 yards I could see the Shell emblem on the funnel, and I grabbed the flare pistol. At 400 yards I was on the point of firing it over his bow to attract his attention when he started a swing to port. He was far too big to make a snappy turn, and cleared our port side by 100 to 150 yards, a distance which seemed a lot less as I stared at his enormous bulk. The name *Halia*, of London, stood out like an ad on the side of a bus as he swept by.

The 14th day was partly cloudy, with a light south-easterly breeze.

130

The place was littered with ships, and at one time we counted 8 of them at once. We were now south of Bishop Rock and near the point where shipping from practically every port in the world converges for the English Channel and Northern Europe—up to 800 ships a day. Just ahead was Track "C," the main shipping lane for fast ships for New York and the Eastern Seaboard, a maritime freeway!

I picked up the Ploneis Consul Transmitter, in Northern France, which provides quite an accurate bearing in these waters, and then a much weaker signal from the radio beacon at Round Island, in the Scillies, a group of islands 30 miles off Land's End. These two cross bearings gave me a fix, which was fortunate, for the sun had gone coy on us just when we needed it most.

At 8:30 p.m. we got a marine forecast from Ilfracombe Radio, threatening Force 6 winds and a cold front. Should we ride it out here, with all this shipping milling around, or run in and have it hit us just off the Scillies? The sooner we got out of these shipping lanes, the less chance of being stomped on by another *Halia*. I decided to head in, and started the diesel, aiming at a point west of the Scillies to round them a few miles off. I took frequent bearings on Ploneis and Round Rock as we went along.

Cutting between the Scillies and Land's End would have saved 20 miles or so, and in good weather I would have done so. But *Torrey Canyon* had tried that a few months before, and had wound up a total loss on the Seven Stones, dumping 100,000 tons of crude oil into the sea. My own plan was to cross the shipping lanes as quickly as possible, west of Bishop Rock, where they all converged and where ships would be keeping a careful watch anyway. Then we would approach the Scillies from the northwest, coming close enough to make a positive landfall before bearing away again to the north or northeast from a known position, and heading for the Cornish coast.

That night we took hourly watches, with cat naps between. Progress was slow into the headwind, and the Round Island beacon crept gradually over to starboard as we drew north of it. By 6 a.m. on the 15th day we were starting our turn to the east, with the beacon on our starboard bow. Visibility was less than 2 miles, but the land was low and we might not see it until we were close, especially in the overcast.

Ploneis was now southeast, which gave me a reasonable idea of the distance from Round Island—if I could trust it! Why do we want to

131

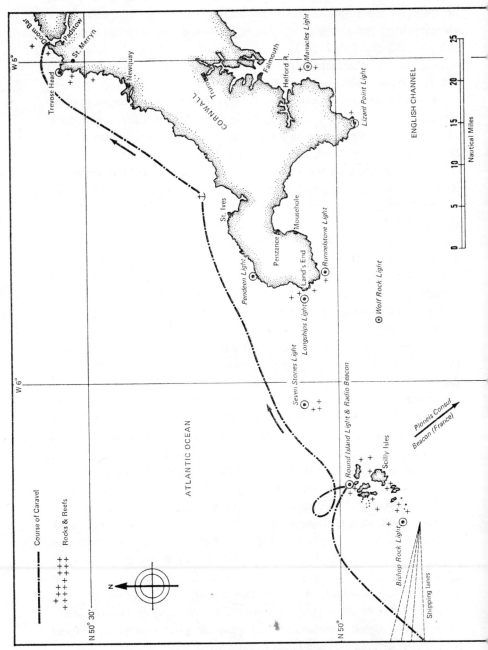

*Land's End and the Scilly Isles: Southwestern approaches to England*

132

trust an instrument less than our own senses? By 9 a.m. we were 9 miles off, and by 10 a.m. this was down to 5 miles. We had turned still further to starboard, and the beacon was now fine on the port bow, pipping away steadily.

Everything seemed to fit, but when you are making a difficult landfall in bad weather and poor visibility, from a last-known position several days old, and onto a coast that has probably claimed more wrecks than any other in the world, there is nothing like a good visual contact. By this time we were all on deck, each with a 20-degree sector to scan.

At 11 a.m. there was still no sign of land, and Ploneis was putting us 2 miles offshore—just about the limit of our visibility. We ought to see it any moment, *if* we were where I thought we were. The wind was still strong, and we were on the port tack. Now the Round Island beacon was dead ahead, and sounded alarmingly close. It shared the frequency with five other beacons, from Scotland to Ushant, and was on the air for only 1 minute out of 6, starting at 2, 8, 14, etc. minutes after the hour. Every 6 minutes it would start up again, the insistent, monotonous signal, "R-R" in Morse, stronger and more strident all the time. "Bip-beep-beep-bip, bip-beep-beep-bip."

At 11:15 a.m. there was still nothing but grey, bleak seas and low, scudding cloud. There was no reading on the depth-sounder, but the seas seemed to be climbing as they felt the bottom. I listened for breakers.

Suddenly, at 11:18 a.m., it was there, very fine on the starboard bow! A mile away, or less!

"LAND HO!"

We all seemed to see it at once. Round Island! The Scillies!

"ENGLAND!"

There was no time to celebrate, and I hauled her around onto the starboard tack and fell away. We had seen it. We had a good, solid position, and in this weather that was all I wanted. For the rest of the day I was satisfied to creep northward, or at least on 340°, which was as close to north as wind and seas would permit. By mid-afternoon we couldn't get higher than 325° in the backing wind, minus whatever drift and leeway there was. Then, satisfied that we had enough offing for safety, and clear of any but local coastal shipping lanes, I hove-to under mizzen, sheeted hard over to reduce flogging.

133

We were drifting towards the Channel again, to the southwest, but now at least I knew where we were, and also the approximate rate of drift. We should be all right unless the wind backed too far and set us into the Scillies, which seemed unlikely.

Darkness fell, with the wind still about 30 knots, and we could see nothing. By the end of my watch, however, visibility had improved somewhat. I could see the loom of the Bishop Rock light, though not the light itself, to the southeast—easily identified by its double flash every 15 seconds. I asked George to wake me if either the wind backed or the light came closer, and he left the same message for Kitty at 2 a.m.

She woke me at 6 a.m. On deck the sun was just rising into a cloudless sky and there was a light breeze from the east. What a fantastic change in 6 hours, but typical of British waters.

We raised both jib and main, and for the second time in 24 hours were soon rounding the Scillies. The gale had set us back quite a way, but this time it was easy, and Round Island was clearly visible as we passed by, close-hauled on the starboard tack and making fair progress on 040°. At 9:50 a.m. we sighted Land's End, and soon after that we could make out what was left of *Torrey Canyon* to the south of us, on the Seven Stones. At 11 a.m. I radioed a telegram to my mother, giving our E.T.A. as the 6 p.m. tide the next day, Monday.

Near the coast we lost the wind and had to motor. By sunset we were off St. Ives, and could just see the red light on Trevose Head, near Padstow, 20 miles up the coast. As the bottom was mostly rock, we sought out the only sandy area shown on the chart, which happened to be in 22 fathoms. In view of the depth, we used the small anchor to hold us from drifting during the night.

Next morning the wind freshened from the southwest, perfect for a run up the coast. We cleaned up ship and I reluctantly shaved off my four-month beard while we waited for low water, to time our arrival for high tide. Small though it was, that anchor was a brute to haul up from 130 feet, but we finally made it, just as a St. Ives fishing boat nosed around curiously.

"Where be 'e goin?"

I told him.

"Paaadstow, eh?" He nodded wisely, to indicate that he had heard tell of the place. Then, as an afterthought, he added by way of dire

134

warning, "Paaadstow be a loong way!" He sounded lugubrious.

I guess it was, at that—all of 21 miles! Another thought seemed to occur to him.

"Wurr be 'e from?"

"Miami!"

He nodded again, dubiously, I thought, as though saying to himself, "Mayammi, ey? Now I wunders wurr that might be. One o' them furrin places, I don't doubt, round t'other side o' Penzance."

We laughed as we hoisted our Canadian flag on the jack-staff, the red ensign courtesy flag on the starboard spreader, and the yellow "Q" flag at the mast-head. Distance is relative.

The seas were building up under the freshening westerly, and this, plus a 2-knot current from the flood tide, sent us along the coast like a cat with its tail on fire. All of which was fortunate, for the tidal range at Padstow, on springs, is 24 feet. As the depth in the harbour is only 16 feet to begin with, this means that you either go in at high tide, or you walk in. Furthermore, there are more than 3,000 charted wrecks around the Cornish coast, and Padstow has had its full share of these, a fact which tends to encourage a somewhat conservative approach when you arrive for the first time. Across the estuary of the Camel River, on which Padstow is located, is a sand bar with a narrow channel, and the seas break on this in an alarming manner. They don't call it the Doom Bar for nothing. Taking all facts into account, and with Shark River still a vivid memory, I wanted to arrive at slack high water, a time when the bar would be relatively harmless.

We were only minutes late as we rounded Trevose Head and warmed up the diesel before dropping the sails. Several local boats came out to escort us in, showing that word of our arrival had got through.

A light rain started, but we hardly noticed it as we followed a boat through to the inner harbour and slowed down carefully. There was a crowd on the quay, my mother among them, waving her handkerchief. Photographers pushed forward as I eased *Caravel* alongside, and lines were thrown ashore.

My mother had a bouquet of flowers for Kitty, and the photographers had her hand them down several times. Then they hoisted her frail figure down onto the deck, with everyone laughing and talking at once.

The B.B.C. did an interview, and next day we were on TV. The local press had a field day, for Padstow is not normally a trans-Atlantic terminal, and even the London *Daily Express* had us on their front page. Reuters put the story on their wire, and soon *The Toronto Telegram* was on the Atlantic telephone for more details.

It was a fantastic climax to a voyage that had lasted, in all, 3½ months from Miami. Sometimes frightening, sometimes pleasant, it had at all times been an adventure. And now, after all the worry and the misgivings, the doubts and the soul-searching, we had made it. It was over. It was a dream come true.

〰〰〰

## LONGSHIPS AND PORTLAND RACE

Padstow is a typical Cornish fishing town, set a mile or so up the Camel River among beautiful rolling hills and wide vistas of rugged coast and moorland. In summer it is jammed with tourists, but in winter life in the narrow, winding streets slows to a crawl. Some of the grey stone buildings date from Norman times, and a nearby church was centuries old when William the Conqueror landed in England in 1066.

We tied up *Caravel* at the stone quay of the inner harbour, well-sheltered from the south-westerly gales which would soon come screaming in from the open Atlantic. Outside the estuary, at Trevose Head, the swell from storms 1,000 miles away pounds against the cliffs, sending salt spray far inland. But the Doom Bar, graveyard of so many ships that tried to enter Padstow in bad weather or at the wrong state of the tide, stops the swell and breakers. Inside, it is relatively quiet.

The tide, though, can surprise you if you are used to the 1 to 3 feet range common in most parts of the world. On springs the entire harbour, and most of the estuary, dries completely. Boats in the harbour settle onto the mud for about 6 hours out of every 12, which gives rise to the problem of plumbing.

Another snag is that if you step ashore at high tide and return several hours later, you find that the deck has now dropped about 20 feet or so. It is assumed that you had the foresight to allow sufficient slack in your

136

dock-warps. Otherwise the result can be ludicrous. But you would also have been wise to tie up opposite one of those steel ladders attached to the wall. Even if you did, it isn't going to be easy to get back on board, unless you are pretty nimble and have no fear of heights. The ladder starts at ground level, and you have to kneel down in the mud and back up to it, navigating over your shoulder and, as you reach the edge, grope around in space for the first rung down. These ladders are often loose or broken and are also slippery from seaweed and oil. With a parcel of groceries or in your best, shore-going clothes, it can be a feat just getting on board at low tide, even without the added problems of darkness, fog or driving rain.

The local school agreed to accept Mary and Nora for the winter, and we were happy to discover that they had not suffered scholastically from their two years before the mast. They also joined the Guides and Brownies and made many friends, as did we all, among the local people. The Cornishman is slow to make friends, but when he does so he is very loyal. Ethnically he is related not to the Englishman, but to the Welshman and the Breton over in France. A Breton sailor we met was surprised to hear one of his own patriotic songs sung as the Welsh national anthem.

Like his neighbour the Devonshireman, the Cornishman has been a natural seaman since the dawn of time, and between them they provided England with her sea dogs and explorers for centuries. He has to be good to survive, for his coast is a sailor's nightmare. Granite cliffs rise hundreds of feet from the rocks and reefs that boil and foam under the pounding of the wild ocean. The coast faces the broad Atlantic, and is swept by the deep depressions that come hurtling in, especially in winter. As the swell from even distant storms feels the bottom, it rises, even in calm weather, to frightening heights. In bad weather, with a south-westerly gale, this becomes a lee shore to make you wake up screaming.

As though gales, an inhospitable coast with few harbours, and the latitude of Labrador and the Aleutians were not enough, tides can exceed 30 feet. When such a flow opposes a southwester even a Cornishman's blood runs cold. Then there is the fog, which doesn't help. And on top of everything else, add one of the heaviest concentrations of shipping in the world. There are times when small-boat sailing off the Cornish coast can be quite a challenging pastime.

Once or twice a week we visited my mother in the neighbouring village of St. Merryn, 2½ miles away. To get there we walked up the winding street from the harbour, past the little stone cottages on the side of the hill, and out onto the country road above. This was narrow, and flanked by tall hedges atop banks of stone which were themselves covered by a canopy of grass, creeper and, for a surprisingly large part of the year, wild flowers. Here and there we stopped at a gate leading into a farm field, to admire the view. Half a mile away was the coast, with its high cliffs and jagged outcrops, its deep fissures and occasional sandy bay far below, its cliff-top paths with views of spectacular beauty and grandeur. All this was accompanied by the sound of surf pounding on the rocks, the soft continuous moan of the wind among the crags and through the long, coarse grass, the cawing and screaming of the wild gulls riding the up-drafts where the sea air met the cliffs.

Trees on this relatively dry north coast of Cornwall were few, and those that did survive leaned to the northeast, weary of fighting the perpetual gales from the southwest. For the wind was everywhere.

Except between the tall hedgerows of this winding country road, often 10 feet high and half as thick. Here we were sheltered, and even in mid-winter could walk in comfort, warmed by the sun but not chilled by the wind. We could have taken a bus, but rarely did. For who looks back with longing on a 20-minute bus ride? Those unhurried strolls through the Cornish countryside will last for ever.

We did have rain, of course, and at times too much. The inside of a boat in England is not the driest place on earth, and if it wasn't the condensation it was the children slopping through mud and bringing wet clothes on board. Electric heat would have been fine, and we applied for a connection to *Caravel*. But this seemed to require an act of Parliament, royal consent, special dispensation from the Archbishop of Canterbury, and approval by the executive council of the Southwest Electricity Board, which has a policy of never saying "Yes" if it can say "No." So we used a kerosene heater and mopped up the condensation every few hours.

In March we rented a car and visited more relatives in 2 weeks than we could have done in 6 months in *Caravel*. April found us ready for the summer cruise, during the course of which we planned to go up the Channel, see London, nip over to Holland and the Rhine, sail north to Denmark, cruise the Baltic and the Norwegian fjords, round the north of Scotland, and return to Padstow in time to fit out and make the Mediter-

138

ranean before winter. Need I say that we didn't quite make it?

To begin with, we found that nobody ever misses the Padstow May Day celebrations.

The story goes that in pre-Roman times some wicked Frenchmen landed one day, bent on murder, rape and loot, while the Padstow men were away fishing. If they had managed to cross the Channel, round Land's End, weather Trevose Head and get across the Doom Bar in safety, with neither chart nor tide tables, I should have thought that they'd have been only too glad to get ashore in one piece, without all that nonsense. However, the Padstow women are said to have dressed up as horses and galloped out to meet the invaders, mouthing horrible threats in the original Celtic. The Frenchmen took off at full speed for home.

The whole thing sounds highly improbable, but the Padstonians put enough credence in it to make it the excuse for a beautiful wingding every May Day. Someone dresses up as an "Oss" and leads a procession around town to the music of an accordion and several other instruments. The tune seems to have no end, and they cover every street in the town several times, while everyone from miles around joins in the fun, singing and dancing in the most uninhibited manner. The parade stops at 6 p.m. The pubs happen to open at 6 p.m. too, which is convenient, for it enables people to adjourn to the Ship Inn, the Golden Lion or the "Doom Bar" in the Harbour Inn to discuss the events of the day over a pint of rough cider or bitter, and to plan an even better one next year.

Shortly before we left, Captain Bob Lott, the ex-harbour master and a real salt, asked us whether he could pilot us round Land's End. He had served his time under sail, many years before, and longed for one last fling. He claimed to have sailed the coast 1,200 times, and we believed him, for he knew every rock by its first name. A partial cripple after a boyhood accident, he was one of the best known and loved personalities in Padstow.

For years he had waged a legal battle with the railway about some land that he claimed belonged to the town of Padstow. As the railway had been nationalized he was, in effect, fighting the Crown. After dusting off centuries-old minutes and acts of Parliament, he won his case and Padstow got its land back.

On May 16th he came on board and we left the estuary on the

139

evening tide. He took the wheel, and for the next 20 hours we couldn't pry him loose.

"If I'm to pilot you I can't sleep below. And if I'm up here I may as well steer."

Off Trevose Head lie the Quies Rocks, which I had previously given a wide berth. But in the gathering dusk he unhesitatingly took us inside. Down the coast in a light norther he identified lights and points on shore, until at about 4 a.m. we were approaching Land's End on the last of the ebb tide, all set to round it and catch the first of the flood up the other side. It was close, and we needed every minute.

Just off Land's End are some awe-inspiring rocks, reefs and islets, some very high and others barely awash. The normal route for anyone in his right mind is well outside the whole rotten mess. In fact the lighthouse there, Longships Light, on the rock of the same name, is designed on the theory that all boats will do just that. It shows a white light to seaward, meaning, "Keep well out, fella," and a red light towards the land, meaning, "Where do you think you're going?"

It was still pitch dark as Bob Lott took *Caravel* round Pendeen Point and past the Brisons, a pair of rocks nearly 100 feet high. There, ahead of us, was the baleful red eye of Longships, blinking its frantic warning at us.

"You going *inside*?" My voice must have sounded plaintive.

His nod was reflected faintly in the glow of the compass light, and his tone suggested that anything else would be out of the question.

"We'll not make the flood otherwise."

Though it was still dark, the 200- and 300-foot cliffs of Land's End, with a reputation as evil as any this side of Cape Horn, were faintly outlined against the pre-dawn paleness of the sky behind. Bob stared into the blackness to starboard and finally grunted in satisfaction.

"There it is—the Shark's Fin! See that low shadow?"

I couldn't, but if he could, that was what mattered. He pointed ahead.

"There's the one to look out for now—Kettle's Bottom. We have to aim midway between that and the Peal, just off Land's End proper."

I could see Kettle's Bottom all right, even in the dark. In fact if my mouth hadn't been so dry I could have spat on it—it was that close. Only yards to port the granite cliffs sprang tall from the water, and I caught a flicker of white at their feet as the surf broke. A verse came to mind.

140

Break, break, break,
On thy cold, grey crags, Oh Sea!
And I would that my tongue could utter
The thoughts that arise in me.

Even Tennyson would have had trouble with the thoughts that were
arising in me right then, as I stared in horror at the silent cliffs sliding
by. This, I thought, is where the steering cables part.

Fine on the port bow was another shadow, towering closer than
ever.

"Armed Knight," murmured Bob, as though introducing me to an
old friend. "We gotta keep a few more yards off here—there's a reef not
quite awash."

I whimpered silently and felt for the depth-sounder switch. His eye
didn't even bother to glance at the dial as the little orange light came on.

"Don't need that thing," he commented disdainfully, as though I had
consulted a prayer wheel. "We got 16 fathoms here." Matter of fact it
was closer to 17, but I didn't argue.

I had long since given up any idea of taking the wheel and was quite
content to leave things as they were. If you ever get to thinking you are
pretty good because you happen to have crossed the Atlantic in a small
boat, I recommend rounding Land's End, inside Longships, in the dark,
with a master mariner at the wheel. It puts things back in perspective
for you.

Then we saw a double flashing white, every 10 seconds. Runnelstone!
He eased to port as we rounded the most westerly tip of England and
headed just outside Runnelstone. In case I thought he was chicken, which
I didn't, he told me why.

"You heading for Mousehole (pronounced Mowzl) or Penzance,
you'll save yourself two three miles inside there. Safe enough, too, if
you keep the rocks close aboard. Then you've got at least 6 fathoms. But
we're heading over for the Lizard, so we don't gain anything."

It was lighter now, and we could see the seas breaking on Runnelstone. We crossed Mount's Bay, rounded both the Lizard and the Man-
acles, and ran up into the Helford River, one of the prettiest in Cornwall, for the night.

In the morning we were off again, following the coast past Dodman
Point, Fowey, Polperro, Looe and Plymouth. Polperro was invisible from
seaward until we had just passed it, when it suddenly opened up—a tiny

141

fishing village hugging the slopes of a narrow gorge and running down to a toy harbour. Far to the south we could just see the famous Eddystone Lighthouse, 140 feet high, over which seas sometimes break during winter gales. Then we passed Yealm Head and Bolt Head before going up the Salcombe River to Kingsbridge, where Bob had to leave us. A few days later we had rounded Start Point and entered the Dart, past the Royal Naval Academy at Dartmouth, and as far as the beautiful Devon village of Dittisham.

Lyme Bay came next, but a brisk easterly pinned us down for several days, so we explored the countryside and made some good friends in Topsham, on the Exe River.

At last we got a fair wind, but darkness fell before we had crossed the big bay and reached Portland Bill.

I remembered the Bill from my school days, but somehow my geography books had skipped over certain points, such as why it had, during the past 3,000 years, claimed so many wrecks. The Coast Pilot tells why.

It is a long peninsula, jutting into the Channel south of Weymouth, with large bays on both sides. South of the Bill, for about 3 miles, is a shallow ledge, and to the east of this is a group of submerged rocks aptly named the Shambles. The fast-flowing tide, whether ebbing or flooding, is pushed to the surface over this ledge, producing the infamous Portland Race, which consists of overfalls, breakers and whirlpools. Even in good weather it takes a powerful engine to get you out of there, and a sailboat is asking for trouble if it goes close.

We sighted the Bill at about 10 p.m., flashing red. As you round it the number of flashes increases from one to four, to help you pinpoint your position, for errors can be costly. We kept the light on the port beam, rounding it at the recommended 5-mile radius. Gradually the compass bearing changed, but for 7 hours straight that red light blinked at us in groups of four, and for days afterwards, in our bunks at night, we could close our eyes and still see it.

Just before dawn I noticed that the Shambles light was moving the wrong way, to starboard instead of to port. We were being carried in towards the Race! We piled on every stitch of canvas and ran the diesel at 2,300 r.p.m., heading due east. Under a strong wind we were making a good 10 knots through the water, and very slowly the Shambles light crept over to port. We were winning.

Half an hour later, and now out of danger, the diesel cut dead. It was a bubble in the fuel line and within minutes it was cleared and the engine running again. But had it happened earlier we should have wound up in the Race. We entered the huge naval harbour at Portland without further trouble, and dropped the hook.

East of Portland Bill is St. Albans Head, with another unpleasant race. We reached this one under power on a dead calm afternoon, and it came as a bit of a shock when the oily water suddenly changed to a seething mass of whirlpools and breakers, far from shore and with nothing to account for it all.

Next came Poole, with its huge, natural harbour, and then through the Solent and along the coast of the Isle of Wight. We were getting strong westerlies now, and had to hole up in one place after another, waiting for weather. Rounding Selsey Bill there was just time to get into Shoreham-by-Sea before things got really bad.

We were made honorary members of the Sussex Yacht Club there, and found hospitality that was embarrassing. It reached the point where we could no longer go into the club bar, for they refused to let us pay for drinks even after we had ordered them. For 11 days the wind hardly dropped below Force 6 or 7, and it was already June 30th. Obviously, if we hoped to reach the Mediterranean this fall we could forget all about the Thames, the Rhine, the Baltic and the Norwegian fjords. Better get back to Cornwall in a hurry.

Kitty's sister Isobel was flying from Toronto to join us for a spell, and we sent a hurried call for her to meet us at Portsmouth instead of London. As soon as the weather permitted, we returned to the Solent and anchored at Fareham, up the river from Portsmouth.

It was at this point that Alec (later Sir Alec) Rose entered the Channel at the end of his epic solo circumnavigation, and we sailed out to the Nab Tower to join the many craft meeting him. We fell in on his port quarter and were a bare 50 yards away when he stepped ashore, to be greeted by a wildly cheering crowd, luncheon with the Queen and a knighthood.

After that we hit a series of easterlies, and made surprisingly good time back to Cornwall. However, rather than face Land's End twice more, we ran up the Truro River and anchored in the heart of Cornwall, a short bus ride from Padstow. The river was beautiful, winding endlessly between hills that were thickly wooded down to the water's edge. Even with our 3-foot draft we could get there only at high tide, for at other times there is a mere trickle between the mud flats.

At Padstow we made plans for the journey south.

143

Victualling up was easy, for we bought in case lots from a whole-saler. We ordered 6 months' supply of food, and it was delivered to the boat.

Convinced that we were now too old to sit up day and night at the wheel, we advertised for a crew of two, and got them with no trouble at all. Forty years ago a young man could go down to the docks and work his passage to any part of the world. But the unions have stopped all that, and now the only way he can do so is in a private yacht. It is now standard practice for students and others, male or female, to crew on a yacht, sharing the watches and other chores and paying $1 or $2 a day for their food. It works well for both sides, and there are usually more applicants than there are berths available. Few are experienced sailors, but the main requirement is the ability to stay awake at nights. The aim is to get people who are congenial and willing to pull their weight.

We selected the two most likely applicants, and were lucky with both. Jane was a twenty-one-year-old blonde with dinghy sailing experience, and Dave, too, had had enough experience to be useful, but not enough for him to want to take over as skipper after 2 days.

I kept in touch with the Royal Air Force at St. Mawgan, and they finally told me of a high coming in about August 23rd. This should give us easterlies for a few days, for we didn't want to have to fight a south-wester across the Bay of Biscay. On the morning of the 24th we slid down-river, past King Harry's Ferry, and into the Channel, with a light northeaster clearing away the coastal haze.

## THE ROCK

As we left the land the wind freshened and a bit of a sea started to build up. By the next afternoon, off the Brest peninsula in Northern France, we found that we had left our sea legs in Cornwall. The Bay of Biscay lived up to its evil reputation, and although the winds didn't go much over Force 5, the seas were short, steep and confused, as they

144

usually are in these waters. Fortunately the wind held fair and we were able to make southing.

On the 4th day, an afternoon sunsight and a Consul radio bearing from Lugo, in Spain, placed us 130 miles from Corunna. Rounding Cape Finisterre, on the northwest corner of Spain, proved slow, due to a contrary current. We kept well out to sea to avoid the coastal shipping, but ran into very light airs.

These continued until the 9th day, so we edged closer to the coast in search of a land or sea breeze, and at midnight we saw the light on Mondego Point, 90 miles north of Lisbon. It was our first sight of land since England.

Next day we had to motor for awhile, to round the Berlengua Islands, which stretch out from the coast in a chain. We cleared them at night, and by dawn they were well astern. The weather was perfect, with light winds and a clear sky, and far to the east we could just see the mountains behind Lisbon.

On the 12th day Dave caught a fish that nobody could identify, even after comparing it with all the illustrations in two fish books. Apparently we had discovered a new species. We cooked it, nibbled it cautiously, and agreed that it was pretty good.

That night, with Dave at the wheel in a Force 3, the mainsail came down with a loud clatter, and the halyard tinkled up to the mast-head. A shackle pin had come out.

In the morning I went up in the bosun's chair, having become slightly more sanguine about such matters since Oswego, N.Y., but my bravado melted rapidly when I got up there. The top of the mast on a trimaran is not the steadiest place in the world, especially in mid-ocean, and by the time I was at the three-quarter point I was ready to quit. We used the topping lift as a halyard instead. By evening the wind was up to Force 6, and rather than put undue strain on the temporary halyard we dropped the main altogether and ran under jib and mizzen. Despite the wind, the sky was clear and starry.

Towards morning the wind died as quickly as it had appeared, and by 10 a.m. we were becalmed. Dave and Jane went over for a swim, towed on a line, with complete disregard for the possibility of sharks. I didn't like the idea, but felt that they knew the risks as well as I did. For my part, I have an understanding with sharks, and it has worked well. I stay out of their ocean, and they stay off my ship. The only time

145

we socialize with them is close to the beach and over clean sand, where they can be seen at a good distance.

We rounded Cape St. Vincent, but didn't see it, and just after sunrise, with a faint breeze coming off the still-invisible land to the north, we picked up the most heavenly scent of pine woods. It was a surprising thing to find, so far out to sea, but when we closed our eyes we could swear that we were tramping through a pine forest with the smell of needles around us.

By noon on the 15th day we were 80 miles from Tangier, but progress was again slow. The wind was now easterly, and gradually strengthening until it was up to Force 6 again. The seas, moreover, were abnormally high and steep, a fact which I put down to the wind bucking the east-flowing current in the Strait of Gibraltar. We pounded badly as we fought our way to windward, and I should probably have given up the fight had the sky not been blue and cloudless. It was difficult to believe that we were really fighting a half-gale.

At 7.30 a.m. the wind suddenly dropped to nothing, and we wallowed in the slop. To the southeast, drifting off the African shore, was a huge bank of low cloud or mist. By 8 a.m. we knew what it was.

Fog!

The Strait is about as busy a 9-mile gap as you will find anywhere, and to be dumped into the middle of it, in a rolling sea and thick fog, can produce ulcers faster than anything I know. We heard a ship's engine to starboard, and the thrump-thrump-thrump of its screw came closer and closer. The direction was impossible to pinpoint in the fog, for the sounds came through the water. So I broke out the little radar detector which howls when it receives a transmission and gives a rough bearing on the source of the signal. But it doesn't tell you how to avoid those 20,000 tons of steel when they are barrelling down on you at 14 knots or so. The main advantage is psychological: it tells you that somebody out there cares enough to turn on their radar. It gives you a feeling of being wanted. It isn't until later that you realize that the existence of a scanning signal is no guarantee that anyone is actually watching that screen of theirs.

I turned on the diesel to get away from the sound of the engines but that only made things worse, for we couldn't hear them any more and could easily have been heading the wrong way for all we knew. So we switched it off, and were relieved to find the sound a little fainter.

146

We just hoped that he could see us on his radar.

Then the wind started again, still from the east, and soon the fog had gone. By mid-morning it was up to Force 7, gusting 8. Entering the Strait in the teeth of that was out of the question, so we fell off on the starboard tack and headed for Cádiz, the nearest port with a big, easy harbour.

It was 1 a.m. next morning before we reached the approaches, and we hove-to outside until daybreak.

Not knowing much about Spanish maritime law, we dutifully flew our "Q" flag and asked for the *Capitánia del Puerto* as soon as we had rafted on to a tug, there being few facilities for visiting yachts in Cádiz. I was directed to the appropriate office and asked several people what one was supposed to do when he entered port. A stout man with glasses on the end of his nose asked me if I wished to speak to the Canadian consul. I gave up and went back on board.

Minutes later a naval rating in spotless whites appeared, smiled, saluted, and gave me a form to fill in—from the *Capitánia,* he explained politely. It called for a mass of details, such as passenger and crew lists. (I never knew whether to include Mary and Nora as passengers, and thus admit to carrying passengers without a licence, or as crew, and thus run afoul of the child labour laws.) It also asked about cargo manifests, names of all personnel who had died since our last port (infectious or non-infectious?) gross and net registered tonnage, draft forward and aft, length, beam, height of upper deck above waterline, date of last de-ratisation certificate, size and working pressure of all boilers, horsepower of main and auxiliary engines, number and type of capstans, deck winches and derricks, and the number and capacity of lifeboats. All questions were, of course, in Spanish, and most of the terms didn't seem to appear in my tourist's phrase book. The naval rating was very helpful, and explained all questions in minute detail. Unfortunately, he did so in rapid Castilian. But I managed to answer everything, in English and in my worst scrawl, on the theory that what they couldn't read they couldn't prove to be false. The main thing seemed to be to fill in every blank space with something.

An hour later another rating brought a duplicate of the form, presented it with a smile and a salute, and answered my protest that I had already filled it in with the comment that two copies were required by the *Capitánia.* I could only assume that the Spanish navy had over-extended itself on ratings and underbought on carbon paper. So I started all over again, trying to remember what I had said the first time, in case someone in Madrid should compare copies one and two.

It was 8 a.m. the next day before the third rating appeared with copy three. This time I couldn't resist it, and gave them information that must have given somebody, somewhere, the impression that the *Queen Elizabeth II* had been in port. Then we went ashore in a hurry, and never did learn whether the good *Capitán* needed a fourth copy.

Cádiz was an interesting city, picturesque and historical, and most of the streets were narrow, designed to produce cooling shade. The main *ramblas* were wide, and shade was produced by trees. The place was obviously prosperous, and we wandered for hours through the narrow arcades and down the broad *avenidas*, resting on the shaded seats in the many parks.

The sight of the old forts guarding the bay reminded us of the part that Cádiz had played in the history of Spain, and indeed of the world. From here the galleons set out for the Americas, to return with their holds crammed with the treasures which made Spain the richest and most powerful nation on earth in her day. One could almost see the ships of the Armada waiting to sail against England and Elizabeth, their captains and crews sworn to the task of wrenching that country from the heretic and returning it to the true church. And one could imagine the little ships of Drake sailing in to "singe the King of Spain's beard" by burning the Cádiz section of the great Armada as it lay at anchor.

Both Dave and Jane had to leave us here, and return to England, which left us free to press on or linger, as the spirit moved us. The local fishermen assured us that the levanter, as these screaming easterlies are called, would end the next day, and so it did. When we sailed at 9:30 a.m. the wind was back in the west, at a nice Force 4.

Gibraltar was rather far for a one-day trip, so we broke the journey at the little fishing port of Barbate, just east of Cape Trafalgar. This gave rise to another history lesson for the children, and we described the significance of the battles of St. Vincent and Trafalgar, telling them of the impact of the latter on the history of Europe, of the loss to Napoleon, and of the death of Nelson. History came alive.

The westerly held nicely as we swung east, with the Spanish Sierras to port and the Atlas Mountains of Africa to starboard. We were carried along by the permanent east-flowing current, and made excellent time

148

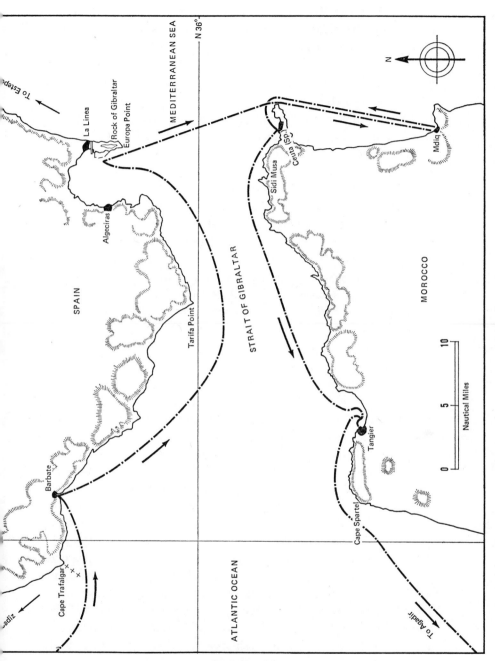

*Strait of Gibraltar*

149

through the Strait. The familiar shape of Gibraltar appeared ahead, and once again the children were given a crash course in British naval history as we turned into Algeciras Bay.

We tied up at the destroyer pens in the navy harbour, and after being cleared by customs—a relaxed experience at Gibraltar—discovered three unpleasant facts.

1. To tie up in the pens cost £4 a week.
2. There was a nasty surge there that may not have bothered a destroyer but it sure disturbed a trimaran.
3. When I went up the mast to retrieve the halyard, I found to my horror that the stainless steel fitting, holding both backstays, had fractured, apparently from fatigue and not recently either, to judge from the discoloration of the metal. The mast was safe enough— provided nobody leaned against it! I remembered the levanter.

We promptly moved to the small-craft anchorage, where repair facilities were available, where the surge was less, and where there was no charge. This anchorage was at the north end of the Rock, between it and the airport runway, and although a nasty swell can still come in from Algeciras Bay in a westerly, as we were to discover later, it was still better than in the pens.

Proctor Masts, when I reported the fracture to them, were most concerned and helpful, and although the mast was four years old they designed a modification to prevent a similar occurrence in the future and asked me to have it made up at their expense. This seemed more than fair of them.

The original plan was to winter in Spain, possibly Alicante, but for several reasons we decided to stay at Gib. For one thing, even in 1932 my schoolboy Spanish wasn't all that hot, and it hadn't improved since. For another, the sight of Lipton's Supermarket, full of familiar brands at low prices, was tempting. Thirdly, the harbour seemed well-protected. And fourthly, the Director of Education, Mr. Harrington, was most courteous and helpful in the matter of schooling. While the children were not entitled to attend a local school, not being residents, it was agreed that if they should appear at classes nobody would throw them into the harbour. So they attended St. Anne's School unofficially and gained immeasurably, not only in academic matters but also from meeting other children (mainly Spanish-speaking), joining in social activities, and adding to their experience of other countries and peoples.

150

That winter was a unique experience that we would not want to have missed. Gibraltar evokes strange emotions, and one can well understand how it can produce either a lump in the throat or a pain in the neck, depending on your most recent experience.

To one of British background, it will always conjure up a picture of a romantic Outpost of Empire, of the naval might that used to be beyond imagination, even if it has grown a bit threadbare in the seventies. With Franco Spain on the other side of a wire fence, and with Morocco a mere 11 miles away and usually visible, the Rock is a minute pocket of England in an alien world. It is strangely pleasant to step ashore and see familiar uniforms, advertisements for products that have been household words since childhood, and other such links with one's youth. It is good to hear the tones of a B.B.C. announcer relayed from London, and the haunting sounds of the "Last Post" coming over the evening air from some garrison bugler.

Its shape must be known to all, but what strikes one most, standing in town or harbour, is its sheer size, a solid mass of limestone 3 miles long and 1,400 feet high, strangely detached from everything around it. At its northern end, known locally as Devil's Tower and as vertical as the wall of a house, it faces Spain defiantly. Generations of British defenders have blasted out gun-ports and connecting galleries across this face, and these still sprout cannon to cover the frontier a few hundred yards away. But they are mere relics, for a far more effective defence is provided by the modern artillery and rocket launchers, backed up by one of the most sophisticated radar and communications networks in the free world, buried deep in the rock itself.

Just south of the border, on a narrow sandy spit of land joining Gibraltar to the mainland, is the airport, and the fill from the many excavations has been used to lengthen the previously quite inadequate runway out into Algeciras Bay. Even now you hold your breath coming in, especially at night, for there is little margin for error. Touch down a few yards too soon, or a bit too far to port or starboard, and you do so on water. Do so a bit late, and you are in the sea at the other end. Modern jets pile on the reverse thrust in a way that makes passengers go pale and causes magazines to slide off knees, but they manage to stop in time. Some World War II bombers, without reverse thrust, didn't quite make it, and there is a lot of scrap aluminum off the end of the runway.

Ethnically, Gibraltar must be the strangest mixture this side of Singa-

151

pore. Main Street is a blend of English, Spanish, Yiddish, Hindustani, Arabic, Russian and, if there happens to be a cruise ship in that day, Brooklynese as well. And there are as many yashmaks as there are mini-skirts. Incidentally, I suppose it had to come eventually, though I hate to think what Mohammed would say—the day of the see-through yashmak has arrived!

Most numerous of all the races are the Spaniards, who wave a Union Jack and insist that they are not Spanish at all, but "Breeteesh," even if many of them can't speak English.

The average American or Canadian, trying to do business in England, eventually takes to drink. But unless he has faced Spanish methods, as practised on the "Rock," he doesn't know what frustrations really are. Along Main Street you can buy saris from India, cameras from Japan, vodka from Russia, ivory from Cambodia or rugs from Persia. But just try to buy a dozen little ¼-inch plain brass washers, or a ball of string, or an air letter form from the post office—just try, that's all! The official motto of Gibraltar should be *"No hay"* (pronounced "no eye"), a widely-used Spanish expression which, loosely translated, means, "Uh uh! We ain't got none!" You hear it before you have even specified your needs, for the store clerks, not in the highest tax bracket even by Gib standards, operate on the theory that the easiest way to get through the day is to discourage all potential customers as they enter the door and persuade them to try somewhere else.

The marina which repaired our mast-head fitting needed some ⅛-inch stainless steel sheet for the job. They didn't have any, of course, but it would arrive on Tuesday from England. I jumped to the ridiculous conclusion that they meant next Tuesday, which they didn't. They meant that when it did arrive it would almost certainly be on a Tuesday. I called in every second day for the next 3 months and finally gave up. An air-mail letter to Proctors, in England, brought the necessary parts within days by air, cut, deburred, drilled and ready to be fitted. It was a pleasure to tell the marina to drop dead.

On the Rock you will suddenly run into a shortage of, say eggs. Not an egg to be had anywhere, all week. Then, out of the blue, every grocery store in town (and they average 7 to the city block) has eggs coming out of its ears and is selling them off cheap before they go bad. All of which makes life interesting, for you never know what is going to disappear next. Meat? Cement? Fourpenny stamps? Tomatoes? Matches?

152

Much of the problem seems to stem from the fact that in Gibraltar a few families have skimmed off the gravy and even today enjoy lucrative monopolies at the expense of the consumer and the grossly underpaid worker. The Saccones, for instance, share the liquor business with the Bagliettos, while the Blands and the Imossis divide up the ship repair business. The Blands have a near exclusive on travel and transportation, and what automotive business there is belongs to the Capurros, who also have the marina work sewn up tight. And so it goes. Most commodities and services are in the hands of a small group, be it lumber or bottled gas, vegetables or crushed stone. The housewives, for instance, tired of the high prices and low quality of their vegetables, formed their own cooperative to bring them in from Tetuan, in Morocco. Prices tumbled overnight until they were told to stop importing without a licence. No, they couldn't get a permit. The cooperative folded and prices doubled again.

The list of such evils is endless, and accounts in large measure for the low wage scale. Most men earn no more than £8 ($20) a week, and must hold two jobs to live. A girl who wanted to crew with us to get away from the Rock was working in a bar six days a week, earning enough for food, or for a room, but not both. So she squandered her wages on food and slept on the beach.

Gibraltar used to be a free port, but is so no longer. A bottle of Bacardi rum, for instance, costs $1 in Ceuta, 11 miles away, but $3.12 in Gibraltar. The result is a brisk import-export business that the customs seem powerless, or unwilling, to stop. We know of one yacht that made two trips a week, returning after dark with liquor which would be unloaded before morning for delivery to the local bars and night-clubs at a 100% profit.

The Strait has always been a traditional smuggling area. One yacht was offered $3,000 to bring a load of cigarettes from Tangier (Morocco) to Ceuta (Spanish Morocco), 25 miles away. The Spaniards try hard to stop this traffic, but the operators use Gibraltar as a haven and trans-shipment base. This makes Franco furious, and he cries that Gib is harbouring smugglers, a claim which is not entirely groundless. He even began patrolling the Strait with an old destroyer that seems to burn soft coal and is known locally as "Smoky Joe." To exceed about 7 knots it has to pump out so much smoke that it can be seen over the horizon, and in anything over a Force 5 wind it takes shelter in Algeciras Bay.

As the winter progressed we began to feel at home on the Rock, and the children loved their life at St. Anne's. It was right on the waterfront and a mere 100-yard row from *Caravel*. They didn't always make it, but the teachers, just by looking at the state of the seas, knew whether to expect them. Although non-Catholics in a Catholic school, they were made most welcome and excused all religious training. At Christmas they were taken into the choir and for weeks *Caravel* rang to the sound of Spanish carols, climaxed by a radio and TV appearance with a solo part for Mary.

But the weather was a problem, for in winter Gibraltar is a place of screaming winds, all either east or west. In a levanter (easterly) the Rock itself, far from affording shelter, actually increased the wind speed as the air rushed round the end of it. It blew for perhaps a minute, with unbelievable fury, and then died suddenly to a flat calm for another minute, while the boat drifted back over its own anchor. Then, with a roar like a train entering a tunnel, it hit us again, lifting us bodily and slamming us back against our anchor-lines. Winds exceeding hurricane force were not uncommon, and on one occasion they were logged at the airport at 112 m.p.h.

Boats dragged anchor and several were wrecked. Fortunately I discovered at the bottom of the harbour, which contains just about everything from Greek amphorae to Ford V-8 blocks, some enormous chain that the Royal Navy had apparently put there at some point in its history. One end of this, to which several smaller chains were attached, was secured to the Rock of Gibraltar, and over the other end they had built the airport runway. All in all it gave the impression of a pretty safe mooring. Getting even one of the smaller chains to the surface to shackle onto it was quite a chore, but with block and tackle we finally made it. And despite ten major storms that winter *Caravel*, with the Rock of Gibraltar securely attached, didn't drag an inch.

And even the storms did us some good, providing both water via the catchment system on the top deck (fresh water, brought into Gib by tanker, is sold by the gallon) and also electric power for the batteries, by way of a wind-generator which I rigged up on the bow. We had our teething problems with this, due to vibration in the screamers. The normal charge rate was 2 amps, and on one occasion it reached 10 amps before the entire assembly shook itself free and took off. Fortunately, the water was only 10 feet deep, and we salvaged it, dried it out, and got it going again. This generator, with its 6-foot propeller, created a

154

minor sensation locally, for it made *Caravel* look more like an aircraft than ever.

As spring approached we began to make our usual overly-ambitious plans for an extended cruise through the entire Mediterranean to the Isles of Greece. We revictualled, refitted, refuelled and wondered whether we should have time to get into the Black Sea and up the Dnieper.

We didn't.

⚜⚜⚜

## COSTA DEL VIENTO

On April 10th we cast off our lines, a process which wasn't quite as easy as it sounds, for we were still firmly secured to those chains on the bottom. Casting off involved a great deal of backbreaking work with blocks, tackle and winches and wasn't completed until nearly midday. We finally got away, and headed south for Europa Point in a light easterly. Here we were delayed again by a patrol boat that waved us well away from the point as we rounded it, yelling something about a firing range. We heard the faint rattle of rifle fire from the Rock, and got the point, making a wide sweep and heading into the Mediterranean for Estepona, 20 miles away.

Here we were puzzled to see that a lighthouse was several miles from the position shown on the Admiralty chart, although it was a well-weathered structure that had obviously been there for many years. Why the Royal Navy doesn't spend $1.25 occasionally for a Spanish chart, to keep itself up to date, I don't know. It wasn't the only inaccuracy that we found.

At Estepona the Guardia Civil came on board, but seemed more interested in the crew list than in possible contraband. Every port in Spain demands this list, but as they all use a different form you can't make them up in advance. Most ports also have a Club Naútico and in some of these, though not all, visiting yachtsmen are welcome. Few members own a yacht, for it seems that in Spain the ownership of a boat

155

over a certain length automatically puts you into a high tax bracket. The result is a lot of sailing dinghies and Boston Whalers, but rarely anything larger. Members are content to lie around all day, soaking up sun and *cerveza*.

Next came Marbella, which turned out to be a tourist trap for West Germans. They charged us 10 pesetas per night for each metre of beam, which is tough on a trimaran 22 feet wide, so we left in the morning, despite a high wind, for Málaga. By noon we were clawing down the mainsail in a Force 7. Fortunately it was astern, and we roared along the coast about a mile offshore. The arid slopes of the sierras swept up to a blue sky, their sides cut by the dried river beds and dotted with almond and olive trees, apparently the only things except cactus that will grow.

What had grown, though, in great profusion along this Costa del Sol, was mile after mile of high-rise apartments and hotels. We sailed past the harbour-less resorts of Fuengirola and Torremolinos, entering Málaga and tying up at the eastern end of the huge harbour.

The city was beautiful and obviously prosperous, with its centre consisting of wide, tree-lined *avenidas*, a lovely park and, strangest of all, an area of old, narrow but well-kept malls from which all traffic had been excluded. These extended a long way, and one could stroll down the shaded alleys and arcades, where the buildings kept out the hot sun but funnelled the cooling breeze. It was delightful.

There was also an efficient and well-stocked *mercado* or municipal market. These are a regular feature of Spanish towns, although the standard of cleanliness and quality varies from place to place. Fruit and vegetables were cheap, plentiful and good. Fish was generally poor, for the Mediterranean does not produce the tasty firm fish that we enjoy in the Atlantic and Pacific, and the Spaniards put up with the most horrible-looking squid, octopus and other soft flabby creatures that defy classification. Actually octopus and squid can taste pretty good, provided you haven't seen them alive on the quay. I never did discover whether the repeated smashing of these onto the quay was to kill them or tenderize them—it doesn't seem to do either very effectively.

Meat was expensive and of poor quality, with little recognizable on sight. Kid was recommended, but hanging from a hook and covered with flies it looked more like a dog than anything else—a disquieting thought! Fortunately we had plenty of canned meat.

There was a fair swell running into the harbour. We put out a stern anchor to hold us off the quay, but this produced an unusual problem next morning. A 20,000-ton freighter came in early, and the tug that had been easing her into the quay near us finished the job and dropped the end of the heavy steel hawser into the water. As the winch-operator on the freighter started to retrieve it, the shackled loop at the end picked up our anchor line and he began to retrieve *Caravel* too, hoisting us rather ignominiously by our rear end.

Everything started to slide forward as I clambered out on deck, wondering what on earth was happening. Another few seconds and we should have been dangling from the hawsehole of that freighter, for the operator didn't even know that he had got a bite. Fortunately the hawser let us go at this point, and our stern fell back into the water with a resounding splash. The only damage, apart from my shattered nerves, was to an inch of the starboard bow where it caught the quay. A spoonful of polyester resin, a dab of paint, and it was repaired. We ate a hurried breakfast and got out of Málaga fast.

By 11 a.m. we were running down-wind like mad, under storm canvas and chased by mounting seas. The cloudless sky, we had already discovered, meant nothing, for in the Mediterranean the fiercest winds can come on an otherwise perfect day. By mid-afternoon we were staggering into the next port, Motril, and glad to be inside.

The location was simply beautiful. At the foot of a wide valley running up into the sierras, the harbour was large but strangely empty. Although equipped to handle many freighters at once, with long, protecting sea walls and modern cranes, it was occupied by only a few fishing boats and several yachts, including *Avila*, belonging to the king of Belgium. A palm-lined road encircled the bay, and behind everything were the high sierras, brown and naked, austerely etched against the blue sky, and dominated by the highest mountain in all of Spain— Mulhacén, with its snowy, 12,000-foot peak. The valley floor was covered with sugar fields, where peasants slashed at the cane with sickle and machete, loading it onto the backs of donkeys. A dozen or so of these heavily-laden creatures, encouraged by a boy with a big stick and a ready repertoire of Spanish invective, carried the cane slowly up the dusty road to the mill.

We stayed at Motril for nearly 2 weeks, attracted by the beauty and the opportunity to work on *Caravel*, and also discouraged from further

157

sailing by the screaming winds that sprang up every day before noon and lasted until dusk. They sent green water and even rocks high over the western breakwater, which was itself 25 feet high. At night it dropped to a flat calm.

Now a week in port can create something of a garbage problem, and Kitty was at last forced to the conclusion that it would have to go over the harbour wall, there being, as far as we could see, no other provision for garbage disposal. So one afternoon when all was quiet during the siesta hour, she stepped ashore with a large box of the stuff, rounded the corner, and ran smack into a Guardia Civil!

Embarrassed at being caught, she smiled sweetly and said, "*Basura!*"

He nodded, but didn't smile back.

"*Donde?*"

This was an easily-recognized attempt to pass the buck, but he wasn't buying. He shrugged his shoulders to indicate that this was her problem.

Accepting this as tacit authority to pollute the whole Mediterranean if she wished, she reached over the wall and consigned the lot to the deep, returning with the empty box for another load. After thus disposing of the entire smelly outrigger-full, she leaned over to examine the result of her handiwork, but instead of the blue Mediterranean she saw a broad expanse of rocky foreshore, well-littered with her all too familiar garbage. There being no tide in the Med, it is probably there yet.

One gradually gets used to the idea that in Spain the way to solve the garbage problem is not to let the stuff accumulate. The moment you finish with a can, fish head, beer bottle, cabbage stalk or cereal carton, you flip it over your left shoulder and make a wish. It will eventually blow away, rust away, or be eaten by a stray cat, and the problem really solves itself.

Two hours or so out of Motril, by bus, is Granada, although it is a hair-raising trip through the mountains with sheer drops of 2,000 feet and no such things as guard rails. We got there in one piece and climbed the heights near the city to the famous Alhambra fortress. This was the palace of the Moorish calif during the Saracen occupation of Spain. It is one of the most beautiful examples of Moorish architecture in the world and presents a vivid picture of what life must have been like for the conquerors in those days, before El Cid drove them out.

A day or so later, with the wind screaming rather less violently than

158

usual, we set out from Motril for the next town, Adra. By mid-afternoon we were limping into harbour under the storm jib alone, and wondering what had hit us.

The harbour was comfortable enough, but the town was as bad as they come, with poverty and filth everywhere. The poor lived in hovels, which they shared with the pigs, goats, hens and numerous children, while the very poor couldn't afford hovels, pigs or goats. They lived in caves in the hillside, and we discovered that in Spain there are still many thousands of cave dwellers.

The main street was unpaved and smelled of garlic, sweat and sewage. Through the centre of town ran a stream, dry at this time of year except for a few stagnant pools of green, slimy water. The *mercado*, surrounded by slums, was far from inviting.

A woman approached, leading her 3-year-old boy by the hand. He was having trouble with a top-heavy ice cream cone, and the contents fell out, flopped into the dirt road at his feet, and started to spread out in the heat. He howled at his loss, and his mother, without a second's hesitation, bent down, scooped up the ice cream with one deft movement, and slapped it back into his cone.

Between Adra and the next port, Almería, was a nasty bit of coast with reefs and shoals, so we took the advice of the Coast Pilot and stood well out. But once again we were hit by a sudden "white squall" before we got in, and I had to fight my way forward and struggle with the wildly flogging mainsail and swinging boom. As I wrestled them, half-blinded with flying spray and unable to keep my balance, Nora watched me from the cockpit while Kitty was at the wheel. She started to bang on the bulkhead in anguish with both fists.

"Oh Mummy, I hate it! I hate it! I hate it!"

The girls were beginning to grow up, and for the first time were able to recognize danger when they saw it.

As we entered port, rounding the breakwater under the diesel, I offered a silent prayer that it wouldn't quit right here, where the seas bounced back from the outer wall and formed a boiling inferno. All went well.

Almería was quite large, and the downtown portion turned out to be pleasant, with wide streets and modern stores. Dominating the city, as at Granada, was the Saracen *alcázar*, or fortress, with lovely shaded gardens and pools with waterfalls. The water for these, apparently,

159

had been carried up by the Spaniards in jars, and one wonders whether the Moorish treatment of the Spaniards may not account, in part, for the behaviour of the latter when they themselves entered the Caribbean and the Americas as *conquistadores* so soon afterwards.

On the slopes of a neighbouring hill was another colony of cave-dwellers, and one morning Kitty and I strolled up this hillside of caves and slum shacks. There was no road, just a winding track. Halfway up was a communal water tap and near the top a communal toilet, too far from most homes to be used, so that the children simply relieved themselves where they stood.

The further we climbed the less comfortable we felt, and we became conscious of looks of curiosity, sometimes of hostility. They recognized us for what we were, tourists intent upon examining their squalor at close range, and we felt guilty. We would nod to a passer-by, with a "*buen di.*" Sometimes they would reply, sometimes not. A huge dog, its ribs pushing through its hungry flanks, growled throatily and stared at us through watery, pale blue eyes. Kitty touched my arm, and we sat in silence on a rock, thinking this was the best way to make the creature lose interest in us.

High above us, at the entrance to a cave, a young girl of about 13, surprisingly well-groomed and in a clean print dress, stared out over town and harbour to where blue sea met blue sky, where a faint smudge told of a ship on the horizon. During the 15 minutes we were there she hardly moved, but gazed out to sea, wrapped in thought. Our hearts went out to her and we both commented later on the hopelessness of her position. About a year older than Mary, she had probably been born in that cave. With little hope of ever escaping from her wretched environment she seemed to be dreaming of lands across the sea, where people lived in houses, and rode in cars, and ate from china plates, and slept in beds, and went to the toilet in private. Somehow the sight of that forlorn little figure, so carefully dressed, touched us more than anything else we saw in Spain.

That night we were hit by a vicious katabatic squall that swept down from the mountains at 1:30 a.m. We dragged anchor and had to use the diesel to hold ourselves until things quietened down and we could reset the anchor.

Over breakfast we held a council of war, and I voiced thoughts that had already occurred to Kitty.

The Mediterranean weather, regardless of the travel brochures, was hopeless for sailing, at least for light displacement craft. The winds came out of a clear blue sky without warning, to scream like a banshee for hours on end and die to nothing at night. So far, it had all been from the west, which was fine. But how on earth were we ever to get back to Gib?

Yachtsmen familiar with the Med had been pessimistic, for every area seemed to have its own breed of explosive winds. Off Southern Spain it was the poniente, the vendevale and the levanter, and off the French coast it was the notorious mistral. Along the African shore it was the sirocco that was the trouble, while Malta suffered from the gregale, the wind that wrecked St. Paul. Further east it was the bora and the maestrale. You couldn't escape them, and from the design of the local fishing boats the only answer seemed to lie in something weighing 100 tons and pushed by 300 horsepower.

Wintering, too, was a problem. Eric Hiscock had told grim tales of winter storms at Rhodes, and we heard gloomy stories of the surge in Valetta harbour. We already knew how Gib could act up.

I badly wanted to see the Med, but not at the expense of never being able to relax and enjoy it. I was getting a little tired of being thrown about by vicious, unpredictable winds and steep, angry seas; tired too of the lack of weather forecasts or even radio communications in our own language, and the absence of the well-organized rescue facilities that were found in North American and British waters. French harbours, we were warned, were very expensive, while Italy suffered from too many boats and too few ports. In Greece there were only 2 months in the year when one could sail in comfort, while both Egypt and Albania were politically difficult and some of the North African countries little better.

We took a long, hard look at the situation and came to the conclusion that we were not here to prove anything, but to enjoy our travels. If we couldn't see the Med in safety, comfort and relaxation, then we might as well return to Gib and make for the Caribbean in the fall. We would explore the Med later, by road.

Gibraltar, however, lay 200 miles up-wind, and it looked as though the only way to get there was to power in easy stages, and at night, when it was calm. After 3 days of almost continuous gales I awoke at 1 a.m. one morning to find a flat calm. I shook Kitty and within minutes we were motoring out and heading west. A westerly started before we reached Adra, but we got in before it rose to gale force.

Another 3 days and we sneaked out at 10 p.m. in another calm,

161

and made Motril under power before breakfast. Gradually, in this way, we managed to reach Gibraltar on June 29th, and picked up our chain again. For all its shortcomings the old Rock seemed like home.

Ahead of us was a long Atlantic crossing, and again we advertised for a crew rather than face 4-on and 4-off for weeks on end. Out of the dozen or so replies we chose two young Glasgow men, Pat and Peter, who were muscular, didn't mind turning night into day, and wanted to cross the Atlantic on the cheap. They paid £50 each to cover their food for 100 days, this being to prevent them from changing their minds and leaving us crewless at the last moment. They also signed an agreement to the effect that they were paying guests, and not paid crew, to remove the possibility of their claiming air fare home when they landed, which they could otherwise do.

Victualling up was simple, and we found that the best thing was to talk Liptons, the only supermarket in town, into a flat 10% discount on everything and give them one order for the lot, which they delivered to the quay. We were also getting smarter on this question of food. In Toronto we had, after drawing up a list of every item needed for 6 months, tried to introduce variety by getting all sorts of fancy things such as lobster, crab, bottled olives, canned breast of chicken and other such exotic items. Never feeling justified in opening these delicacies, we would find them in the bilge 2 years later, rusty and blown. Now we were buying corned beef, canned sausage and similar basics by the case, and thus at a low price. Kitty had learned that there are a dozen ways to dress up corned beef with various sauces, curries and dried soups, to say nothing of using it as a cold cut or in sandwiches or in a meat pie or casserole. The stuff may be lowly, but at sea it is worth its weight in gold, as are, for instance, canned salmon and tuna. The trick is to buy large quantities of a relatively few items that can be served in many different ways.

There will always be problems, of course. Take yeast, for instance. Liptons didn't have any at all, and the bakery used only the fresh kind that needs refrigeration. Nobody in Gibraltar had any dried yeast, and up to 3 hours before sailing we were resigned to a bread-free diet for the next few months. But at the eleventh hour we found a wholesaler down a back street who had a room full of it. Hungrily we bought four 1-pound cans, determined never to run short again. We never did, either. In fact we have just thrown away the last of the first can, as too stale.

162

Anyone want to buy 9 pounds of dried yeast, wholesale? No, my mathematics are not wrong. What happened was this. A month later we met a freighter awaiting lengthy repairs in dry dock, and they gave us a lot of surplus food. It included, yes, six 1-pound cans of dried yeast!

The plan was to sail from Gib fairly early, be hauled for scraping and painting at Mdiq, Morocco, where the prices were lower than at Gib, head out of the Strait and down to the Canaries before the October gales started, then wait for November when the hurricanes would be over in the Atlantic. At this point I was still under the illusion that you can come to terms with weather, and didn't realize that before the October gales come the September storms, the August tempests, and the July cyclones. To be on the safe side I notified Lloyd's of London, who had insured us, of the impending plan.

I expected to be charged about the same additional premium as on the west-east passage, namely $40, on top of the premium we had already paid. They had surcharged the standard rate when we left England for the Med, and now wanted an extra $71 for the trip from Gib to the Canaries, and then a further $600 for the passage to Barbados. I thought maybe the decimal point was in the wrong place, and questioned it, asking how they arrived at this figure. They thought my attitude most ungentlemanly and flatly refused to insure me again on either side of the Atlantic, let alone in the middle. At those prices it was pretty academic anyway; it would be cheaper to sink.

We later discovered that other yachts, both monohull and multihull, had been asked additional premiums as high as $1,000, and we were delighted to learn that in each case the yachtsmen's reply had, despite minor variations in phraseology, been in essence the same.

"Turn blue!"

♥♥♥

## OF MOSQUES AND MINARETS

With much blowing of horns and waving to friends on shore and in other boats, the morning of September 8th found us motoring across the

163

Strait to where the misty outline of Sidi Musa stood guard on the African shore. By mid-afternoon we were tied up in the little town of Mdiq.

It has a sheltered harbour, a fact which has so far remained a secret from the British Admiralty, who still show it in both charts and Coast Pilot as an open roadstead. The town itself, however, hasn't changed much in the past 3,000 years, except for the odd Coke sign and gas station. Open sewers meander in a charming way through the dirt streets. The term "dirt streets" in Morocco means something quite different from "dirt road" in North America, for they use the word "dirt" in a far more literal sense. After a brief look at the local *sukh* or market, Kitty opened some canned hamburger for supper.

Our 22-foot beam was just too much for the Mdiq slip, so we explored the town and sailed north again, for Ceuta, to await the east wind that we needed to get out of the Strait.

The Strait of Gibraltar is a mere 30 miles long and 8 miles wide at the narrowest point. Coming in, a year before, we had made it in 4 hours plus. Going out, it again took us 4 hours plus—plus a couple of weeks! For we discovered that there is more to sailing through that channel than meets the eye.[*]

Firstly, the evaporation rate in the Med is so great that the combined flow of all its rivers—Rhône, Nile, Danube, Dnieper, etc.—makes up only one-third of it. The rest has to come in through Gibraltar in the form of a permanent east-flowing current which reaches 4 knots in the middle, although at the edges there is a slight in-and-out cyclic tide.

Secondly, the Western Mediterranean is a basin, surrounded by mountains on all sides. Given a high pressure system inside and a depression in the Atlantic, or vice versa, the rush of air through that 8-mile funnel is considerable, as anyone who has wintered a sailboat in Gibraltar knows to his cost. And it always blows due east or west, never north or south.

Coming in, you wait for a westerly, and with that and the current sweeping you along your main problem is to stop before you reach Israel at the other end. Going out is another story. To oppose wind and current in a sailboat is obviously impossible, especially that sort of wind and that kind of current. But a powerful wind against a 4-knot current

---

[*]Refer to the Strait of Gibraltar chart on page 149.

sets up the sort of seas that make sailors take up chicken farming. This situation in the Strait undoubtedly accounts for the reluctance of the ancient Greeks, Romans, Egyptians and others ever to leave the Med by sea. They took one look through the Pillars of Hercules and turned back in a hurry. Things haven't improved much since.

In Ceuta, after stocking up on such basics as rum and Spanish wine, we settled down to our paperbacks while waiting for an east wind— unfortunately at 30 pesetas a day harbour dues! After 10 days of this the wind finally died down during the night and dawn found us casting off before the fat little man in the grey uniform could come waddling along the quay for his fee. We hoped that we could get through the Strait before the wind swung into high gear from the east.

An hour later it was up to Force 6, and by the time we reached the narrows, opposite Tarifa Point, it was blowing at a sustained 7. Off Tangier, which is 5 miles from the end, it was gusting Force 9 and doing things to the incoming seas that you normally see only in movies. We ran into Tangier with our tail between our hulls and breathed a sigh of relief as we tied up in the beautifully sheltered inner harbour at the Tangier Yacht Club, where they promptly made us honorary members.

With all due respects to the T.Y.C., the city is largely a tourist trap, and what the Moroccans didn't already know about fleecing tourists the French soon taught them. The *kasbah* is colourful and interesting, but apart from the odd item of native handiwork there are few bargains, and certainly none among the watches, cameras and perfume displayed everywhere.

One thing that fascinated the girls, however, was the *mullah*, if that is his correct title, calling the faithful to prayer from the minaret on the mosque. But I couldn't help noticing that one no longer saw the white-robed figure up there. All you see, through the binoculars, is a group of loudspeakers, but no *mullah*. Either he is downstairs in his office, at a microphone or, worse still, the whole thing is on tape and activated by a time-switch. The prophet, I suspect, would never have approved of all this.

After a couple of days the wind eased and, fearing that if we waited too long it might start in again from the west, we left on the 24th. It was still pretty dusty outside, but it was astern, and within the hour we were off Cape Spartel, very glad to be out of the Mediterranean and into the Atlantic. Already the seas had changed. They were no longer the short, steep vicious creatures of the Strait and the Med, but the longer, easier swell of the ocean. They seemed more benign.

Bound for the Canary Islands, 700 miles down the African coast, we could either port-hop or head out and make a non-stop passage of it. The Africa Pilot is a bit pessimistic about this coast. Of the major port of Casablanca it reads, "Vessels berthed in Casablanca should use extra hawsers owing to the heavy swell which sets into the harbour, even in fine weather. In the event of bad weather, vessels should be ready to leave at short notice."

Without insurance, or even with it for that matter, I didn't fancy being forced out to sea in a gale because the harbour wasn't safe. As it happened, two other yachts we knew didn't have a copy of the Pilot, and foolishly went in. They found the harbour beautifully protected, were treated like visiting royalty, and gave us a glowing account of the place.

But we didn't know all this, and with Pat and Peter on board to steer at night, the offshore route seemed the more attractive.

The first day out from land we had a plague of flies—just ordinary house flies. For every one we swatted, 50 more would appear, until every nook and crevice was piled high with cadavers. Possibly they were blown offshore and figured that *Caravel* was their last chance before Cape Cod.

Then came the tuna fleet, if indeed that's what it was! It was night, and the first thing we saw was a group of lights that seemed to be trawlers, so we veered off to starboard to avoid them. Then came more lights, mere pinpricks on the water. Suddenly they were only yards away, and floating on buoys that appeared to be supporting tuna netting. We kept edging further and further to the west in an attempt to outflank the seemingly endless line of lights, and it took us nearly 2 hours to round them and get back onto course. As close as I could judge, this enormous net, hanging from floats, stretched in a circle *5 miles across*. This indicated a net 15 miles long, with a fleet of a dozen or so trawlers in attendance.

The passage down the coast, some 50 miles offshore, was otherwise uneventful, and the weather quite pleasant. Off Agadir, however, it started to blow hard from the north, and the seas began to build up. A day or so in port looked pretty good, especially as Agadir seemed to be one of the few places down the African coast that didn't give their

166

Lordships in Whitehall ulcers. It was also the scene of a notorious earthquake in 1960, and the last port before the Canaries. So we turned off and aimed for where I hoped Cap Ghir would be.

We made the landfall all right, but Cap Ghir is apparently renowned for its high winds and heavy seas. After identifying the Cape we turned south for Agadir, roaring along in the near-gale. We almost got fouled up in another, though much smaller, tuna net complex, and finally found Agadir just on dusk. It was pitch dark by the time we got our lines ashore.

The city was a surprise in every way. The earthquake had flattened it completely, leaving only two buildings standing, a movie house and the Standard Oil Building. A mountain, with the old *kasbah* on top, had collapsed onto the town, and 15,000 people had been buried alive in 15 seconds.

Agadir lies at the foot of the Atlas Mountains, and this can hardly have been the first earthquake in its history. Nor will it be the last. But in rebuilding it they have used the best architectural brains and engineering techniques available. It is as modern as tomorrow, with broad, tree-lined avenues and prestressed concrete buildings that are clearly designed to be quake-proof. Even the main post office is beautiful, set off in a huge piazza for maximum effect, while the *marché* looks more like Lincoln Centre than a municipal market. But the most beautiful building of all is the new mosque, isolated from the neighbouring buildings by acres of paved sidewalk and flower beds. Dead white against the dazzling blue African sky, it rises in perfect proportion from the ground to the graceful minaret itself, combining modernistic simplicity with the beauty of classical Moorish design.

South of the harbour was a clean, white beach, and it was here that we took *Caravel* at high tide, to beach her and attend to her ablutions. At low water we scraped and painted her bottom. It took several days but had to be done, for with such a long ocean passage ahead of us we couldn't afford to start off with a fouled hull.

The trip across to the Canaries was largely uneventful, and at 45 miles from the coast we could still see the Atlas Mountains faintly—our last contact with the African mainland. There was a fair amount of traffic about, but chiefly trawlers, and on the morning of the 14th we picked up the radio beacon at Arrecife, on the island of Lanzarote.

The island was poorly lighted, and as we couldn't hope to reach

167

Arrecife (meaning "reef") that day, we hove-to, well offshore, and deployed our huge, 24-foot parachute-type sea anchor. We had never used it before, and opinions seem divided as to whether they do more harm than good under storm conditions. But the weather was fine, and all we asked of it was that it hold us away from the inhospitable coast until dawn. We lay head-to-sea all night, very comfortably, and at dawn didn't seem to have moved an inch. Later in the day we entered Arrecife to find that three old friends were already at anchor there. They were Frank Caspar in *Elsie* (last seen in the Azores, 2 years before), Mike and Irene Wright in *Beyond*, and Jonathan and Bobbie Standley in *Mary Poppins*.

Mike was English by birth, but his wife, Irene, though born in Russia, had lived in France since infancy. They lived in the States, had gone to England to buy *Beyond*, and were now sailing her back with their 10-year-old boy, Jimmy, and a little French poodle, Sarah.

Jonathan Standley was also English by birth, though he had become a Toronto doctor, and his blonde wife, Bobbie, from Belleville, Ontario, was an ex-nurse. Unfortunately even their combined medical skill was not enough to overcome seasickness, which can be quite a problem if you have a small boat and a wanderlust.

Lanzarote was as close to being a desert island as they come, consisting of several hundred extinct volcanoes, a few live ones, and a terrain which is 100% barren. We saw hardly a tree or a blade of grass. There is no manufacturing, and the small tourist industry seems to be having trouble getting off the ground. A few goats almost starve in the lava and scrub.

One evening, with the crews of *Beyond*, *Mary Poppins* and *Caravel* all sitting around and telling tall tales over short drinks, the conversation got around to the impending voyage. It was the first time across for both the Wrights and the Standleys, and they were naturally a trifle apprehensive. I was apprehensive too, but as a veteran of one previous crossing was supposed to be nonchalant about it all. Also, although they both knew the rudiments of celestial navigation, neither had ever taken a sight.

To cut a long story short, we decided to go in convoy. Mike had enough spares and equipment to start a shipyard, Jonathan was a doctor, and I was assumed to be able to navigate.

Sitting around the cabin table in Arrecife we became quite enthusi-

168

astic about the idea, and even convinced ourselves that if we pulled it off it would be something of a record. For as far as any of us could remember, it been done by three sailing boats only once before, and they were the *Santa Maria,* the *Pinta* and the *Niña,* back in 1492.

The following morning I figured out a course designed to produce not the shortest, but the easiest route across, and we called this the "Optimum Track," a term which impressed everyone and sounded like something out of N.A.S.A. If we lost each other, which I felt to be not entirely unlikely somewhere in the next 3,000 miles, we would rendezvous at the next of a series of points along the line. That, at least, was the theory.

Radio communications were a "must," and here things got a little complicated. *Caravel* and *Beyond* both had radio telephones with a range of over 200 miles on the 2 MHz band, although these used a lot of battery power on "transmit." *Caravel* also had a portable D.F. (Direction Finding) receiver, and could thus determine the direction of *Beyond*'s signal, although she herself had no D.F. set. *Mary Poppins* had no transmitter at all, but did have a D.F. set and could also receive the transmissions of both of the other two boats.

We, however, happened to have a pair of v.h.f. walkie-talkie sets operating on the 27 MHz band, but these had a range of only 5 miles. Feeding from the ship's batteries, though, they used very little power and could be used all day with negligible battery consumption. So I lent one of these to *Mary Poppins* and kept the other. *Beyond,* on their all-wave receiver, could listen to this conversation but could not reply. The net result of all this was that we had a sort of 3-way radio hook-up amongst all ships. The only requirement was that for *Mary Poppins* to make herself heard she must be within 5 miles of at least one other ship. At the same time she could get a D.F. bearing on both of the other two. *Caravel* could get one on *Beyond* only, and she in turn could not get one at all.

We set up schedules of radio times and frequencies, and agreed to stay on Greenwich Mean Time the whole way across, to avoid confusion.

For various reasons each vessel was to travel independently through the Canaries, and would rendezvous at the final jump-off point, La Gomera. We decided to go first to Santa Cruz on the island of Tenerife, mainly because the alternative fitting-out port, Las Palmas, had a bad

169

reputation among yachtsmen. It was large and exposed, filthy with oil and garbage, and inhospitable to yachtsmen. At the yacht club they even refused visitors permission to tie up their dinghy while collecting mail.

Santa Cruz is certainly more hospitable, though equally polluted with oil and has no place for yachts. The city and the entire island are, however, lovely. Their prosperity is based on tourism, a thriving banana and other fruit industry, and the fact that ocean vessels call in there to refuel on their way to most ports of the world. The climate is near-perfect, and if you don't mind living in a Spanish-speaking community then Tenerife is a wonderful place to live.

As the water there was plentiful and good, we decided to fill up our tanks and also every possible container on board. Unfortunately, the water supply on the quay was designed for 45,000-ton ships, and the pipe they handed to me, a good 4 inches in diameter, obviously wasn't going to fit into our filler cap. They finally came up with a reducing nozzle, but this also had the effect of increasing the muzzle velocity, not inconsiderable in the first place, to frightening proportions. I could foresee difficulties if that guy on the quay should be a bit careless with the valve, and I tried to warn him to take it easy.

"*Muy, muy pocito; pocitito* in fact! *Muy despacio!*"

He nodded understandingly, and held his palms close together, as though in prayer, to indicate that he would open it just a teensy weensy bit and try not to blow us out of the water. Only half-convinced, I went below and held the nozzle firmly, with both hands, into the now empty forward tank.

"*Ahora,*" I said to Nora, who was in the cockpit to relay urgent messages ashore.

There was a momentary pause as she gave him the okay, and the huge, canvas-covered hose leaped around the cabin like a boa constrictor with a stomach ache. The brass nozzle made like both barrels of a 12-bore, and the tank beneath my feet roared explosively. Water shot in, but much of it came out round the nozzle just as violently and over me. That tank held 55 U.S. gallons, and as near as I could judge it was going to be full in about 3½ seconds. I had no way of estimating how much it now contained, but it was obvious that when it did reach capacity, any second now, the result was going to be spectacular in the extreme.

"*Cesa*," I screamed, and Nora, sensing the urgency of the situation, passed on the instructions with even greater emphasis. He apparently got the idea, for the roaring suddenly subsided and the boa constrictor lay down again. I shone a flashlight into the tank, and saw that it was about two-thirds full. This, I could see, was going to call for some split-second timing during the closing stages of the operation.

By now there was quite a crowd on the quay, and an assortment of truck drivers, deck hands and stevedores were all offering advice to the water engineer—in voluble Spanish.

However, he seemed to be developing a more delicate sense of touch as he went along, and the next blast added a mere 20 gallons or so. Unfortunately, we needed only 15, and the rest went all over the galley, the bunks and myself.

We filled the plastic jugs on deck, where the surplus could go straight into the harbour, for it takes a remarkably short squirt to fill a 5-gallon jug by these means.

After that we pumped out the bilges, mopped up the cabin, changed into dry clothes, and hung the bedding on deck to dry. Then we made a brief stop at another quay for diesel fuel, which they fortunately dispense from a much less enthusiastic source, and, later in the afternoon, left for the little town of San Sebastian on La Gomera. It was an overnight trip, and we arrived next day to find that *Beyond* and *Mary Poppins* were awaiting our arrival. It was a tiny harbour, with not much room to swing, so we put a line ashore and a bow-anchor out to hold us off the rocks.

The convoy had formed.

# HOMEWARD BOUND

# NIGHT ON BALD MOUNTAIN

The choice of La Gomera as a starting point turned out to be an appropriate one. At Santa Cruz we had met Helen Stansbury, an American who lived there and was writing a book around the personal life of Columbus. She filled us in on a few details.

It seemed that Christofo had a thing going with the wife of the Spanish governor of La Gomera, and made a point of dropping in there to fill up his water and wine casks, and doubtless to say a fond farewell. He also attended Mass at the little stone church up the street before leading his three caravels out of the harbour on what was destined to be an important trip for all concerned.

A plaque on the wall records this, and also the fact that Hernando Cortés called in and celebrated Mass on his way over to set his foot upon a "Peak in Darien." Even Sir Walter Raleigh, on his famous voyage of discovery, called in at La Gomera, though the plaque makes no mention of this Protestant heretic ever attending Mass there.

At any rate, we felt that if La Gomera was good enough for Columbus and Raleigh, it must surely be good enough for us, a view which was confirmed next day when we met and were escorted round the town by a girl called Maria. She turned out to be a direct descendent of the original governor's wife who entertained Columbus so royally.

On the evening of November 12th we had a final dinner on board *Caravel*, and reviewed plans for the passage. Then someone discovered that tomorrow was the 13th and there was a long silence. Mike pointed out that if we stayed over until the 14th, that would mean sailing on a Friday, which could be even worse. We finally settled on the 13th.

As it happened, the problem solved itself, for while we did set out on the 13th we had hardly cleared the island before *Beyond's* generator packed in, throwing out a lot of smoke but no amps, so we all turned back. While Mike spent Saturday on his generator, which he managed to fix, Maria was taking us round town in an attempt to find a compass. Ours had developed air bubbles and in case I couldn't stop the leak I wanted a spare. All we could find was one of those little auto things

175

that stick onto the windshield with a suction cup. I hoped we shouldn't have to find Barbados on that.

We were now all set, and at 11 a.m. on the 16th, somewhat against my better judgement (sailing on a Sunday could be worse than on a Friday) all three boats raised their anchors. In light airs and under full sail we fell into a loose sort of formation on a course of 235°.

By late afternoon we were pretty well strung out, but at dusk we closed up and switched on mast-head lights, of which *Beyond* had two, one above the other, and could always be identified at night. We chatted away on v.h.f. to conserve battery power, although Mike, of course, had to use his main transmitter. It was all very cosy.

For the first few days the weather stayed fair, which was fortunate, for even under ideal conditions we found that keeping station was a lot more complicated than we had expected. Each vessel and crew had different characteristics.

With a full crew we were able to steer manually, 24 hours a day. But trimarans, if hit by a squall, don't lie down and spill the wind as monohulls do, and the helmsman has to take instant action or risk losing mast and rigging. With a green crew, I deemed it wise to drop the mainsail, or at least reef it well down, before turning the wheel over to them at night.

*Mary Poppins*, on the other hand, was a racing sloop and while too small for a full crew she could carry her sails better in a blow. Instead of a crew, Jonathan had a self-steering vane, a device which automatically steers the vessel on a predetermined angle relative to the wind. She steered better under full sail, and Jonathan didn't like to reef if he could avoid it. Thus he tended to maintain a better average speed at night. In addition to this, if the wind should veer, say 30°, during the night, *Mary Poppins* would naturally follow it blindly. Pat or Peter, at the wheel of *Caravel*, wouldn't know whether to hold their course and lose *Mary Poppins* or follow her on a course they knew to be wrong and lose *Beyond*. I told them to ignore *Mary Poppins'* digressions, on the theory that Jonathan would discover the wind-shift when he woke up and set a correcting course. If all else failed, he could come back on a radio bearing. Somehow he always returned to the fold, though we never knew whether he would do so from port or starboard, ahead or astern.

*Beyond*'s problems were quite different. She was also short-handed,

176

with only Mike, Irene and little Jimmy, but had no self-steerer. So Jimmy did a 5-hour spell during the day, and for the rest of the time Mike and Irene did 2-on and 2-off. Though younger than we were, I still don't know how they managed it, on top of the other chores: cooking, maintenance, repairs, washing up, sail handling and so on.

Also, *Beyond* was slower than either *Caravel* or *Mary Poppins* in light to moderate airs, and her sails were old and had to be treated carefully in strong winds. But she did have a powerful diesel, and if she dropped astern during the night, which she often did, she could usually power up to us again by noon. Things were a bit chaotic around dawn, and the 8 a.m. radio call was generally devoted to getting all ships back into the same bit of ocean again and to smoothing the ruffled feathers of Jonathan, who seemed to become frustrated over the problems of a convoy.

*Beyond*'s engine, only newly installed, began to vibrate, and a few days out the two front mounting brackets fractured. Fortunately it was dead calm at the time, and we were able to pass over some hardened aluminum angle from our old outboard brackets. He cut this, drilled it, and made a pair of jury feet. But he still had to keep his engine at high speed to smooth out the vibration.

Meanwhile, Kitty had taken advantage of the calm weather to clear out and restow her galley cupboards, only to discover that half of her cake and other mixes had weevils in them. On similar occasions in the past she had removed them secretly with a sieve, but this time Peter was there when she found them and announced the fact in a loud voice, so overboard they had to go. Jonathan saw the line of cartons floating astern and asked if we were going to throw a party. Kitty explained the reason for it all, and Bobbie promptly went below to check her own stock.

Weevils had long been a problem on board, and we tackled it by putting all flour and mixes in screw-top plastic jars, so that the creatures would at least be limited geographically. We were later told that one or two bay leaves in a jar will prevent weevils. We tried it, a year ago, and haven't seen one since.

That night there wasn't a breath of wind, and as we had a full crew to stand watch anyway, I suggested that *Mary Poppins* secure on to us with a 300-foot line and that they get some sleep. They were delighted, and passed us the end of their "umbilical," as Bobbie called it. As the

177

sun sank lower Jonathan started his tape recorder and we all sat on deck, sipping cocktails and listening to the strains of *Swan Lake* drifting over the water. Somehow it didn't seem like mid-ocean at all, and we felt we were cheating.

After dark we heard a pod of whales, puffing and snorting in the darkness, but they took no notice of us.

The lack of wind persisted for several days, and while we had been warned to expect this, it was disappointing not to make better progress. The weather was getting warmer, too, and both Pat and Peter would swim around the boat as we drifted aimlessly. But this sport came to an abrupt end when Peter saw a huge basking shark glide by. After that he would hardly use salt water to clean his teeth, let alone to swim in.

That afternoon we caught five dolphins in quick succession, on tackle consisting of a hook wired onto a beer-can opener. These fish make excellent eating, but are poor losers and tend to be bad-tempered when hauled on board. They are heavy, strong and very active, and with five of them in the cockpit at one time, splattering their blood far and wide, steering an accurate compass course wasn't easy. Before long the place looked like a slaughter house after a busy day.

Kitty de-gutted them, and as there was more than we could eat I radioed the other ships to "come and get it." We handed out fillets in a long-handled net as they came by, a procedure which we came to employ quite often, passing over anything from bran muffins to paperbacks. It was always a tense moment, however, especially with *Beyond*, for she had a heavy metal hull and rolled badly. While we never did actually touch, her ponderous bow came within inches on one occasion before Irene managed to grab the electronic gear that I was handing across and Mike was able to haul away before the next roll.

On the 8th day the wind freshened at last, but was almost dead ahead and we couldn't steer any less than 265°, as against the 230° that we wanted. During the afternoon it rose to Force 5, gusting 6, from the southwest, and we wallowed rather badly. Rather than fight it all night I decided to heave-to, and *Beyond* promptly did the same. Jonathan was lowering his main when he was hit in the face with a flying winch handle. He had some nasty lacerations, but insisted there was no concussion. *Mary Poppins* was several miles away and by the time we had powered over to her it was pitch dark. They had backed their jib and turned in, so we did the same.

178

In the morning we discussed strategy, and I suggested that we heave-to on the starboard tack, so that any forereaching would be to the south rather than the west. The further south we went, the better the chances of picking up the elusive trades.

It was the 12th day before the wind finally veered. The seas lengthened and decayed, and the skies cleared a little.

By noon on the 15th day we were 818 miles from La Gomera, with *Mary Poppins* out of sight somewhere ahead and *Beyond* hull-down astern and suffering from a broken spreader. At dawn on the 16th day *Mary Poppins* was just visible to starboard, but *Beyond* had vanished behind shortly after midnight, according to Pat, and hadn't been seen since. At 8 a.m., however, Mike reported 5 knots under his big genoa, and hoped to catch us soon.

We were losing sight of each other so often that I found it surprising that we were still able to keep in touch and regain visual contact. By taking careful note of the last-known bearing, and then comparing courses and log readings by radio, we somehow managed to come back into that tiny radius of visibility, usually about 3 miles or so.

On the 17th day, with the wind now round to the E.S.E. at Force 6, *Caravel* was making 6 knots all night under reduced sail, but at dawn we had lost the other ships. Assuming that they were both behind us, we dropped the main altogether, and still made a fair speed under jib and mizzen, though in a more sedate manner despite the rather wild, following seas. To the northwest, right across the horizon, lay a huge bank of cumulus and cumulo-nimbus.

At 10 a.m. we raised *Beyond* on the 2 MHz band, and arranged that if we failed to make contact at the scheduled time we should keep trying at each hour thereafter. There was a lot of lightning about, producing bad static, and Mike's signal was weak. Of *Mary Poppins*, whose v.h.f. range was only 5 miles under good conditions, there wasn't a sign, although we assumed that she was receiving our 2 MHz transmissions. So I gave her a slow count to 30 to enable her to get a bearing on us.

Mike said he had been hove-to from 2 a.m. to 9 a.m., so that with our 6-knot speed during the same period he must by now be about 40 miles astern. It was agreed that we should proceed under much reduced sail, while *Beyond* made her best speed on 270°. I carried only the storm jib, and bunched this in halfway up with a line, to reduce the area still more. Even so, we were logging 3½ knots, as against *Beyond*'s four.

179

No sights were possible, and by 2 p.m. the sky to the north and west was as heavy and threatening as I have ever seen, on land or sea, before or since. Huge anvil heads rose to 20,000 and 25,000 feet, with protuberances hanging below. The whole scene was like the front door to hell, and with a near-gale behind us there was nowhere we could go but straight into it. Radio reception became impossible, due to static. I wished that I could have seen an isobar map of the North Atlantic, and thus get some idea of the overall weather pattern. But all we could see was our own tiny patch of ocean. Just what lay ahead, I didn't know, and wasn't sure that I wanted to, either, if that sky was an indication.

It was not until months later that we learned that what we were looking at was, in fact, the bar of a tropical cyclone, which had developed out of what is known as an easterly wave. This cyclone apparently died out before reaching the western part of the Atlantic, and was never classified as a hurricane, although we have no doubt at all but that locally the winds in it were well over hurricane force.

At the time, however, I was very puzzled about it, for the few facts which we could deduce, relating to wind strength and direction and to barometric pressures, seemed to fit into no recognizable weather phenomena that I had ever known. I didn't like the look of things at all.

At 6 p.m. we did manage to speak to *Beyond* again, but the static made a D.F. bearing impossible. So I hove-to under backed storm jib, and settled down to wait for whatever the night might bring. It brought plenty!

At 10 p.m. a huge thunderhead rolled in, and the squall, lasting about 40 minutes, contained both rain and wind in large quantities. The tiny jib just couldn't hold our bow to the sea. It fell off, and we pounded badly, being flung violently from side to side, on the starboard tack. For the first time ever, in deep water, seas broke over her deck and flooded the cockpit (although even then it was only the occasional rogue sea that did so).

When the squall passed, I dropped the storm jib and raised the mizzen, sheeting it hard over. But it shook like a crazy thing, and the entire mizzen mast started to dance around. If another squall came, and we left any canvas on it at all, we should lose it. So we dropped the mizzen sail and lay under bare poles.

Throughout the night there was a series of squalls, each more violent

180

than the last, and accompanied not only by torrential rain but also continuous lightning and thunder. There was, quite literally, no darkness at all between flashes, for it seemed that at any given moment in time there were several flashes occurring at once, all blending together. It was impossible to see anything anyway, either through the windshield or with one's head outside, impossible even to separate air from water, or rain from spume. Watches were pointless, so we lashed the wheel and all lay huddled together on the cabin sole, amidships, where the movement was less extreme.

Nobody said much. We just squeezed ourselves in, waiting for something to happen. Occasionally one of us would stagger into the cockpit and stare out into the night, seeing nothing. I suppose we all wondered whether *Caravel* could stand it, but nobody voiced the thought.

Between 5 and 6 in the morning, an hour or so before dawn (we were still using G.M.T.), there came the most violent squall of all, with the wind screaming in from the southeast. There was no way of even guessing at its strength, especially in the dark. All we knew was that it was far worse than anything any of us had ever experienced or even imagined.

*Caravel* was flung about like a cork, and I just lay there and wondered whether she was going to break up. It didn't seem possible for any man-made object to survive such a battering. At times I could feel her lift, not with the hard kick of water under her, but the feel of air, as the wind got under her and tried to raise her bodily. Until now I had been worried that she might be overloaded; now it seemed that her very weight might serve to prevent her from being picked up from the water by the screaming wind under her wings, like a parked aircraft in a tornado.

The one redeeming feature of the holocaust was the fact that the seas, despite the wind, didn't seem to be getting any worse. The rain tended to flatten them if only slightly, and the wind, I suppose, was whipping the tops away as they formed, thus limiting the height. My own vivid recollection is of the pounding, for I feared that we should break up. Kitty remembers most of all the lightning. I had already shackled a chain to the mast, looping it around a shroud and dropping the end into the water, as a lightning conductor. Whether this would do any good if we were struck, I don't know, although I suspect that most

181

of the lightning was from cloud to cloud, rather than cloud to sea; otherwise we could hardly have escaped being struck. The air mass must have been very unstable to a considerable height.

Dawn came slowly, and found us still huddled together on the cabin sole, wishing that we could just take a pill and wake up when it was all over. Kitty still refers to the experience as the "Night on Bald Mountain."

Such conditions, fortunately, rarely last very long, and although each squall had so far been worse than the last, it turned out that the 6 a.m. one was, in fact, the worst. Although we got several more, none was quite as ferocious as that one.

As the grey light grew stronger, the seas looked frightening indeed, enormous monsters that rolled relentlessly across the face of the world. It was as though the ocean was gasping for breath after its struggles of the past 12 hours, and the seas still contained enough energy to flick *Caravel* contemptuously aside as they passed. Above, great masses of cloud rushed by, while below them spume and rain and mist obscured everything more than a few yards away. Things were actually better than during the night—they just seemed worse now that we could see them.

We bobbed around helplessly in our plywood cockleshell, still alive and apparently not even damaged. In fact the only damage we suffered that night, other than to our nerves, was that the mast-head tell-tale, an 18-inch piece of ribbon to indicate the wind direction, had vanished.

Our horizon, even when we rose on the crest of a sea, was only yards away. The world consisted of a tiny saucer of wild, turbulent ocean, a patch of scudding cloud, and *Caravel*.

Of *Mary Poppins* and *Beyond* there was, of course, not a trace, either visually or by radio. Our convoy of three pathetically tiny, flimsy sailboats, daring to challenge the awesome fury of an Atlantic cyclone, had been torn apart. Somewhere, if they were still afloat, and up to 100 miles in any direction, were two other minute specks, also floundering helplessly and glad to see the dawn. We thought of Jonathan and Bobbie, and of Mike, Irene and Jimmy, and we wondered whether they were still alive, and, if so, how their little craft were faring.

By dead reckoning we were 1,000 nautical miles from La Gomera, and 2,000 from Barbados.

And very much alone!

# SEARCH FOR *BEYOND*

By 10 a.m. it was clear that the worst was over. There had been no more squalls to match the 6 o'clock one, and the wind was down to Force 8 or 9. The clouds seemed higher. There was still no word from *Beyond*, but the static level had improved, and it seemed to me that if she was still afloat and anywhere within 100 miles or so, then we ought to be getting some sort of signal from her. I didn't even try to reach *Mary Poppins* on v.h.f., for in these seas she could be in the next trough and not read us, reception being limited to line of sight. I assumed, however, that if all was well on board her, she was probably receiving our 2 MHz transmissions.

About noon, we did, in fact raise *Beyond*, and were relieved to know that she had survived. Her signal was not good, but was enough for a sloppy D.F. bearing. This put her at either 144° or the reciprocal, 324°, from us. In theory we should have been able to eliminate this 180° ambiguity, but we found the so-called "sense" reading unreliable, especially with a weak signal. *Beyond* had neither seen nor heard anything of *Mary Poppins*, and it seemed that we were the last vessel to sight her, at dawn on the 16th day.

The sky now cleared rapidly, and by early afternoon I was able to get a sight, although this was, because of the poor horizon, very approximate. I asked Mike to take a reading too, and to radio it to me. He had not had much chance to practise with his sextant, and in any event had no reduction tables for our range of latitudes. But I hoped that a comparison of the two readings would at least indicate which ship was the further north, and by roughly how much. His reading was 42°-28', as against our 42°-38', which suggested that he was about 10 miles further north than we were. It did not, of course, give any indication of our relative positions in the east-west plane, but did tend to support the 324° radio bearing, as opposed to the 144° one. I assumed provisionally that *Beyond* was about 15 miles northwest of us.

Mike was still hove-to, and when I suggested that he remain so while we ran down-wind towards him, he was only too happy to agree,

183

for the seas were still very high indeed. We were to sail on 270°, namely due west, rather than aiming straight for *Beyond*, for two reasons. Firstly, our base course was roughly southwest, and there was no point in going any further north of this than was necessary. And secondly, if we put *Beyond* on our starboard hand, instead of ahead, her changing bearing would give us a clue as to her position. If she were on 324°, her bearing should increase rapidly as we passed to the south of her, while if she were on 144°, the bearing should decrease slowly.

When the sun was far enough west, later in the afternoon, I took another sight, although again the height of the seas made accuracy impossible. For what it was worth, it put us about 19°-47′ north, 30°-08′ west, and I duly entered this in the log and radioed it to both Mike and, if they should be reading us, *Mary Poppins* as well. Not wanting to pass *Beyond* during the night, I suggested that she get under way if possible. She did so, moving slowly on a closing course of 240°. We kept a careful lookout to starboard all night, but failed to raise any light.

The 19th day was still squally, with a strong southeast wind, a heavy rolling sea and lots of cumulus and rain. *Beyond* came in at 9 a.m. G.M.T., but her signal seemed weaker. Her bearing was 320°, but was too sloppy to be meaningful, and I began to hunt around for other means of establishing our relative positions. If we could both take visual bearings on the same object! There was a small patch of blue sky to the north, a Dutchman's-breeches, and I described the shape to Mike. He said he could see it, and we both took compass bearings on it. These confirmed that he was further north than we were, and on this assumption we came onto 320° while he steered at 250°.

At 11 a.m. his radio bearing was 350°, and the 26° increase from the original 324° was, I felt, enough to confirm our assumption, namely that he was northwest of us. We were probably close enough to make visual contact when the weather improved. I asked Mike to heave-to again, while we headed towards him on 350°, and he did so.

An hour later, however, his bearing was more sloppy than ever, and each reported the other's signal becoming weaker, just when they should have been getting strong. For the first time, despite the combined evidence of the radio bearings, the patch of blue sky, and other factors, I began to have doubts. Was our original assumption of 324° wrong? Was it 180° out? It all hinged on yesterday's comparative sunsights, which

184

put *Beyond* further north than *Caravel*. But the seas had been quite high, and it would have been easy, especially for a relative beginner, to mistake the top of a distant sea, at the moment of the sight, for the true horizon, and thus to get an unnaturally low reading. Such an error would make it appear that *Beyond* was further north than she actually was, and the difference could well be 10 to 20 miles.

I searched the sky for some easily-identifiable cloud formation that we could use as a reference point, and for a while we seemed to have one. Mike and I both took bearings on a peculiarly-shaped cumulus with a lump on the top, low on the horizon. But then he reported that the top had become detached and was drifting away, whereas from our position it was still firmly attached. Obviously we were not talking about the same cloud. If only a jet would pass overhead and leave a contrail. Even the sound of an aircraft would help. But there was nothing.

Half an hour later Mike came on the air (we were now leaving receivers on continuously during daylight, for with transistors the current drain on a receiver is negligible). He reported a small squall, with rain falling from it, off to his starboard. Could we see it? Actually I could see two of them, one with slanting rain below it and the other too far off to be sure. It was all rather frustrating, for there was nothing fixed, solid or identifiable. At one point Mike came on excitedly and announced that we were just ahead of him. He had sighted an orange-coloured box that we must have tossed overboard. I was sorry to disillusion him, but it wasn't ours.

From the strength of our respective signals, however, it was clear that we were getting further apart, rather than closer. So we agreed to work on the assumption that *Beyond* was, in fact, southeast of *Caravel*. They turned west and we swung south. My respect for Columbus, who had managed all this without radio, was increasing hourly.

At 4:30 p.m., just as we were reaching the conclusion that our signals were getting a bit stronger, we picked up a three-cornered conversation between the yachts *Stormvogel*, *Bollero* and *Ariel*, and we promptly joined in too. Transoceanic yachts usually do this, exchange positions, weather reports, and light-hearted banter. It is a pleasant and useful custom, especially useful if one should later be overdue. We all arranged to come on again at 10:30 a.m. next day, although I didn't expect to maintain contact for very long. They were already west of us and *Stormvogel* was reporting 220 miles a day. I asked how much sail

185

she was carrying, and she said 4,500 square feet. Ours amounted to about 550 with the main up and half of that with it down. Boats like that give me an inferiority complex.

All this time, of course, there wasn't a peep out of *Mary Poppins*. I kept calling *Beyond* on v.h.f., as well as on 2 MHz, on the theory that if she ever heard me we must be not over 10 miles apart, and probably a lot less. And had Jonathan picked up my v.h.f. signal he would certainly have returned it. It followed that if he was still alive he was more than 10 miles away. As I worked out our position each day I gave it to Mike on 2 MHz, and also quoted our course and speed, so that if Jonathan heard this, which he should if he was within 250 miles, he could attempt an interception if he wished. I also gave him a slow count to 30, to enable him to get a D.F. bearing on us if he was reading us.

On the other hand, Jonathan had certainly found convoy work very frustrating, and even before the storm I had considered it possible that he would, at some point along the line, decide to go it alone. It now seemed quite likely that he would make no serious attempt to reform. But I felt that Mike, on the other hand, with less navigational experience and no reduction tables, short-handed and with no self-steering gear, with a badly vibrating engine, uncertain generator, old sails of doubtful strength, and several other mechanical problems, really did need *Caravel* in a way that *Mary Poppins* did not. Also, both Mike and Irene seemed almost pathetically anxious to find us again, and agreed unquestioningly to every suggestion that I made about strategy. To abandon them and little Jimmy would have been unthinkable.

At 10:30 a.m. *Stormvogel*, *Bollero* and *Ariel* were all noticeably fainter as they galloped off westward, and *Beyond* and *Caravel* went on to what we hoped were converging courses, with the object of making westing while we hunted for each other.

The following morning we spoke to both *Stormvogel* and *Bollero* for the last time. They were now 300 miles away and at extreme range.

At 6 p.m. Mike's voice boomed in, reporting excellent strength from us on his "S" (incoming signal) meter, and in calm weather we both powered towards the other's transmitter, sure that we should make visual contact very soon. By 11 p.m. there was still no sign of any light. There was cloud, however, at about 3,000 feet, which should reflect light a fair

186

distance. On an agreed signal I fired off a white flare. It glowed plainly on the clouds as it arched over and fell into the sea.

"Did you see it?"

"Negative, Fred. Not a glimmer!"

The ocean seemed to be just too big. I worked it out that with a range of visibility from deck level of about 3 miles, and even if we knew for a fact that *Beyond* was within 50 miles radius, the chances against a sighting were still 277 to 1. It seemed hopeless.

At 9 a.m. on the 23rd day, *Beyond*'s radio bearing was S.S.E., and we were becalmed. As she sat still, we motored for an hour, to see whether we could detect any change in bearing. If there was any, it was very slight. We must be further apart than we thought, for even at 30 miles range an hour's sail should have a more noticeable difference. I tried him on v.h.f., but he couldn't read me. Then, just as I was about to switch off, I heard a faint voice, barely audible through the background static.

*"Mary Poppins, Mary Poppins, Mary Poppins, Mary Poppins."*

It was like a voice from the dead!

"Hello *Mary Poppins. Caravel, Caravel.* We read you! We read you! Come in!"

Mike also heard it, but neither of us heard it again. She must have been outside normal range, and it had probably been freak reception. But it did prove two things. Bobbie and Jonathan were alive, and they were still looking for us.

At noon both Mike and I took transit sights, which give latitude but not longitude, and on this occasion conditions were good and the sights reliable. They showed with a fair degree of certainty that *Beyond* was some 28 to 30 miles further north than *Caravel,* thus confirming the original assumptions just after the hurricane, which we had already decided were all wrong. How could this be? When we sailed north, *Beyond*'s signal became weaker.

As a double-check, we took two more sights, 10 minutes later, and while these were not at local high noon, they were close enough to confirm that the first ones had at least been reasonable. For the first time we now had some really solid navigational data to go on. Based on this, we swept aside all previous assumptions and started afresh. *Beyond* went onto 260° and *Caravel* onto 270°, gradually closing courses. We were, of course, not forgetting that the primary objective was to get to Barbados, and not to play Hide and Seek all around the Atlantic Ocean. So we kept as close to the base course as possible, with only minor variations as we tried to close each other.

It was at this point that our crewmen, Pat and Peter, complained that we were wasting too much time looking for *Beyond*, and that each day lost was costing them $1.25 for their food. I agreed to give them their food free for the extra days involved, but flatly refused to leave *Beyond* alone, or even to discuss the matter further. The situation was unfortunate, and led to a strained atmosphere for some days.

At 6 p.m. we compared sextant readings again, with the sun almost due west. Mike's reading was a mere 2′ higher than mine, meaning that he was 2 miles further west than *Caravel*. Plotting both noon and 6 p.m. sights, he ought to be 33 miles away, on a bearing of 327°, or roughly northwest.

By this time I was convinced that the general principle of comparative sights offered the best hope of success. Then someone, and I can't even remember who, suggested a refinement which was so obvious that I don't know why we didn't think of it before.

Mike and I would take sights, with the two radios manned by Irene and Kitty respectively. While he took his sight, I would follow the sun carefully with my own fine adjustment, and when he was satisfied with his sight he would shout "Mark." Irene would instantly relay this to Kitty by radio, and she would relay it to me via one of the girls in the cockpit. I would leave my sextant reading at that, and start my stopwatch. The whole operation was squeezed into less than 2 seconds from Mike's sight to mine. Down below, Mike would give me his reading, and with my tables I would sit down and reduce both sights, getting lines of position for both *Beyond* and *Caravel*. Several hours later we would repeat the whole procedure, and wound up with a definite position for both vessels.

At 2:15 G.M.T. a second pair of "simulsights," as we called them, placed *Beyond* a mere 10 miles away on 253°, or about W.S.W. A D.F. bearing confirmed that this was reasonable, but there was still no contact on v.h.f. Their 2 MHz signal, however, was coming in like C.B.S., and I suggested that he sit tight while we powered towards him.

At 4:30 p.m. there was still no visual or v.h.f. contact, but his D.F.

bearing was a good, solid one, and put him squarely on 240°. I asked him to stay where he was for another 2 hours, while we went onto 240° and headed straight for his signal. He had to be just over that horizon.

At 5:20 Mike's voice came screaming in.

*"Caravel, Caravel, Caravel. WE CAN SEE YOU!"*

"What bearing, Mike?"

"One-ten true! Jimmy has been up the ratlines for the past hour, and he can see your mast."

I climbed our own ratlines with the binoculars, and swept the horizon from west to northwest. At first I couldn't see anything. Then I saw it, but it vanished. Then I got it again and lost it as *Caravel* yawed. Finally I pinpointed it in relation to a low-lying cloud, a tiny needle on the horizon.

*Beyond!*

After a search lasting 8 days and 1 hour, a search covering a hundred thousand square miles of vast, empty ocean,* we had found *Beyond* again. Seldom in my life have I felt as good as I did at that moment.

It was actually 7 p.m. before we reached them, and by that time, judging from the way Mike and Irene were waving, dancing, shouting, laughing and wisecracking, I suspect that they had started to celebrate the reunion within 30 seconds of the original sighting. Certainly no land-fall was ever quite as exciting, quite as soul-satisfying, as that crazy meeting in mid-Atlantic, at Latitude 18°-20′ north, Longitude 36°-17′ west.

By 7:30 p.m. we had settled onto 250° true, on a broad reach, with a Force 4 from the E.S.E. At dark we fell into close formation, *Beyond* a mere 100 yards away on our starboard beam and her double mast-head lights glowing comfortingly in the velvet blackness.

That night the wind went up to Force 6, and we romped along under reduced sail. At 9 a.m. next morning, while handing the mainsail, I was thrown against the boom and thought for a while that I had frac-tured a rib. But it turned out to be only a bruise, and was the closest that any of us came to injury in *Caravel* during the entire passage.

We proved to have found not only *Beyond*, but also the trades, at long last, for the wind now settled into the easterly quadrant and blew steadily at about Force 5. We began to log 105 to 125 miles a day and,

---

*The search area covered roughly a rectangle, 200 miles wide by 500 miles long.

189

equally important, were able to lay an exact course for Barbados. Though still north of our Optimum Track we were closing it steadily.

The temperature, too, was improving, and reached the 80's every day. We felt disgustingly smug as U.S. and Canadian weather reports spoke of record low temperatures, blizzard conditions and travellers' warnings from the Rockies to the Eastern Seaboard.

Then we lost *Beyond!*

At 11 p.m. on the 29th day her lights suddenly fell astern and disappeared, and I was unable to raise her by radio. In the morning we learned that Mike had suddenly lost our light (it was never as strong as his), and assumed that we had heaved-to. Unable to raise us for the reason that we had switched off our receiver for the night, he hove-to himself. As *Beyond* was obviously dead astern, a fact which the D.F. receiver confirmed, we didn't worry unduly, but agreed that we would slow down while he made his best speed.

The weather, however, was deteriorating, and, with the wind dead astern, steering became unstable. *Beyond* rolled badly.

Next day the noon sight put us 605 miles from Barbados, and by this time the seas were high and the odd rogue ran to 12 feet or so.

By the 32nd day *Beyond* still hadn't caught up, and D.F. bearings were becoming difficult due to our yawing up to 30° each way.

Then the skies cleared and the seas began to die down a little. We went back to simulsights, which put *Beyond* 14 miles away, on 025°. Barbados was 490 miles ahead.

We used the twin jibs, and made a steady 5 knots, while Mike carried his main and a boomed-out genoa, closing at 5½ knots.

At 10:30 the next night I saw a faint light on 060°, and 15 minutes later another one beneath it. *Beyond!* I told Mike at once, for he couldn't see us as we were dead up the moon's path from him.

On the morning of the 34th day he reported water coming from his engine block—not the happiest of discoveries in mid-ocean. This meant no propulsion and very little radio power, so we agreed that *Caravel* would do all the talking and Mike would limit himself to "yes" and "no." However, a little thing like a cracked block didn't phase him for long, and within hours he had driven a sliver of wood to plug the hole. We were able to chatter like crazy again.

By noon on the 35th day we had 190 miles to go, but *Beyond*'s generator started to belch smoke again, and idle talk was once more rationed as he fell back onto his little Honda generator. Then our own charge rate dropped to zero and the temperature shot up to 200. A fan belt had disintegrated, but we had a spare and were soon running again.

The 36th day found us 99 miles from the island at noon, and I started to take almost running sights, to update our position and reduce errors to a minimum.

On the morning of the 37th day I took the earliest possible sight, with the sun a mere 7° above the horizon, to establish our longitude, and thus our distance from the island. The line of position was almost touching the circle of maximum visibility around Ragged Point, the nearest point on Barbados. And I wondered how many navigators, during the past 500 years, had sailed over this identical section of the sea bed, staring at this same western horizon, watching for that same point of land to appear after the long, gruelling run from Europe.

"You know," I announced dramatically as I put down my pencil, "it's just possible that we might see land any minute, if it's not too hazy ahead."

"I hate to disappoint you," remarked Kitty, pricking my ego with a grin while the children, with whom she had already shared her secret, hugged themselves with delight at the thought of scoring one over Daddy. "I spotted it 15 minutes ago, fine on the starboard bow. I didn't want to say anything until you had finished your sight."

We all dashed on deck and there, faintly against the western horizon, was the low, shadowy outline of something. It could be a cloud—no, it was too hard. It was Mount Hillaby, on Barbados.

We closed the land at a surprising rate because of the following current and the powerful trade wind astern, easing just far enough to the south to clear the reefs. Then we rounded up and entered the aptly-named Carlisle Bay. With *Beyond* only yards away, we entered the bay at 1:30 p.m., dropping the anchor in pale green water. We had arrived, 37 days out of La Gomera, after covering a distance which, measured between noon positions, totalled 2,842 nautical miles. Allowing for our many course changes, the actual distance must have been 3,000 miles.

Anchored nearby was *Mary Poppins*, and we at last learned what had happened to her.

On the 17th day she had, like ourselves, hove-to as conditions deteriorated in the afternoon, and they suffered the worst night of their lives. They were both violently seasick, and *Mary Poppins* developed

191

deck leaks until everything below was saturated. They bounced around all night and at dawn were so glad to be alive that they couldn't have cared less for convoys. They failed to raise us on v.h.f. and just left the main receiver on.

They heard us talking on 2 MHz, and realized that we too had survived. When the seas died down later they were able to get reasonable bearings on both *Beyond* and *Caravel*, and to triangulate and avoid the 180° error which so confused us for a week. When Jonathan heard us come to the wrong conclusion on this point and head off in the opposite direction to each other, he was fit to be tied, but couldn't, of course, tell us about it. He heard us jabbering away about clouds and squalls and floating boxes, and would bleat plaintively into his walkie-talkie, but nobody could hear him. He even saw the loom of our flare on the clouds, but lacked the fuel reserve to power up-wind to us.

Getting our position and course at least once a day by radio, interception should not have been difficult, except for the fact that this presupposed a knowledge of his own position too. He could take a simple transit (latitude only) sight, and during the first few days out of La Gomera had compared his own latitude readings with ours. They were close. This would enable him to find Barbados simply by getting onto the same latitude as the island, that is 13°, and heading west on that latitude until he reached it. But it is not, of course, possible to intercept a moving vessel by these means. His problem was that without regular "timed" sights he could not find us, even though he knew where we were, and without a radio transmitter he could not enable anyone else to find him.

On the 23rd day he heard my reply on v.h.f. and knew that we had heard him, but was still unable to intercept. He also heard Mike's announcement that Jimmy had seen us, and for a while this made him more determined than ever to rejoin us. But he failed, and eventually he saw Barbados and ran in.

*Mary Poppins* reached Carlisle Bay 12 hours ahead of us.

I am still not certain whether the convoy system is a good one for small craft, though certain conclusions do seem valid:
1. The very presence of another boat is a good thing, psychologically and for practical reasons. A yacht faces many hazards in mid-ocean—sickness and accident, fire, mechanical failure to engine or rigging,

192

hitting floating logs, being run down, and so on. The thought of mutual aid is a comforting one.

2. For this added insurance, plus the company of other humans, one has to pay the price of a much lower average speed. For not only is a convoy's speed that of the slowest ship, but in the case of yachts a lot more time is lost through course changes, waiting while a boat makes repairs, reforming after lost contacts at night or in bad weather, and so on. And several vessels of widely differing characteristics and crew personalities don't always want to follow the same strategy, or carry the same sail, or heave-to at the same time. Nor do they react to heavy weather in the same way. In my view, if *Beyond, Mary Poppins* and *Caravel* had all sailed independently of each other we should have cut our time from 37 days to about 27. If time is critical, go it alone.

3. Good radio communications are essential, and should consist of a 2 MHz radio-telephone for all ships (it is surprising how many yachts cross the ocean without being able to shout for help), plus v.h.f. for short-range use, plus a good D.F. receiver. And all ships must be able to navigate by sunsights.

My own conclusion is that while convoys are a good idea, it is not necessary, nor even desirable, for yachts to stay within visual range. It is better to stay in line abreast, and from 5 to 50 miles apart. They can maintain radio contact once a day, exchange positions and log readings, agree on a course, and keep track of each other's D.F. bearing in order to stay in line. Each is available to the others if needed, and no time is lost trying to stay within that impossibly small radius of visibility.

The other aspect of the passage that seems worthy of comment is the weather—the only really important topic at sea. The Pilot Charts for November and December show the northeast trades as holding good for about 90% of the time, with only minor variations. Yet we found no trades until mid-December. Boats leaving the Canaries in November, as we did, made runs of from 30 to over 40 days, while those leaving in December logged from 19 to 27 days, with beautiful weather and following trades all the way. Nor is this, apparently, unusual, for we learn now that the old hands avoid leaving until the end of November, for this very reason. Why do I always learn these things too late?

The Pilot Charts also do not indicate the area of calms up to 500 miles southwest of the Canaries, although here again this seems well-known to the old-timers.

193

And then, of course, there was the hurricane, or tropical cyclone, or easterly wave—call it what you will. A storm by any other name is just as unpleasant. It came as a nasty surprise to everyone, except Murphy!

\[\msymbol\]

# IN THE WAKE OF THE BUCCANEERS

Having reached Barbados and the western hemisphere we somehow felt that Toronto was just around the corner. So it came as something of a shock to discover that while the journey from Gibraltar had been 3,900 miles, we still had 4,100 to go, so that we were not yet halfway. I don't know why I figure out these statistics—they only depress me. It was the same at Horta, in the Azores, when I discovered that after travelling from Toronto to Miami, on through the Bahamas to Bermuda, and then across 2,000 miles of the Atlantic to the Azores, we were still closer to Canada than we were to England.

However, after sailing on both sides of the Atlantic there is no doubt, in our minds, but that the western side is more attractive, from the point of view of the cruising yachtsman, than is the European. The Mediterranean weather is unpredictable, with the winds either blowing like fury or not at all, with short, steep seas and with differences of language and politics that cannot fail to present problems at times. In Northern Europe the season is short and a combination of high tides, frequent gales and fogs, heavy traffic and congested harbours all tend to make sailing less pleasant.

In the Bahamas-Caribbean, on the other hand, the climate is near-perfect, except for the hurricanes, and if you use your head and follow a few sensible rules these are not the threat that one imagines. The trades are brisk, in winter, but not dangerous, and there are adequate harbours, breath-taking scenery and the knowledge that help is always there for the asking by radio, in English.

There is, of course, the problem of race in some islands, and no matter how liberal your views on this subject you can't escape the fact that, especially in the towns, you are liable to find yourself resented, or

194

worse, just because you are white. But even this problem is far from universal, and is worse in the independent ex-British islands of Grenada, St. Vincent and Antigua than in the French and Dutch islands. Trinidad and Jamaica are notoriously bad in this respect, but in the more remote islands of the Bahamas, such as Caicos and Crooked Island, the people are warm, friendly and hospitable.

Barbados is pleasant, but unfortunately it lies 80 miles east of the main chain of the Windward Islands, dead up-wind—for sailboats an impossible trip. The down-wind run, on the other hand, from Bridgetown to Bequia, is easy enough, if somewhat exhilarating, and the difficulty is to swing round and enter Admiralty Bay on the west side. Miss it, and you're liable to wind up in Costa Rica. Nearly all of the towns and harbours, by the way, are on the westerly, or sheltered side of these islands. The eastern side is invariably a mass of reefs and a dead lee shore. The native fishermen do venture out there in dugout canoes, but it's not for me.

Bequia is a nice place, and Lully's is one of the best marine hardware stores in the Windwards, although I still can't figure out why they built it on the top of a hill instead of on the waterfront. I badly needed charts, so I panted up the goat path. Yes, they did have charts of every island, but had nowhere to store them so they hadn't unpacked them and couldn't sell me any.

Not wanting to miss any islands, we first headed south for Grenada, planning to turn round there and touch every one to the north. St. George's, the capital, turned out to be a well-sheltered port on a beautiful island, but we had already been warned that the government was solidly Black Power and the customs tough on all whites. So we declared everything, but drew the line at paying overtime rates at 3:45 p.m. An argument developed, and I told them we would stay in quarantine overnight. They could come and clear us in the morning. They backed down.

St. George's does have a well-equipped supermarket right on the quay. You tie up your dinghy across the road. If you are wise, though, you'll leave one person to watch it, for the small boys who do so for a fee can be vindictive if they consider the fee too small. But at that they are not as bad as the Haitian watchmen who undertake to watch your yacht overnight. If they don't do so, the water witches will rise from the bottom and saw the boat in half.

195

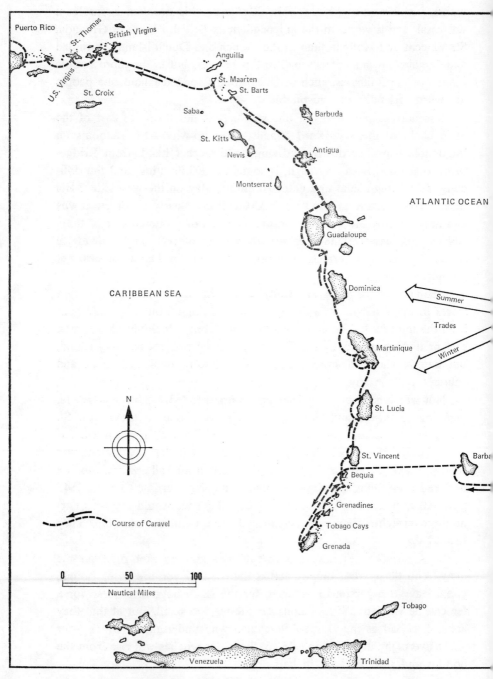

*Islands of the Caribbean, from Trinidad to the Virgin Islands*

196

Water witches do not, apparently, get this far south, although cockroaches do, and in large numbers. You soon learn not to take a cardboard carton or paper bag below with your groceries, but to open everything on deck and pass them in one at a time. We never did have any serious infestation of these creatures, and found just the odd one that we were able to discourage effectively with a spray can. But *Mary Poppins* brought on board a carton which proved to contain a dozen cans of beer and at least twice that many cockroaches.

When we turned north, through the Grenadines, we found that in winter the trades not only blow at 25 to 30 knots, but they also do so from well north of east, so that one heads straight into them. We pocketed our pride and plugged away on the diesel, staggering from one beautiful anchorage to the next. This was January, but in the spring and summer the sailing here would be perfect. The children had a wonderful time gathering shells, beachcombing and using the snorkel. We had to restrict swimming to midday and near the shore, where any sharks could be more easily seen.

Carriacou and Union Island crept by, and then Mayero, where sunken treasure is said still to exist. At Cannouan we ran across the Canadian survey ship *Baffin*, charting the island apparently under an aid program. Then came Mustique, a beautiful island owned by the Tennant family (Scottish brewers), who run an experimental farm there. Some time after we left this island the French luxury liner *Antilles* tried to round the north end but cut the corner a shade too close and wound up on the reef. All 650 passengers and crew got away safely, but the ship was a total loss.

At Bequia I made another fruitless trip up the goat track for charts. We then went on to Kingstown, St. Vincent, where the anti-white feeling seemed particularly strong. Not only did we not dare to leave the dinghy unattended ashore, but we had to chain it to *Caravel* overnight.

All of the larger islands are high and lush, the very peaks themselves covered with dense tropical growth, and the sides slashed by rivers and waterfalls. While the eastern side is swept by the trades, there is little wind on the western, other than the occasional squall tumbling down the valleys. It is pleasant to lie at anchor in the palm-lined bays in calm water. Offshore, though, the current runs up the west side, to be met by the wind sweeping round the north end, creating a wind against current situation off the northwest corner that can be unpleasant for small craft heading north. We learned to avoid this to some extent by hugging the

197

shore and motoring as far to the east as possible before bearing off close-hauled for the next island. Even so, with both wind and current sweeping us to the west between the islands, it was a struggle to maintain easting.

At the north end of St. Lucia is Pigeon Island, with a lovely anchorage. From the top of a hill you can see Martinique to the north with Diamond Rock off its southwest corner, just south of Fort-de-France Bay. In Napoleonic times the British somehow managed to get men and cannon up the sheer face during the night, and the next morning the French awoke to the embarrassing realization that every ship entering or leaving their main West Indies port was seen by the British and reported to watchers on Pigeon Island. Their lordships at the Admiralty were delighted, and called it *H.M.S. Diamond Rock*. It took the French nearly 2 years to recapture it, and when British naval vessels today fire a salute as they pass by, they try not to notice. But when a French flagship made an official visit to Fort-de-France a few years ago, the admiral could hardly help noticing that some British students, the night before, had scaled the rock and hoisted a huge Union Jack on the top.

*"Sacré bleu!"*

Fort-de-France turned out to be fascinating, with no race problem at all. Here the affluent society was much in evidence for black and white alike. The coloured people were mainly Creoles, and they spoke French, wore Parisian clothes, and drove Citröens, in marked contrast to the natives of the ex-British islands to both north and south, who still blamed "Whitey" for their poverty and squalor. Somewhere, one felt, there was a lesson to be learned here.

At the north end of Martinique we paused at St. Pierre, but only overnight, for the anchorage was an exposed one and liable to turn nasty. Dominating the town was Mount Pelée, the volcano that blew its top in 1902, killing all in St. Pierre except one man. He was protected from the intense heat by being in the deep stone basement of the local jail—in the death cell! Mount Pelée is still active, and the present-day inhabitants of St. Pierre live in its shadow. One wonders why.

Next came Dominica, where the people, exclusively black, were friendly but very poor. We took the dinghy up one of the rivers, and in a deep pool among the rocks we bathed and washed our clothes in luxuriantly soft, fresh water, under a canopy of tropical growth and to the sound of jungle birds.

Here the island chain bent noticeably towards the west, so that the sail between islands became easier until at last it was a down-wind run.

Bourg des Saintes, just south of Guadeloupe, was French again, so I rowed ashore to enter customs. It was siesta time, but at the closed door of the customs house a passer-by suggested that if I "frapped" hard enough the *douanier* would appear. I did *frappe*, but all I got was a querulous voice demanding to know who went there. In my best schoolboy French (circa 1929), I announced that I was a foreign yacht, entering. This brought forth a much longer but less intelligible reply in some rapid-fire patois that was way out of my league. I waited for 5 minutes, in the hope that it had all boiled down to "I'll be right there," but apparently it didn't, so I rowed back to *Caravel*. If they weren't interested in me, I didn't propose to be pushy.

It was a mistake to say even a word in French; I should have shouted something in Welsh or Russian, to make him appear out of sheer curiosity. Say *"Bon jour"* to a French official, however, and you have committed yourself to a long harangue in his own language. The best plan, I find, is to address them in impeccable B.B.C. English, and say, "Look, fella! Let's talk English, shall we?" Most of them know this much English, and it renders them speechless with rage, so that you have regained the initiative. If all else fails, let your wife handle them, still in English of course. This brings out their chivalry, and if things should still get out of hand, she can always slap their face, which you can't.

Guadeloupe turned out to be short of good harbours on the west coast, but we did stop for a few days at Deshaye before heading across the big northern gulf to Port Louis, our jump-off point for Antigua. The route over to Port Louis skirts some of the worst reefs you'll find anywhere, and if Port Louis is a port I'm Elizabeth Taylor. There isn't even a jetty, let alone a harbour, and for days we lay at anchor, wallowing in a ground swell that was just on the point of breaking. We did not dare to take the dinghy ashore through the surf. When hunger finally did drive us in search of a supermarket, we went in our bathing suits, with our clothes in a waterproof sail-bag.

The passage over to Antigua was easy enough, but finding English Harbour, on the south coast, was another matter. Nelson selected the place as the base for his West Indies squadron because it was difficult to spot from the sea, a feature which makes for an interesting exercise in pilotage even today. Another problem is that with current and trades

199

sweeping you to the west, you have to make your landfall on the southeast portion, find English Harbour first time, and nip in quick, or you've had it. We aimed at what we thought was it, but bore away again hurriedly as we found ourselves among reef breakers. Then I noticed a fair-sized schooner sailing right out of a high cliff, which struck me as sort of unusual. It was English Harbour!

Inside, it was beautiful, and historically fascinating. Nelson's dockyard is now being renovated, and is almost as it was in his day: sail loft, spar shed, carpenters' shop, pitch kettles, careening windlass—all are there. We tied up at the old stone quay where centuries of British sloops, frigates, corvettes and ships of the line had tied up before us, and where Nelson himself had stepped ashore. Half-buried in the ruins of what had apparently once been the officers' mess we found the bottoms and necks of several very old, hand-blown glass bottles, some round and some square, the uneven glass black and pitted. What toasts to the health of King George or to the damnation of "Boney" had been drunk from the contents of these bottles? Who had washed, eaten and drunk from the bowls, platters and jugs of which these broken remnants of pottery had once been a part?

Unfortunately, anti-white feeling in Antigua was strong, and we slept with a loaded rifle handy and didn't dare go out of sight of *Caravel* after dark. The position of the few white residents was shaky, and the dogs of white yachtsmen were poisoned with strychnine. We left for St. Barts, feeling rather sad.

Most free ports around the world pay only lip service to the expression, using it merely to attract tourist dollars for goods that can be bought for nearly the same price at home. But the French island of St. Barts is a genuine free port. It has no customs, and bargains are real. Mount Gay Barbados rum, for example, costs $7.50 U.S. per case of 12 fifths, and liquor, naturally enough, is the basis for the island's economy. One store sells shoes and liquor, another hardware and liquor, and a third ready-to-wear and liquor. It is inevitable that the Caribbean charter boats, which buy in large quantities, should drop by once a year to stock up for the season. At one island we saw a native schooner at anchor in a secluded bay, its cargo of St. Barts liquor being unloaded by men, women and children over a period of 3 days, in broad daylight and with not a customs man in sight. The good people on St. Barts don't go in for smuggling—they just sell to those who do.

The neighbouring island of St. Maarten is half-French, half-Dutch.

We called at the Dutch half, and found them trying to sell duty-free items to the tourists. The prices were good, too, but it was like trying to run a grocery store next door to the A. & P.

We passed up Anguilla as being flat, uninteresting, and, of recent years, politically unstable, and while we could see Nevis, St. Kitts and Saba away to port, they were not on our route. So we headed for the British Virgins, or B.V.I., an overnight trip to the northwest.

This chain of islands forms an oval, some 25 miles long by 5 wide, surrounding the Sir Francis Drake Channel, which must rate as one of the finest cruising grounds in the world. Most of the islands are uninhabited or only sparsely so, and the channel is fully protected from the ocean swell, yet open to the trades, which seem less strong than they are further south. The scenery is just beautiful and every island has one or more perfect bays as anchorages. You can drop your hook in a different spot every night. Swimming, beachcombing, exploring, cookouts on the beach, or just lazing around in the sun are all to be enjoyed. There isn't much to do at night (once the sun has sunk in a fiery glow, to throw the mountains of St. John and the clouds above in a pink haze), and if you can't stand the sight of all this as you sit on deck and sip your rum punch before supper, then you can always sail down-wind to St. Thomas and sample the faster tempo of life over there in the American Virgins.

One of these islands in the B.V.I. is Norman Island, which is said to have inspired Robert Louis Stevenson's *Treasure Island*. When the girls heard this they promptly reread the book. As we headed towards it, 2 days later, they were already identifying Spyglass Hill and even the tall tree on the shoulder. Hardly was the anchor down in the clear water before they were pulling for the shore in search of adventure and pieces of eight. It didn't take them long to unearth the ruins of an old building.

"Mummy! Daddy! Quick! It's the stockade, where they fought Long John Silver and the pirates."

We explored the island, avoiding the wild cattle which roam freely and are considered dangerous, and the girls were becoming so pirate-conscious that it was difficult to explain to them the difference between fact and fiction. This wasn't helped any when we learned that the owner of this uninhabited island actually did find treasure in a cave some years ago.

By now the trades were astern, and it was a lovely run from St.

201

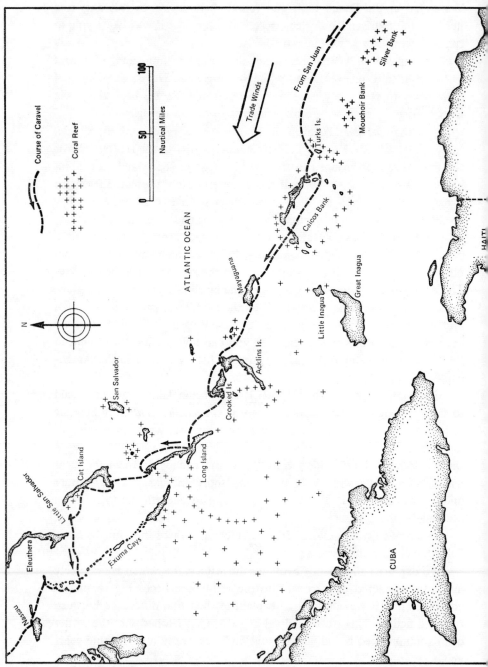

*Southern Bahamas, from Grand Turk Island to Nassau (New Providence Island)*

202

Thomas, via Culebra Island, to Fajardo, at the eastern end of Puerto Rico. The north coast of this island has a bad reputation, but the day we rounded it it was in a good mood, and there was so little wind that we had to power along to the huge harbour at San Juan.

Here we were faced with two alternatives, neither of which was very attractive. Between Puerto Rico and the Bahamas lie the infamous Silver and Mouchoir Banks, consisting of extensive coral reefs— unmarked, unlighted and awash. To go to starboard of these would mean a 4-day trip, taking us close along the windward side where the slightest error in navigation could be disastrous.

The other route lay west along the north coasts of the Dominican Republic and Haiti, and thence north between some small and badly charted Bahamian islets. Recent reports out of the Dominican Republic were that the best way for a visiting yachtsman to stay out of jail was to grease every palm that presented itself. In Haiti a businessman we knew had been trying to persuade us for years to visit there. He knew "Papa Doc" Duvalier personally, and assured us that we should be safe. But I was sceptical, and remembered the experiences of other visiting yachtsmen. Also, if the dictator should topple overnight—always a possibility —the more remote one's connection with him, the better!

We were still trying to reach a decision, in San Juan, when the news broke that Papa Doc's navy had mutinied and was shelling his palace at Port-au-Prince. This sort of thing had happened before, and it always made him irritable. So we decided on Plan "A" in the belief that if the choice lay between Papa Doc and the Silver Bank, then the latter was, at this point, probably the more friendly and hospitable of the two.

Moreover, the problem of 4 nights offshore was solved when we ran into Richard, who lived in New York and was homesick. As a crewman he was all right except that he:

1. Was a self-styled hippie, with whom I was continually arguing.
2. Had a glass eye. I don't think I'm all that prejudiced against glass eyes, as such, but the problem was that when he went to sleep, on the seat in the main cabin, he never closed it. We had the impression that he was staring at us with one eye all the time, even when the other one was asleep. It was all rather unsettling, especially as we couldn't remember which one was glass and which was real.

The ride from San Juan was a rough one, with the winds strong and

203

on the beam, but we made good time. I didn't sleep much until we were well past the Silver Bank, but we did clear it all right, and on the third night we raised the light on Grand Turk. There being no good anchorages there, we carried on for South Caicos, to discover that this group, though geographically part of the Bahamas, is legally part of Jamaica, of all places.

After 5,000 miles of deep water it was a change to cross the shallow Caicos Bank, although we didn't realize just how shallow it was until we started to bump our way across the nearly 40 miles of sandy, though uneven bottom, dodging around the dark patches that might be coral heads or merely clumps of harmless grass. Anchoring overnight at Providenciales, the island on the north side of the bank, we left early in the morning, aiming for the narrow gap in the otherwise continuous reef that blocked our passage some 5 miles offshore. We could see the line of breakers from several miles away, and the gap looked very narrow indeed. But this side of the reef there were no heads within 12 feet of the surface, at least according to the chart. I've got news for them: there's one just under 3 feet! If you've ever had a Boeing 747 land on your roof with its wheels up, you know what it sounds like to scrape over a coral head. Luckily, we only skinned the fibreglass from our skeg. It could have been a lot worse.

After anchoring for the night off Mayaguana we continued past the French Cays and the Northeast Breaker, an isolated, unmarked and dangerous reef off Acklins Island that is almost invisible in calm weather. But now the heavy seas were breaking over it, and we carefully went down-wind of it. The entrance to Atwood Harbour, on Acklins, is tricky, again due to a reef with a narrow gap. It was also the first "harbour" we had even seen that was completely uninhabited.

Richard walked to a village a mile or two away, and returned to say that he was flying home on the weekly plane. As we no longer needed a crewman, we made polite sounds of regret but were secretly glad that he had decided to fly.

Next day, May 20th, we were anchored in a very exposed spot off Landrail Point, on Crooked Island, when we managed to pick up Miami for the first time. The opening words were rather sobering.

"And here again are those coordinates for Hurricane Alma, which is expected to hit the Cayman Islands tonight."

Oh boy! Just what we need, here on an open beach in one of the most isolated islands in the western hemisphere! This accounted for the cirrus cloud this morning, the threatening sky this afternoon, and the deteriorating weather. What was it they said about hurricanes? "June, too soon!" And this was May 20th!

The chart showed a channel between the cays at French Wells, a few miles south. Not much shelter, but out here it would be suicide, so down we went. A mile north of the inlet, with a strong offshore wind, the bottom became thickly studded with coral heads. Closer inshore, the water, while more shallow, seemed to be solid green, indicating a clean, sandy bottom. I went in, but found that it had been an optical illusion, for now that the angle of the eye with the water was steeper we could see that the place was a mass of heads, with scores of them reaching just above the surface. Fingers of coral seemed to be clutching at us. We were trapped, unless we could feel our way out again into deeper water. Unfortunately, the wind was carrying us out, so that even with the diesel it was impossible to stop without drifting out of control.

I conned from high in the ratlines, while Nora stood in the pulpit as an extra pair of eyes. Kitty took the wheel and Mary relayed my messages to her, for she couldn't hear my voice above the diesel at her feet.

"Port a bit—more—hard over—too late, we're drifting. 1,500 astern and right rudder. That's it—steady—neutral—now ahead—more power —2,000 ahead and port rudder—FULL AHEAD!"

We drifted crabwise, right over a black patch, and I waited for the crunch. It didn't come. We had cleared it.

"Now 1,200 ahead and wheel central—starboard—not too much— now over to port and 1,750 ahead."

For a good half-mile it was like this, twisting and turning like a snake, while all around us the fingers of coral pierced the surface like gulls scattered across the water. It was a miracle that we didn't hit any and that at no point were we caught in a cul-de-sac, unable to find a way through, yet with no room to turn round before drifting onto a head. Gradually they thinned out and the black, brown and purple patches, looking like an underwater forest of trees and jagged peaks, became more scattered. The green water slowly turned to a light blue, and then a darker blue. We were out!

An hour later we were anchored at French Wells, which consisted of two low islands with a 200-yard wide channel between them, an

205

abandoned house with a well, and some mangrove swamps. As a hurricane hole it would be better, though not much better, than the open sea, and if Alma should come all we could do would be to put out the heavy storm anchor and go ashore, to take shelter in the empty house or among the mangroves. We couldn't stay on board *Caravel*.

But fortunately Alma died in infancy, as do most very early hurricanes, and within days she dwindled to a tropical storm, hit the mainland, and fizzled out completely.

Grateful for our escape, we made our way out to deeper water and headed for Clarence Town, on Long Island. We then rounded the northern tip of Cape Santa Maria and anchored off Calabash Bay, a 2-mile strip of white, virgin coral sand. Then it was over to Cat Island and on to the uninhabited and rather beautiful Little San Salvador before crossing to the Exumas.

These islands are renowned for their beauty, and we glided among them for days, stopping here and there to let the girls run off some of their surplus energy ashore and to collect shells and have fun. At Southwest Allans Cay we beached *Caravel* to scrape and paint her bottom between tides, and to inspect the damage from the coral head at Providenciales. Despite the sound it had made inside the boat, this turned out to be quite minor. We also managed to spot several of the 2-foot long iguanas which inhabit this island and which are almost extinct in this hemisphere. They seemed to be quite harmless and very timid, which was more than could be said for the 8-foot hammerhead shark that someone had caught, killed and left in the shallows to scare the daylight out of us when we waded by and saw it.

Now it was but a short sail to Nassau, and the circle was completed as we crossed the path of our outward passage of April 1967. A few days later and we were in Miami, where it was a delight to meet old friends again.

The journey up the Waterway was uneventful enough, although several things were different. It was summer, and the banks were in full leaf, while in some places the water was thick with pleasure boats. We had bridge problems, too, for in the New Jersey section many of the bascules had been replaced by 35-foot fixed bridges, without even a notice to warn boats of the clearance. New Jersey seems to care little for sailboats, and on several occasions we had to turn back for many miles and head out to sea to avoid an unexpected bridge.

206

One thing that we had learned since 1965, however, was that if one plans things carefully one can find a suitable anchorage every night. As a result, we travelled from Miami to Toronto without paying a cent for dockage.

The Erie Canal was as lovely as ever, and we felt like old hands as we negotiated the locks. In Lake Ontario we kept to the south shore until Olcott, and then cut across for Toronto, sailing close under Scarborough Bluffs to see whether our house was still there. We entered Toronto harbour on August 23rd.

"Where have you come from?" asked the customs officer as he filled in Form A-6.

"Bronte," I replied.

"Bronte? Then you don't need to. . . ."

"By way of New York, Miami, England, Gibraltar, Spain, Morocco, the Caribbean, Puerto Rico, the Bahamas, the Intra-Coastal Waterway and Olcott, N.Y.," I added with a grin.

He went back to Form A-6 with a disapproving frown.

Customs officers, I find, are in some ways like the Coast Guard—salt of the earth, you know, but not much sense of humour.

❦❦❦

# THE SEA WAS MEANT FOR SAILING

Looking back over the past 5 years, I find myself faced with one fundamental question, which in turn poses others.

Was Operation Palm Tree a good idea in the first place?

For myself, most decidedly, yes! It enabled me to break the deadly sequence of "cradle-to-school-to-desk-to-grave." And I have finally done something which was at least unusual and interesting, and, I hope, worthwhile.

For my family, I believe that it was worthwhile for them too. None of them would want to repeat some of the incidents of the past 5 years, but each is proud and happy to have been through it all once. We have experienced things which, these days, are given to very few. We

207

have felt the gratitude of having not conquered but rather survived the ocean in all its fury, in a small boat. We have known the thrill of a landfall after many weeks alone at sea, the beauty of a tropical lagoon, the excitement of a "green flash"—that last razor-thin sliver of sun as it sinks into a tropical sea from a dead clear sky, and in the last split second turns green. And we have known that steady, ceaseless thrusting of our own bow, lifting and plunging as it slices through the water for mile after mile after endless mile, under the gentle, but relentless pressure of wind against sail, the bow that takes you like a faithful old hound, pulling, guiding, leading you to a distant shore.

These things are unforgettable. They are things that no money can buy. They are free, but you have to reach out and seize them with your own hands. And when I weigh them against five years of peddling insurance, to make a few more dollars in order to pay a bit more tax, I know that there can be only one answer—for myself, at least, and I sincerely hope for Kitty and the girls.

For Mary and Nora will never be the same people again. Academically, they have accelerated since they left their school desks, to say nothing of two winters spent in other schools abroad. But that is a small part of the story. They have experienced so many things that will stay with them forever. They can't tell you the names of the current pop stars, and they don't recognize the TV cartoon characters. To them, drugs are aspirin and penicillin. When a geography book speaks of a desert, their mind goes back to the foothills of the Atlas Mountains in Morocco. When it refers to a volcano they visualize Mount Pelée or the island of Lanzarote. And when it describes a tropical hurricane, they shudder and remember the "Night on Bald Mountain" off the Cape Verde Islands. There is no generation gap—how can there be when we have shared so many experiences?

They are now back at school, making new friends and getting the more advanced, orthodox education that we feel is essential for them. But nothing can ever take away the past 5 years, the experience of 3 continents, 28 countries, and 20,000 miles of ocean.

Yes, it has to have been worthwhile, and any one of a hundred incidents would alone have made it so—the day we raised the Texas Tower, the day we met *Echo*, the day we found *Beyond*, and a thousand days between.

Not that cruising has been all fun, by any means, for ocean cruising

208

and week-end sailing are worlds apart, and incidents such as the one at Gun Cay we simply try to forget. For 5 years we have hardly ever been able to relax completely and, with few exceptions, even at anchor in a snug harbour, danger has never been very far away. Every time we dropped the hook and went to sleep it was with the knowledge that we might be wakened before dawn by a howling wind, a dragging anchor and a lee shore. For a breathless calm can become a screaming gale in minutes, day or night, winter or summer, in the Florida Keys, a Spanish harbour, or a Cornish fishing village. One is never so close to the weather, in all its moods, as in a small boat. Nor does it ever seem so violent as when one is at its mercy, trying to hand a vicious, flogging mainsail in a sudden 3 a.m. squall. One can never say "Safe at last," but only "Safe for the present!"

Why, then, if things were such a success, do we not embark on another 5 years and see, perhaps, the Pacific? For several reasons. Firstly, we could never repeat the experience. No landfall is ever like the first, there is only one first love in a life, one first day at school, one first of anything. Secondly, the girls now need social contacts, a high school education, a junior prom, amateur dramatics, debating clubs and dates. They mustn't become female beachcombers. And thirdly, we want to explore Europe, and beyond . . . by truck-camper.

The obvious question arises: would I recommend that others do what we did? Based on our own experience, the answer has to be "yes," although I must qualify this by pointing out that ocean cruising is not everyone's idea of fun. Indeed, you can pick up yacht bargains in Barbados and Hawaii from sailors who were so disillusioned after one ocean crossing that they sold their boat to the first bidder, flew home and took up golf. But if it is something that you want to do, a dream that you have nurtured for years, then by all means do it. If you don't, you'll grow old regretting it, for in the words of Anton Chekhov, "Life does not come again. If you have not lived it during the days that were given to you once only, then write it down as lost."

There are fewer serious barriers than you imagine, other than a lack of desire. If you are married, your wife needs the courage to adopt a way of life that is even more foreign to her than it is to you, but most wives are stronger than their husbands anyway. Children of high school age are a problem, on two counts. Firstly their education has reached the point where it is no longer a part-time occupation. And secondly, teen-agers do not seem to adapt readily to ocean cruising, and it would be wrong to try to force them. Later on they can accompany you or not, as they wish, and young children, even toddlers, are no problem at all. We have known new-born babies and 90-year-old grandmothers to make successful ocean passages.

Financially, it costs far less to live afloat than in suburbia, although we always duck the "How much does it cost?" question for the sole reason that it all depends, as it does ashore, on the standard which you want to maintain. Perhaps a very simple rule of thumb might be to estimate your costs for food and clothes, and double it to allow for boat maintenance and extras. This won't allow for sickness or emergencies, of course, nor for the cost of your vessel, but it should cover fuel and normal expenses. We certainly don't recommend it, but we have met many families with no income at all except what they earn casually as they travel.

It is unlikely that you are physically unfit for cruising, that is if you have one or more arms, legs and eyes. Bob Lott has been a cripple since boyhood, but is a skilled and competent sailor. And we know an ex-bomber pilot from World War II who sails the Mediterranean in his own sloop, with one hand and a steel hook, the result of a 2,000-pound bomb that went off over Germany—before he managed to drop it.

I suppose the one thing that scares off the would-be cruising sailor more than anything else is the thought of storms in mid-ocean. Indeed, it can be a frightening experience. Yet strangely enough such storms are rarely a serious danger to cruising boats, especially in the latitudes and seasons that you are likely to be sailing. The Denmark Strait in February, of course, is something else again. But most well-constructed boats will ride out a storm with little or no damage, provided the skipper doesn't interfere too much. Indeed, the main danger from a storm comes not from the sea, but from the land, and the further you are from the latter in bad weather, the safer you are.

The most common cause of fatalities, in small boats at sea, is falling overboard, outnumbering all other causes combined. The other hazards include sundry accidents, fire, explosion and collision, and here again the latter is less likely to happen in mid-ocean than in coastal waters. The best way to stay alive at sea is to exercise infinite foresight, adopt the more conservative of any two alternatives, be prepared for the most unlikely mishap, and be equipped with the tools and materials for every conceivable repair.

In *Caravel* I once set out in a hurry and failed to coil and stow the dock warps. One was washed overboard in heavy seas and fouled the propeller, so that we had to enter port in bad weather with no power. It was a simple oversight, but it could so easily have been fatal. If you ever do die at sea, it will probably be the result not of some dramatic hurricane, but of some equally trivial mistake. Since that day we have a check list of about forty items, on a clipboard, that must be done before we sail. It is so easy to coil a line in harbour; so difficult to recover it from a fouled screw in a seaway.

Remember always that the ocean is like a beautiful woman. She can sparkle with gaiety or be austere and morose. She can be languorously seductive or serene and dignified. And she can erupt in violent rage. Love her, treat her with understanding, adapt to her many moods, and she will bear you to the ends of the earth. But ignore her, or take her for granted, and she will kill you.

What, then, of *Caravel*? At this writing it is a question we try to avoid. We cannot use her for several years, yet how could we sell her to some stranger who doesn't know her strengths and her weaknesses? Could you sell your child? Perhaps we can lease her to someone who longs to do what we did but who lacks the $35,000 to buy a new boat, someone who could rent her and give her his loving care. For we hope to live in her again, in a few years, and until then shall probably keep her on the shore. Meanwhile, we plan to put the girls through high school and to prepare for another voyage of discovery, but this time on wheels.

Operation Hedgerow!

# APPENDIX
## CELESTIAL NAVIGATION — THE EASY WAY

There are many inshore yachtsmen, and not a few offshore cruising men —and women—who would love to learn celestial navigation but who have never managed to do so. The reason, often enough, is that as soon as they pick up a book on the subject, or enrol in night classes, they are faced with such a barrage of technical expressions, Greek and mathematical symbols, that they become discouraged. Most teachers and authors want to cover the subject in depth and often go out of their way to complicate things.

Admittedly, celestial navigation is a science, almost an art, and to master it completely demands considerable study and a keener brain than mine. But it is possible, indeed it is easy, to find your position at sea under normal conditions to within 3 or 4 miles—without mastering the subject completely, without a Ph.D. in advanced mathematics, without being able to identify a lot of stars, and without a lot of expensive equipment.

The most difficult thing that the professional navigator had to learn at Annapolis or Dartmouth was to solve curved triangles by spherical trigonometry and logarithms, and this is something you don't pick up casually while waiting for a bus. Fortunately it is no longer necessary, for the amateur can achieve much the same results with the modern Sight Reduction tables, without any calculations more complicated than addition and subtraction. Furthermore, although the method involves over 20 separate, though easy, mathematical steps, it isn't necessary to remember them, for a worksheet solves the problem nicely. All we do is go down the page and fill in the blanks.

Celestial navigation, when reduced to the basic needs of the cruising yachtsman, really is that easy, a fact which doesn't seem to have been widely publicized. It is for this reason that, despite the remark in the preface that this book was in no sense a manual of seamanship, I feel constrained to include an appendix on the subject. When *Caravel* sailed down the Hudson and out to sea, I did not own a sextant; nor should I have known which end to look through if I had been given one.

212

Yet the system outlined below, which was developed for the crews of World War II bombers who had to do their figuring when they were cold, tired, scared, and lost over enemy territory with people shooting at them, enabled us to hit every landfall with fair accuracy. On the return east-west crossing, Nora, at age ten, was actually reducing sights by herself, and on one occasion caught an error in my calculations before I did, a fact, incidentally, which she still relates with obvious relish to all and sundry. I mention it to show that the whole thing is within the capacity of a child, if that is at all encouraging.

### EQUIPMENT REQUIRED

MARINE SEXTANT If you have $400 to $500 to spare, by all means get yourself a Plath or the equivalent. If you don't, then a quite adequate plastic job will cost from $15 to $25. I prefer the English Ebbco. Incidentally, don't get a surplus aircraft or "bubble" type unless you know sextants. Some can be modified for marine use, but many are quite unsuitable.

CHRONOMETER Again, you can pay a lot for a deluxe model, or you can do as I did and use a $15 Timex wrist watch, checking it daily against the radio. I have yet to see a chronometer that can match the radio time pips for accuracy.

STOPWATCH Don't get a yachting timer; they read backwards and are all wrong for our purpose. You also pay for that word "yachting." Get an ordinary stopwatch from a department or surplus store.

DIVIDERS The longer the better, and preferably with screw adjustment.

PLASTIC PROTRACTOR For laying off angles. I use a U.S. Navy one, which is perfect. It cost me 10¢ in a Miami surplus store.

RULER A solid, straight one, preferably 18-inch.

POLAROID SUNGLASSES The filters on a $25 sextant don't take the glare off the sun's path. These do.

PLOTTING SHEETS These are blank charts showing latitude and longitude only. You can use either the large, regular type, good for only a limited range of latitudes, or the smaller and cheaper universal type, in pads of 50. But these need certain preparation before use, so it might be wise to learn on the regular ones and change over later. (This and the next three items are all available through chart agents.)

NAUTICAL ALMANAC (for the current year) This is a sort of celestial

213

bus schedule, showing the position of sun, moon, planets and nearly 200 stars for every second of the year. It is published jointly by the American and British governments.

SIGHT REDUCTION TABLES FOR AIR NAVIGATION (Volumes II and III only. Volume I is for stars and won't be needed unless and until you go on to starsights later.) This is published jointly by the governments of the U.S. (as HO-249) and Great Britain (as AP-3270).

AMERICAN PRACTICAL NAVIGATOR By Bowditch. (U.S. publication HO-9). This isn't essential, but once you have seen a copy you'll never sail without one. It's the yachtsman's Bible.

BASIC PRINCIPLES

Celestial navigation is based on the angle of the sun (or other heavenly body) above the horizontal, and except for noting the time this is the only observation that we shall make. We do so with a marine sextant, a simple but ingenious instrument which allows us to see both the sun and the horizon simultaneously, through mirrors. By rotating one of these mirrors, we bring the image of the sun down until it appears to sit on the horizon, as though at sunset. A special scale then measures the angle through which we have lowered it. Despite a heaving deck and hazy cloud cover, it is amazingly accurate.

Although we could use any heavenly body, we are aiming at simplicity, and shall confine ourselves to sunsights. And while it is possible to take a sight, reduce it and plot it, all without knowing what we are doing, I feel that it is worthwhile, at this point, to pause and review the principle of *circles of equal altitude*, which is the root of the whole thing.

Imagine a tall TV tower in the middle of a big field. Stand under it, and the top is dead overhead. In other words, the sextant reading (angle above the horizontal) is 90°. Now walk away in any direction for 100 yards, face the tower, and take another sextant reading of the top of the tower. It is obviously lower. Let's say that it is now 80°. Note that it is the distance of 100 yards, and not the direction, that determines the new angle. Any point on a circle of 100 yards radius will produce the same 80° reading. Conversely, if the angle is 80°, then we are somewhere on a circle of which the centre is the tower and the radius 100 yards. This has become the circle of equal altitude (meaning equal sextant read-

214

ing). We can refer to it as our *circle of position*, because we know that we are somewhere on it, even if we don't know where.

Now let us assume that the tower moves across the field at a known speed and direction (as does the sun). If we take another sight later, noting the exact time, we can plot another circle, again with a known centre and radius, and know that we are on that one too. Now if we are on 2 circles, it follows that we must be at 1 of the 2 points where they intersect. In theory, we won't know which of these 2 points is our position, but in practice there is never any doubt for they will be many thousands of miles apart.

That, then, is the basis of celestial navigation. Take 2 sextant readings several hours apart and thus determine that we are on 2 intersecting circles of position. While the lines are obviously curved we shall be concerned with such a small portion of them that we can, without appreciable error, assume them to be straight lines. So we shall hereafter refer to them merely as *lines of position*. Each sunsight will produce 1 line of position, and where these intersect will be our actual position.

Like most theories, it doesn't work out quite the same in practice. For a variety of reasons that we don't need to go into here, what we actually do is to turn the whole thing around and work backwards. First we establish an *assumed position*, which may or may not be accurate, it doesn't matter. From this we figure out by means of the almanac and tables what our sextant reading should have been if this assumed position had been correct. The difference between what it should have been and what it is tells us the extent of the error in our assumed position, so that we can then correct it. That may sound a rather silly manner of going about things, but just take my word for it—it really is a lot simpler that way.

The basic steps in finding our position are, then:

A. Take a sextant reading and enter both it and the time on the work sheet.

B. Enter the assumed position on the work sheet, based on the estimated position from dead reckoning. (Note that errors up to 50 miles or so don't matter, and substantially larger ones will become apparent as we go along.)

C. Use the almanac and tables to determine what the sextant reading ought to be, based on this assumed position.

D. Compare the theoretical sextant reading with the actual one. The difference indicates the extent of the error in the assumed position.

E. Plot the assumed position, plot the necessary correction, and draw in the first line of position.

F. Several hours later (when the sun has moved to a suitable new position) repeat steps A through E, thus producing a second line of position. Where it intersects the first one is the ship's actual position.

Don't read past this point until you are completely satisfied that you fully understand all that has gone before. If in doubt, don't cheat, but go back and read it over again and again, until it all makes sense.

### TAKING THE SIGHT

As shortly before the sight as convenient, check the chronometer against the radio time pips, and note the error. Take your sextant and stopwatch on deck. Find a suitable place, facing the sun, with your lower body supported and the upper free to move. I like to sit against the cabin roof with my feet apart, so that I have both hands free for the sextant. Make sure the stopwatch is stopped and at zero.

Taking a sight is like riding a bicycle or ice-skating, completely impossible when you first try it but dead easy when you get the hang of it. Practice makes perfect, so keep at it, on land or water, until you know in your bones that your sights are good ones. The most common problems are:

1. Mistaking a large, distant swell for the true horizon. This can put you out 10 miles or more.

2. The sextant is out of the vertical in the left-right plane. Swing it slowly from left to right, like a pendulum, and notice how the sun rises above the horizon as you leave the vertical.

Remember that you want the sun just to kiss the horizon, which is easier than it sounds, for even when seen through thin cloud the sun is converted by the lens and filters into a large and sharply defined coloured disc.

The moment you are satisfied with the sight, start the stopwatch and go below, putting the sextant aside until you have attended to the matter of time first. When the second hand of the chronometer reaches a whole minute, stop the stopwatch, note the chronometer time, and proceed with the items on the work sheet in the order indicated in the notes below.

216

WORK SHEET

ine:

(1) GMT by Chronometer (in whole minutes) — *11 - 23 - 00*

(2) Chronometer Error (+ if slow, − if fast) — *32 (+)*

(3) Corrected Chronometer Time — *11 - 23 - 32*

(4) Stop-watch elapsed time (always −) — *2 - 09 (−)*

(5) Actual time of sight by GMT — *11 - 21 - 23*

(6) GHA Sun for whole hours in (5) *11 hrs.* — *345° - 53.3′*

(7) GHA Sun for mins & secs in (5) *21ᵐ - 23ˢ* — *5° - 20.8′*

(8) GHA Sun for actual GMT of sight. — *351° - 14.1′*

(9) aλ (+ if east, − if west) — *68° - 14.1′ (−)*

10) LHA Sun — *283°*

11) aL (north or south) — *N. 21°*

12) Decl Sun (north or south) — *N. 17° - 03′*

13) Hc for whole degrees of Decl Sun — *17° - 48′*

14) d for odd mins of Decl Sun — *01′ (+)*

15) Hc (Height by calculation) — *17° - 49′*

16) Hs (Height by sextant, uncorrected) — *17° - 26′*

17) Index Error, if any (+ or −) —

18) Dip (Height of Eye correction) (always −) — *02.4′ (−)*

19) Combined SD & Refr correction (+ or −) — *13.0′ (+)*

20) Ho (Height by observation, corrected) — *17° - 39′*

21) Intercept (Difference between Hc on 15 and Ho on 20) — *10′ (miles)*

22) Enter 360° here only if necessary —

23) Z — *078°*

24) Zn (Equals either Z or 360 minus Z) — *078° + 180° = 258°*

25) Miles and Base Course. — *10 ‖ 325° T*

217

This work sheet is based on an actual sight taken on board *Caravel* on the morning of May 8th, 1970, one day out from San Juan and bound for the Caicos Islands. The dead reckoning position was about Latitude 21 north, Longitude 68 west, and the sun was low in the sky and just north of east. The Walker Log showed 107 miles and our base course was 325° true, at about 4 knots.

*Work-sheet*

*Line*

(1) Always keep chronometer on *G.M.T.*, regardless of local time. When we returned to it, after the sight, the next whole minute was 11-23-00 *G.M.T.*, and it was at this moment that we stopped the stopwatch. After entering this line, move ahead to line (16).

(16) This is the actual sextant reading taken from the instrument itself. Note this and put the sextant away safely. Then return to line (2).

(2) Determine this error at least once a day by radio, and keep a running record. DO NOT attempt to reset the chronometer to the correct time during the voyage. Just note the extent of the error on the work sheet. Ours happened to be 32 seconds slow, so we entered + 32 seconds.

(3) Enter corrected chronometer time.

(4) Elapsed time between the moment of sight and the moment that we stopped the stopwatch. Stopwatch shows this to be 2 minutes 09 seconds.

(5) Actual time of sight, by *G.M.T.*

(6) *Greenwich Hour Angle of the Sun* at 11 hours *G.M.T.* In navigation we assume that the sun travels around the earth instead of the other way about. It does so towards the west at the rate of 15° of longitude per hour, and its position at any point in time, always measured in a WESTERLY direction from Greenwich in degrees, is known as the *Greenwich Hour Angle*. This information is given in the almanac, and in the present case we turn to the 1970 edition, on the page for May 8th, and refer to 11 hours under the column headed "Sun." The *GHA* is here shown as 345°-53.3′ (west of Greenwich, of course). We enter this on line (6).

(7) This page of the almanac shows only the whole hours, and to interpolate for the odd minutes and seconds we turn to the buff

218

pages at the back. Here we find that in 21 minutes 23 seconds the sun always moves through 5°-20.8′, so we enter this on line (7) and add it to the figure on line (6).

(8) The total is shown on this line as 351°-14.1′, and this is the *GHA Sun* at the actual moment of the sight.

(9) What we want to know, however, is not how far the sun was west of Greenwich, but how far it was west of our Assumed Position. To arrive at this we must allow for our *a*λ, which means Assumed Longitude, adding it if we are east of Greenwich and subtracting it if we are west. (Pause for a minute and make sure that you can see why this is so.) We are about 68° west, and if the sun was about 345° west of Greenwich, it must be 345° minus 68° west of us. So we deduct this 68° from the *GHA Sun*. However, things will be a whole lot simpler, mathematically, if the answer should happen to be in whole degrees, and as this is unlikely without a little help, we cheat a bit and assume our longitude to be not 68° but 68°-14.1′. Now our *a*λ happens to have the same number of odd minutes as does the *GHA*. Cunning, eh?

(10) We now find that the sun was exactly 283° west of our assumed position, so we call this, logically enough, the *Local Hour Angle of the Sun*, or *LHA Sun*, as opposed to the *Greenwich* Hour Angle. Enter this.

(11) *aL* means simply *Assumed Latitude*. We always assume it to be in whole degrees and it may, of course, be either north or south of the equator. In this case we enter North 21°.

(12) This refers to the *Declination of the Sun*, and means simply the distance that the sun is north or south of the equator at that particular time. We know that this varies between about 23½° north (in June) and 23½° south (in December). The almanac tells us the exact angle, on the same page as the *GHA* but under the next column to the right. Once more, as it is shown only for the whole hours we must interpolate for the odd minutes and seconds. However, the difference in this case is quite small and can usually be determined on sight without even using your fingers. The nearest minute is close enough, and in our case it worked out at North 17°-03′.

Look again at lines (10), (11) and (12). These values all relate to the position of the sun, in either the north-south or the east-west plane,

219

relative to the assumed position of the ship. It now becomes possible, using these 3 values, to obtain from the Sight Reduction Tables both the *Hc* (which means Height by Calculation and is what the sextant reading ought to be) and also the *Zn* (which is the direction of the sun and is thus the direction of the centre of our *Circle of Position*.) As the circumference of a circle is at right angles to the radius, it follows that the Line of Position must be at right angles to *Zn*.

It is hardly necessary here to describe the exact method of looking up this information in the tables, for these instructions are covered fully in the introduction to the tables themselves. Suffice it to say that, using the three values in our particular example, namely *LHA Sun, aL* and *Decl Sun*, we are presented with the following group of figures in the tables:

| Hc | d | Z |
|----|----|----|
| 17°-48′ | +17′ | 78° |

At this point, jump ahead to line (23) on the work sheet.

(23) Enter the value for *Z* as being 78°. This is NOT the same as *Zn*, which is what we really want, but there is a simple formula for converting it. In North Latitudes this is:

If *LHA* is greater than 180°, *Zn* equals *Z*.

If *LHA* is less than 180°, *Zn* equals 360° minus *Z*.

(The formula for South Latitudes is different. See the tables.)

(24) In our case the *LHA* is 283°, so that *Zn* equals *Z* and we simply repeat the same 78° on line (24). Had *LHA* been less than 180° we should have entered 360° on line (22) and subtracted *Z* from it. Now return to line (13).

(13) The tables show *Hc* for only whole degrees of *Decl Sun*, and the figure of 17°-48′ now entered on this line is the *Hc* for a *Decl Sun* of 17°.

(14) The *d* refers to the difference in *Hc* for the next whole degree of *Decl Sun*, namely for the difference between 17° and 18°. So we have to interpolate for the odd 3′, adding 3/60 × 17° on line (14). To avoid having to figure this out (I promised nothing but addition and subtraction), Table 4 in the back of the book does this for us, producing a figure of 1′. Note, however, that the *d* factor can be either (+) or (−). The table shows which, and in this case it happens to be (+).

(15) This gives us a final *Hc* of 17°-49′, which is our theoretical sex-

220

tant reading. We now want the actual one so that we can compare the two.

(16) We already entered this from the instrument itself, but before we can make use of it we have to make several corrections and these are:

(17) *Index Error.* This is the "built-in" inaccuracy of the sextant itself, and on expensive models is shown on the case. On the cheaper models we simply adjust it to zero occasionally with a little screw and let it go at that. So here we assume no index error.

(18) Even on a small boat your eye is above the water, so that the horizon is slightly below you, producing a small but significant error of about 3 miles. The correction is shown in the table headed *Dip* on the inside of the front cover of the almanac. For our Height of Eye of about 6 feet above the water, which is pretty close for most small craft, the correction is 2.4′. This factor is always subtracted, and we enter it on line (18).

(19) On the same page is another correction table headed *Sun,* and this combines 2 items in one. Firstly, although all almanac figures are based on the centre of the sun, this is pretty hard to estimate when taking a sight, so we use the more easily defined bottom edge, or *lower limb.* We must thus allow for the *SD* or *Semi-diameter,* which varies slightly between summer and winter. And secondly, because the light from the sun bends as it enters our atmosphere, we must allow for this *Refraction,* which varies with the angle of the sun—the lower the sun in the sky, the greater the refraction error. From this combined table we find that the correction for an angle of about 17½°, in May, is + 13.0′. (It may be + or −.) So we enter this figure too.

(20) After all of these corrections we find that the *Corrected Hs,* which we now call *Ho* (Height by Observation), is 17°-39′, and we enter this on line (20). At last we have a final value for both the actual and theoretical sextant readings, and can thus compare them and determine the extent of the error in our Assumed Position.

(21) Deduct *Hc* (on line 15) from *Ho* (on line 20), entering the difference on line (21).

If this is not possible, because *Hc* happens to be greater than *Ho,* don't panic. Just deduct *Ho* from *Hc* instead, again showing the

221

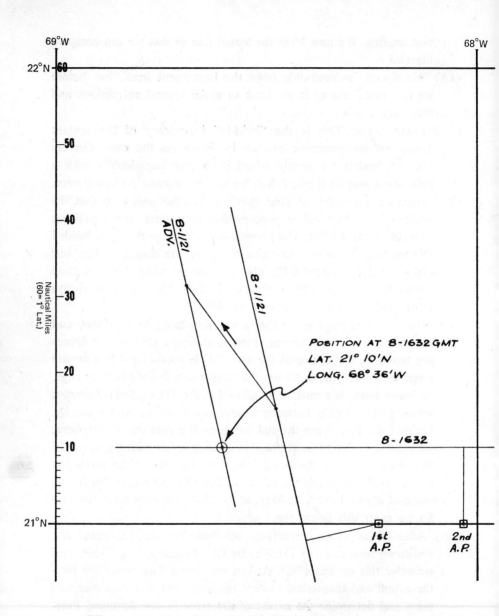

69°W                                                          68°W

22°N

Nautical Miles
(60= 1° Lat.)

—50

—40

8-1121
ADV.

8 - 1121

—30

POSITION AT 8-1632 GMT
LAT. 21° 10'N
LONG. 68° 36'W

—20

8-1632

—10

21°N

1st
A.P.

2nd
A.P.

difference on line (21), but in this latter event you must ALSO
CHANGE *Zn*, on line (24) to its reciprocal by adding or subtracting 180°. In the present case, *Hc* is, in fact, the greater, so
we deduct *Ho* from it, entering the difference of 10' (which is the
same as 10 nautical miles) on line (21). We also add 180° (as
we cannot subtract it) to *Zn*, thus producing a revised *Zn* of 258°.

222

Again, don't worry about this bit of arithmetical juggling at this stage. The reason will become apparent after a few sights.

(25) Enter here the mileage at the time of the sight, from your Walker Log, Sumlog, or other type of odometer. Also enter the average true course (not magnetic) made good after allowing for tacks, leeway, drift and so on. The purpose of this is to tell you how far you have travelled, and in what direction, between the 2 sights. In our case the entries read 107 miles on a course of 325° true.

If you are wondering, at this point, how it is possible to finish today's sights before it is time to take tomorrow's, don't get discouraged. You may not believe it, but after a few days of actual sights at sea you will run through this entire work sheet in not more than 10 minutes, eventually discarding it altogether as kid stuff and using the inside of a cigarette package.

PLOTTING THE SIGHT

We are now ready for this stage of the operation, and shall need the plotting sheet covering latitudes 17° to 24°. The meridians of longitude are already drawn in, but not numbered. Based on our probable position it seems to make sense to number the one on the extreme right as 67° west, and the others 68°, 69°, and so on. Date the sheet, for posterity, and you are ready to go.

The first step is to plot the Assumed Position (Lat. 21 north, Long. 68°-14.1' west), with a dot in a little square. Set your dividers at 10 miles (line 21), using the scale of 60 miles to the degree of latitude on the chart. (Note that on this plotting sheet, as on all relatively small-scale Mercator projection charts, the degrees of latitude are more widely spaced as you go further from the equator, so you must measure mileages at about the same latitude as the area concerned, and not too far north or south of it.)

With the protractor, lay off a line through the Assumed Position at the same angle as Zn, in this case 258°, and mark off the 10 miles along it. Through this point draw a line at right angles to the Zn line, that is at 168° and 348°, and in length perhaps a degree of longitude or so.

This is the first Line of Position, and at 11:21:23 G.M.T. the ship was somewhere on this line. We identify this line as 8-1121 (the 8th at 11:21 hrs), as shown in the diagram. We then proceed with the second one, based on a further sight taken about 5 hours later. In point of fact it was taken at 1632 hrs *G.M.T.*, and as this was just about local noon the resultant *Line of Position* runs east-west. There is just one more step to be taken before we can get an actual fix from these lines.

The time of the first sight was 1121, and that of the second 1632. During the intervening five hours the ship had, of course, moved, and a comparison of the figures on lines (25) of the two work sheets shows that she had travelled 21 miles on a course of 325° true. We must advance the first Line of Position accordingly.

To do this we take any point on the first Line of Position, marking it with a dot. Through this dot we draw a line in the direction travelled (325°) and of length 21 miles. Through this latter point we now draw another line, parallel to the Line of Position and long enough to intersect the second (1632 hours) Line of Position. The point of intersection between the advanced 1121 line and the 1632 line is the *actual position* of the ship at the time of the second sight, namely 1632 hrs *G.M.T.* Measure off the latitude and longitude, and there is the fix.

THE TRANSIT SIGHT

There is, in fact, a simplified refinement to this system which is worth remembering. Having taken a morning sight when the sun is close to due east, thus producing a Line of Position that runs north-south and is consequently the longitude, start the second one a few minutes before local high noon. As the sun creeps up through the last few minutes of arc towards its zenith, follow it up with the sextant. It will pause for several minutes at high noon before starting its slow descent, but do NOT follow it down. Leave the sextant at the highest reading reached, for it is this figure that you want. Don't bother about timing the sight to seconds. Just note the time to within 15 minutes or so, for Declination purposes.

Correct this maximum reading for Dip, Semi-diameter and so on, as before, and then subtract the corrected reading from 90°. To the result add the Declination of the sun if both this and your latitude are the same name (i.e. both north or both south), and subtract it if one is north and the other south.

The result is your latitude!

"Look Ma! No GHA!"

This is a quick and easy way to determine latitude, and if a cloud happens to get in the way just on high noon (Murphy's Law), take a "timed" sight a little later.

Nobody is going to pretend that you can, whatever the system, learn celestial navigation in the time that it takes you to read this appendix. Indeed, I never promised to teach you celestial navigation at all, but merely how to find your position at sea from sunsights, which is not quite the same thing. But if you can get away on your own somewhere, turn off the TV, and go through the whole thing again, slowly, digesting each paragraph before going on to the next, it will fall into place and make sense. And when it does, it will strike you as the smartest idea since the rudder.

Some experts will, I know, criticize me for advocating a simplified system based on sunsights alone and a plastic sextant. This latter will not be suitable for star sights. But while we all prefer a Cadillac, some of us have to settle for a Volkswagen, and while I have no desire to sell you on a Volks, I do want to show you that, until you can afford a Cadillac, a Volks is a lot better than walking.

And the amazing thing about this "quick and easy" method, when you get around to trying it out in practice, far out of sight of land, is that it does work surprisingly well. When you make your first ocean landfall, after days or weeks at sea, and discover that the place really is right there, within a couple of miles or so of where you figured it to be, nobody will be more amazed, or delighted, than yourself.

One final word of advice, though! When the crew expresses equal surprise, be nonchalant. Look at your watch with a frown, and mutter, "Hm, should have sighted that several minutes ago. I seem to be slipping."

You don't want them to think that just anyone can navigate, do you?

# GLOSSARY

ABEAM To either side of the ship, and about level with it.

AFT Towards the stern, or behind the vessel.

A-HULL To lie a-hull means to let the vessel drift and assume her natural position, without sails or power.

AMIDSHIPS Neither forward nor aft. It can also mean neither to port nor to starboard, but in the middle.

ANEMOMETER An instrument for measuring the speed of the wind.

ANVIL-HEAD The top of a cumulo-nimbus cloud.

AUXILIARY In this context, a sailboat with an engine for occasional use.

AZIMUTH SCALE A circular scale, calibrated in degrees or compass points, and used to indicate bearings.

BACK, TO 1. The wind is said to back when it changes direction against the sun, i.e., anti-clockwise in the northern hemisphere and clockwise in the southern. The opposite of veer.

2. Sails are said to be backed when they are on the wrong side, thus ceasing to drive the vessel forward. This may be done accidentally or intentionally. (*See* heave-to.)

BACKSTAY The cable supporting the mast from the stern.

BACKWASH The pressure of waves or a current bouncing back from a sea wall or from rocks.

BAR 1. A sandbank, usually across the mouth of a river or inlet, on which incoming seas sometimes break dangerously.

2. A solid mass of cumulo-nimbus cloud across the horizon and heralding a hurricane.

BASCULE The roadbed of a bridge that tilts up to allow ships to pass. It also refers to an entire bridge of that type.

BASE COURSE The normal course, as opposed to a temporary one.

BEAM 1. The width (of a vessel).

2. "On the beam" means to one side, and neither ahead nor astern.

BEAM REACH A course which puts the wind on the beam.

BEAM SEAS Seas or waves that hit the vessel from the beam.

BEARING The direction of an object from the observer, expressed in either degrees or compass points. It can be a true bearing (measured from the true north), or a magnetic bearing (measured from the magnetic north), or a relative bearing (measured from the ship's bow).

BEAUFORT SCALE OF WIND SPEEDS

| Force | Speed in knots* | Description** American | British | Seas | Height*** in feet |
|---|---|---|---|---|---|
| 0 | 0- 1 | Light | Calm | Calm | 0 |
| 1 | 1- 3 | Light | Light air | Smooth | 0- 1 |
| 2 | 4- 6 | Light | Light breeze | Slight | 1- 3 |
| 3 | 7-10 | Gentle | Gentle breeze | Moderate | 3- 5 |
| 4 | 11-16 | Moderate | Moderate breeze | Rough | 5- 8 |
| 5 | 17-21 | Fresh | Fresh breeze | Rough | 5- 8 |
| 6 | 22-27 | Strong | Strong breeze | Rough | 5- 8 |
| 7 | 28-33 | Strong | Near gale | Very rough | 8-12 |
| 8 | 34-40 | Gale | Gale | Very rough | 8-12 |
| 9 | 41-47 | Gale | Strong gale | High | 12-20 |
| 10 | 48-55 | Whole gale | Storm | Very high | 20-40 |
| 11 | 56-63 | Whole gale | Violent storm | Mountainous | 40-up |
| 12 | 64-71 | Hurricane | Hurricane | Phenomenal | |
| 13 | 72-80 | | | | |
| 14 | 81-89 | | | | |
| 15 | 90-99 | | | | |
| 16 | 100-108 | | | | |
| 17 | 109-118 | | | | |

*To convert knots to m.p.h., add about one-seventh.
**Descriptions vary between countries and authorities.
***These are very approximate, as the height of seas depends on many variables in addition to wind speed.

BILGE PUMP A pump (hand or power) used to remove water from the lowest part of the vessel.

BLOCK Nautical term for a pulley.

BOOM In modern yachts, the heavy spar attached to the base of the mast, to which the foot of the sail is secured.

BOSUN Short for boatswain. The man responsible for the general repairs and maintenance of the vessel at sea.

BOTTOM The outside of the hull, below water.

BOW 1. The forward end of the vessel.

2. "On the bow" means not dead ahead, but rather to one side, although forward of the beam. "Fine on the bow" means close to dead ahead, while "broad on the bow" means further away towards the beam.

227

BOWDITCH *The American Practical Navigator*, an American publication widely used by yachtsmen and named after its original author.

BREAK OUT, TO To open up, unpack or unstow, for immediate use.

BREAST ANCHOR An anchor set to one side of the vessel, usually to hold her away from the quay in an onshore wind.

BROACH, TO To be overtaken by a large following sea and turned sideways, usually the result of sailing down-wind too fast under gale conditions. In extreme cases it can result in the vessel rolling over.

BUOY 1. A floating device, anchored to the bottom, which by its shape and colour is an aid to navigation.

2. To buoy an anchor is to attach a float to it by a line.

BUTANE A bottled gas, similar to propane.

CAN A black, cylindrical buoy.

CARAVEL A general type of sailing craft common in the Middle Ages, partly square-rigged and partly fore-and-aft rigged. Of no set design, but they had certain characteristics in common.

CAREEN, TO To pull a vessel onto her side in shallow water, in order to scrape, paint or repair her bottom.

CATALYTIC HEATER A flameless heater that burns gasoline at temperatures below those of flame, and is thus safe for use in the presence of inflammable vapours.

CATAMARAN Originally any multihulled vessel (Catu-tied together, and Maran-logs), but now used only for two-hulled boats.

CAVITATE, TO A ship's propeller is said to cavitate when it loses efficiency by sucking down air from the surface and thus pushes back froth instead of solid water.

CHAIN LOCKER A stowage space, usually in the bow, for anchor chain.

CHOCKS Metal fittings which act as guides for anchor or dock warps where these pass over the edge of the deck.

CHOP Waves, usually steep, that are bad enough to be unpleasant but are not really rough.

CIRRUS High clouds of ice crystals, light and feathery in appearance. Often the first sign of approaching bad weather. "Mackerel sky and mares' tails/Make tall ships carry low sails."

CLEAT A metal fitting around which a line can be quickly and easily secured. The line is then said to be cleated.

CLEW The bottom corner of a sail, furthest from the mast or stay on which it is carried.

CLOSE, TO To close anything is to draw closer to it.

CLOSE-HAULED Describes a vessel that is sailing close into the wind, that is, with the sails hauled in close.

COAST PILOT A book describing a particular coastal area, with reference to weather, currents, hazards, port facilities, etc.

COCKPIT The steering or control area of a small craft. It is usually open, but may be enclosed.

COLD FRONT Part of a low pressure weather system, and normally a sign that the low is moving away. Indicated by a drop in temperature, a rise in pressure and a veering wind.

COMBER A huge sea with a curling top.

CON, TO To control a vessel, by signals to the helmsman, from a high vantage point where dangers ahead can be more easily seen.

CONFUSED Seas coming from several directions at once and interacting with each other so that they are no longer regular in size or shape. Unpleasant.

CONSOL (American name, Consolan) A system of radio navigational aid in which a transmitter on shore sends out a series of dots and dashes. By counting these the navigator can determine his bearing from the transmitter.

CORAL HEAD A patch of coral rising steeply from the bottom and shallow enough to be a serious hazard. In good light it is usually visible as a dark patch.

COTTER PIN A soft metal pin, split down the middle, used to lock nuts or turnbuckles to prevent them from becoming accidentally unscrewed.

COURSE May be expressed in either degrees or compass points. May be true (based on the true north), magnetic (based on the magnetic north), or compass (magnetic but without any allowance for the ship's compass error.) (See swing.)

COURTESY FLAG The flag of the host country, flown as a courtesy by a visiting foreign vessel.

CQR A type of anchor, also known as a plow anchor. In our view a good, all-round anchor for yachts.

CREAM, TO A colloquialism, meaning to sail quickly enough to cause a creamy wake.

229

CUMULO-NIMBUS A huge cloud with a flattened anvil-head, rising to great height. It results from strong vertical movement of warm, unstable air, and can produce rain, hail, thunder, lightning and high winds.

CUMULUS A low-to-medium height cloud consisting of lumps rather than a continuous layer.

DANFORTH A popular type of anchor. Suitable for general-purpose use in sand or firm mud, but in our view not strong enough for heavy conditions.

DATUM An arbitrary level from which tide heights are measured, and usually quoted on charts.

DEAD RECKONING The estimating of a ship's position, based on its last-known position and its movements since then.

DE-BURR To clean the rough edges from metal after cutting or drilling.

DECK-HEAD Nautical term for ceiling.

DEPTH-SOUNDER An instrument which indicates, usually on a dial, the depth of water under a vessel.

D.F. RADIO Direction finding receiver. One that can determine the direction of an incoming signal.

DIURNAL LOW The normal barometric pressure varies slightly during the day, being about .03 inches lower at 4 a.m. and 4 p.m. (diurnal low) than at 10 a.m. and 10 p.m. (diurnal high). This should be allowed for when interpreting barometric readings.

DOCK WARPS Lines for securing a vessel to the quay.

DOCUMENTED A vessel is said to be documented when its ownership and other details are registered with its central or federal government, as opposed to being licensed by a state or local authority.

DODGERS Canvas screens for protection against the weather, often at the sides of the cockpit.

DRAFT Minimum depth of water in which a vessel can float.

DRAMAMINE Trade name of an American brand of anti-nausea pill. Other brands are Gravol (Canadian) and Marzine (British).

EASTERLY WAVE A pressure irregularity along the southern side of the Azores High. It creates locally severe conditions and can develop into a tropical cyclone.

EASTING Movement towards the east.

EBB (noun or verb) The state of the tide when going out.

230

ECHO The identification letter (E) of the U.S.-manned weather ship between Bermuda and the Azores. There are nine such ships, operated by various governments, in the North Atlantic.

EMBAYED Trapped in a bay and unable to escape to open water because of strong onshore winds and seas.

EPOXY A synthetic resin which makes an excellent glue. Superior to, but more expensive than, Polyester resin.

E.T.A. Estimated Time of Arrival.

FACE In this context, the sloping side of a sea or wave, such as the leading face or the after face.

FANTAIL A small deck area at the extreme stern of the vessel.

FATHOM A nautical measurement of depth. Six feet.

FATIGUE The tendency of metals to become brittle and to break, due to age, vibration or repeated bending.

FIN In this context, a blade extending below the centre of the outrigger keel to help the vessel to turn.

FLOOD (noun or verb) The state of the tide when coming in, but before reaching high water.

FO'C'SLE Short for forecastle. Originally a high structure at the bow, but nowadays the foremost quarters of the ship.

FORCE OF WIND See Beaufort Scale.

FORE-GUY A line holding the boom forward and preventing it from jibing or swinging across unintentionally.

FORE-PEAK A space in the extreme bow, too small for anything but stowage. Forward of, or part of, the fo'c'sle.

FORE-REACH, TO To creep forward slowly when lying a-hull, or when hove-to.

FORESTAY The cable supporting the mast from the bow. Also used to carry the foresail or jib.

FREEBOARD Measurement of the height of the main deck above the water or, in the case of an open boat, the height of the gunwale.

FRONTAL SYSTEM The various fronts associated with a low pressure system.

GALLEY Nautical term for kitchen.

GASKET A layer of soft material between two metal faces, to make a watertight or airtight joint between them.

GC1A Model number of *Caravel's* all-wave radio receiver.

GENOA A large foresail to replace the normal working jib either when racing or in light airs.

G.M.T. Greenwich Mean Time. Five hours ahead of Eastern Standard.

GREAT CIRCLE ROUTE The most direct route between any 2 points on the earth's surface, but not necessarily the most suitable for sailing or the easiest to follow.

GREEN WATER Solid water, as opposed to mere spray or splash.

GROUND SWELL A long ocean swell, resulting from a storm perhaps thousands of miles away, that has reached shallow water near the coast.

GUNK-HOLE, TO To explore the shallow places along a coast.

HALYARD A line running through a block at the top of the mast and used to haul sails, etc. aloft.

HAND, TO To lower a sail and furl it.

HANGING LOCKER A cupboard in which clothes are hung.

HATCH The cover protecting the entrance to either a cabin or a stowage compartment. From this it has come to mean the stowage space itself.

HAUL, TO A boat is said to be hauled when removed from the water for work below the waterline or for winter storage.

HAWSE HOLE The hole near the bow of a larger ship through which the anchor chain and dock warps are fed.

HEAD 1. A marine-type toilet.

2. Top of the cylinder in a gasoline or diesel engine.

3. The ship's bow.

HEAD SEAS Seas that are meeting the ship head-on.

HEADING The direction in which the ship is actually pointing, though not necessarily travelling.

HEAT EXCHANGER Part of the engine's cooling system. Equivalent to a car's radiator, except that instead of being cooled by air passing through it, sea water ("raw" water) is used.

HEAVE-TO, TO This means to hold a vessel almost head to wind and at near zero speed, usually to ride out bad weather. In a sailboat it is done by backing the sail and lashing the helm. The vessel should then lie comfortably without attention.

HEEL, TO A vessel is said to heel when she lies over to one side under pressure from the wind.

232

HIGH A high pressure system producing generally fair weather and, in the northern hemisphere, a clockwise wind circulation.

HIKE, TO To lean out of a small sailboat on the windward side in order to counteract heel.

HOOK Slang term for the anchor.

HULL-DOWN A ship is said to be hull-down when it is far enough away for the hull itself to be below the horizon and only the superstructure visible.

IRONS A sailboat is in irons when allowed to come too close into the wind so that she loses all forward speed and cannot be steered back onto course.

ISOBAR MAP A weather map showing the lines of equal barometric pressure. It gives a good weather picture for the next 24 to 48 hours.

JIB The foremost sail.

JIBE, TO To turn too far down-wind and thus allow the sails and booms to swing over to the other side. It can be either an intentional, controlled manoeuvre or an accidental one, and the latter can be dangerous. The fore-guy prevents an accidental jibe.

JURY (adjective) Of a temporary or emergency nature, such as "jury steering."

KATABATIC A coastal wind near mountains. Dense, cool air in the mountains tumbles down coastal valleys and causes violent offshore winds.

KEEL The main member along the bottom of a boat. In many sailboats it also refers to the deep, ballasted structure below it.

KETCH A two-masted sailboat in which the after mast (mizzen) is the smaller and is located forward of the post on which the rudder is mounted. *See* also yawl, schooner and sloop.

KEYS U.S. spelling for Cays. Small, low islands, specifically off the Florida coast.

kHz Abbreviation for kilohertz, a measurement of the frequency of radio waves. 1 kHz = 1,000 cycles per second. (*See* MHz.)

KNOT A measurement of speed, not of distance. One nautical mile per hour. Equivalent to about 1.15 statute m.p.h.

LAND BREEZE A breeze blowing from the land to the sea.

233

LAT. Short for latitude. The distance in degrees north or south of the equator.

LATITUDE SIGHT A sun- or starsight telling the ship's latitude.

LEE In a down-wind direction, or on the down-wind or sheltered side of the ship. The following derive from it:

1. To turn to leeward (looard) means to turn down-wind.
2. To make leeway (pronounced as spelled) is to drift down-wind.
3. To get a lee from something, or to be in the lee of it, means to be sheltered by it.
4. A lee shore is down-wind, and thus a danger.
5. The lee side of a ship is the down-wind or sheltered side.

LEVANTER An east wind, usually strong, off the south coast of Spain.

LIFT BRIDGE A bridge in which the moveable span remains horizontal but is raised at each end by cables and counterweights to allow ships to pass.

LIGHT DISPLACEMENT A hull of generally light construction but designed to ride *in* the water, as opposed to a planing hull which rises onto the surface at higher speeds.

LIGHTSHIP A ship, moored to the bottom, and used as a floating light-house. They are gradually being replaced by smaller, automatic navigational aids.

LINE Rope that has been cut from its coil for use.

LINE OF POSITION A line drawn on a chart in the knowledge that the ship is at some unknown point on it.

LOCK A device for moving ships from one level in a canal to a higher or lower one to follow the changing contours of the land.

LOG 1. An instrument for measuring the distance that a ship travels through the water. An odometer.

2. A ship's official diary. The written record of events.

3. As a verb, to record a certain speed or distance.

LONG. Short for longitude. The distance in degrees, east or west of Greenwich (England).

LONGITUDE SIGHT A sun- or starsight telling the ship's longitude.

LOOM Reflected glow in the sky of a powerful light or mass of lights, visible when the light itself is still below the horizon.

LOW A low pressure system, generally associated with bad weather and, in the northern hemisphere, an anti-clockwise wind circulation.

LUFF (verb) To sail closer to the wind. It has also come to mean sailing

234

too close to the wind, so that the sails cease to drive and just flap like flags.

(noun) The forward edge of a sail.

MAIN Of a sloop, the after sail. Of a ketch, yawl or schooner, either the taller mast or the principal sail carried thereon.

MANGROVE A tropical tree that grows in shallow salt water, with thick leaves and tough wood. The name means to "walk forward," because of the tree's continuous action of throwing down roots in the water.

MARIE CELESTE An American sailing ship found abandoned near the Azores Islands, drifting, but intact, and with a meal half-eaten. No survivors were ever found and the reason for deserting the ship so suddenly is a classical mystery of the sea. The current theory is that they thought her to be sinking after being hit by a waterspout.

MET. Short for meteorological.

MHz Abbreviation for Megahertz, a measurement of the frequency of radio waves. 1 MHz = 1,000,000 cycles per second = 1,000 kHz.

MISTRAL A katabatic wind off the French Mediterranean coast. It comes down from the Alps, usually in winter, and is often very violent. It can appear without warning and on a cloudless day.

MIZZEN The smaller mast at the stern of a ketch or yawl, or the sail carried thereon.

MONOHULL Any vessel with one hull.

MOOR, TO To secure a vessel by two or more anchors. From this it has come to mean securing it to the bottom by any means other than by a single anchor, such as to a mooring buoy.

MULTIHULL Any vessel with two or more hulls.

NAUTICAL ALMANAC An annual publication providing certain navigational and nautical information, including the position of the sun, moon, stars and planets for every second of the year.

NEAPS Those tides which occur at half-moon (new and old) and which produce the minimum rise and fall. The opposite of springs.

NORTHING Movement towards the north.

NUN A red, conical floating buoy.

ODOMETER An instrument measuring distance travelled.

OFFING Distance from the coast.

235

OPTIMUM TRACK A word coined by ourselves to refer to the most efficient and most easily-sailed route, though not necessarily the shortest or the rhumb line route.

OUTRIGGER Sometimes called a float or pontoon. The outer hulls of a trimaran.

OVERFALLS Breaking seas, often at a distance from shore, caused by either a shallow ledge or the interaction of opposing currents.

PAINTER The line securing a dinghy by its bow.

PASSAGE A one-way journey by sea from one point to another. A series of passages is a voyage.

PILLARS OF HERCULES The two hills said by the ancients to guard the entrance to the Mediterranean—the Rock of Gibraltar on the north side and Monte Hacho on the African shore.

PILOT CHART A small-scale, strategic chart giving details of weather, currents, shipping lanes, etc.

PITCH KETTLE A large iron pot used to melt pitch for the caulking of wooden ships.

PLOTTING CHART A chart showing latitude and longitude, but no land masses, and used to plot positions at sea.

PLOW A type of anchor, so-called for its shape. Same as CQR.

POLYESTER RESIN The synthetic resin commonly used in fibreglass.

PORT On the left hand, facing forward.

PORT TACK Sailing with the wind on the port side.

PRIMUS A brand name for a portable stove, burning in this case kerosene under pressure.

PROPANE A bottled gas used for cooking and refrigeration.

PULPIT Rails around the bow, to protect the man working there.

QUARTER That part of the ship to one side or other of the stern. From this are derived:
1. Quarter deck. The deck to one side of the stern.
2. On the quarter, meaning aft of the beam but not dead astern.

Q-FLAG The yellow signalling flag representing the letter "Q," and called the Quarantine flag. It is flown when entering port from a foreign country and means, in effect, "I am entering your country from abroad. I have no contagious disease on board and request clearance by your customs, Immigration and Health authorities." It

236

does not, as is sometimes thought, mean that there is disease on board, but just the opposite.

RADIO BEACON A radio station transmitting nothing but its identification letters in Morse code. The navigator determines its bearing on his D.F. receiver and thus establishes his line of position.

RAISE, TO To sight, or make contact with by radio.

RANGE MARKERS A pair of markers, usually posts on shore or on the bottom in shallow water, with the farther one always higher than the nearer. When they are in line, as seen from the vessel, the boat is in the correct channel.

RATLINES Rope or wooden steps up the standing rigging, to enable a seaman to go aloft.

RAW WATER Sea water used for engine cooling, as opposed to the fresh water in the closed system of the water jacket itself.

REACH (noun) To sail on a reach is to do so with the wind approximately on the beam. In a close reach, the wind is forward of the beam, but not so far that the vessel is close-hauled. A beam reach means that the wind is on the beam. A broad reach means that it is aft of the beam but not so far as to constitute a run.

REDUCE A SIGHT, TO To perform the mathematical calculations involved after a sun- or starsight.

REEF (noun) A line or layer of rocks or coral, shallow enough to be a hazard.
(verb) To reduce the effective area of a sail by mechanical means, such as roller reefing.

RELATIVE BEARING See under bearing.

RHUMB LINE The simplest, but not the shortest route. On a standard Mercator projection chart it shows as a straight line, but on the earth's surface it is actually a curve.

RIG Term used to describe the general mast and sail configuration.

RIGGING (RUNNING) The lines used to adjust the position of sails, booms, etc.

RIGGING (STANDING) Cables supporting the masts.

ROADSTEAD A port or anchorage offering no protection, either natural or man-made. The vessel must anchor off a fully-exposed coast.

ROGUE SEA A sea substantially higher than the other seas being experienced.

237

ROLLER REEFING A geared device for rotating the boom in order to roll the sail around it and thus reduce the effective area in heavy weather.

ROPE Cordage while still on the coil and not cut up for use.

ROTOR In this context, that part of the Walker Log which is towed astern.

RUN (verb) To sail before the wind.
(noun) The direction of sailing which puts the wind well aft.

SCHOONER A fore-and-aft rigged vessel with two or more masts, of which the forward one is not the tallest.

SCREW Ship's propeller.

SEA ANCHOR A drogue-like device dragged through the water to reduce drift, especially in heavy weather, by its resistance.

SEA BREEZE A breeze blowing from sea to the land.

SEAS Almost synonymous with waves, except that a sea is generally larger and higher than a wave. Both terms apply only while they are being acted upon by the wind. Thereafter they become swells.

SHACKLE A U-shaped fitting, the opening of which can be closed by a threaded pin screwed through two eyes. It is used for joining lengths of chain and for securing a wide variety of cables, blocks and fittings.

SHACKLE PIN The threaded pin in the above.

SHEAVE The rotating portion of a block or pulley.

SHEET The line controlling the position of a sail or boom.

SHOAL (noun or adjective) Shallow.
(verb) To become more shallow.

SHORT AND STEEP Seas that are both close together and have a steep face. They produce an uncomfortable ride when heading into them.

SHROUD Cable supporting the mast from port or starboard.

SKEG A heavy structure below the after portion of the keel, and often the lowest part of the vessel. The propeller shaft runs through it.

SLACK WATER The point of tide when all flow has ceased but the reverse flow has not yet started.

SLIP (noun) A sloping track used to haul boats from the water.

SLOOP A fore-and-aft rigged sailboat with one mast.

SLOP Unpleasant sea conditions, with short, steep, confused seas.

238

SLOW COUNT A spoken count sent out by radio to enable the receiving operator to get an accurate bearing by D.F.

SNAPS (of a sail) Small fittings on the luff of a jib for attachment to the forestay.

SOUTHING Movement towards the south.

SPARS In general, all masts and booms.

SPINNAKER A large, balloon-like foresail used as a down-wind sail, especially when racing.

SPREADER A short cross member, part way up the mast, used to form a diamond-stay to stiffen the mast.

SPRINGS Those tides which occur just after new and full moon, and which produce the greatest rise and fall.

STABILITY The ability of a boat to remain upright.

STARBOARD On the right hand, looking forward.

STARBOARD TACK Sailing with the wind on the starboard side.

STAYS Cables supporting the mast from bow or stern.

STEP (verb) To put up the mast.
(noun) The base on which the mast sits.

STERN BITT Heavy fitting on the stern for an anchor or stern warp.

STINK POT A term used by sailing fans to describe any engine.

STORM ANCHOR A heavy anchor used under storm conditions.

STORM JIB A small but strong jib used as a storm sail.

STRINGER A longitudinal member which stiffens the skin of the hull.

STRUT A fitting which supports the propeller shaft, aft of the skeg.

STUFFING BOX A gland through which the propeller shaft enters the water. It should leak very slightly, and be tightened if it leaks too much.

SUMLOG Trade name of an instrument measuring speed and distance through the water.

SURFING Sailing down-wind in heavy, following seas, fast enough to be carried along on the leading face, as though on a surfboard.

SURGE An uncomfortable swell in a harbour or anchorage.

SWELL Residual seas that are no longer acted upon by the wind and are decaying.

SWING, TO To swing a compass is to check the extent of its error when facing different directions.

SWING BRIDGE A bridge in which the roadbed rotates horizontally about a central point, to allow ships to pass.

239

TACK, TO To sail a zigzag course, with the wind first on one side and then on the other, due to an inability to sail directly into the wind.

TELLTALE A short length of coloured ribbon, tied in an exposed place, to show the direction of the wind.

TEXAS TOWER A steel structure standing on the sea bottom and extending above the surface. Named after the offshore Texas oil rigs.

THROTTLE Engine speed control.

TIDAL RANGE Difference in height between high and low water.

TIDE TABLES Tables forecasting the height and times of high and low tide at various places for each day of the year.

TOPPING LIFT The line supporting the end of the boom from the top of the mast.

TOPSIDES Sides of the hull above the water but below the deck.

TRADE WINDS Belts of generally easterly wind blowing with considerable constancy over the oceans near the edges of the tropical zones, both north and south.

TRANSDUCER That part of an electronic depth-sounder which protrudes through the hull and does the sensing.

TRAWL A tubular fishing net towed by trawlers.

TRIANGULATE, TO To determine positions by the forming and solving of triangles.

TRIATIC STAY Cable joining the tops of the masts for mutual support.

TROUGH That part of a low pressure system, between the fronts, that normally contains the strongest winds.

TRUE In this context relating to courses, it means based on the true north, as opposed to the magnetic north.

TURNBUCKLE A fitting used to vary the length of a cable by a screw adjustment, or to disconnect it.

TWIN JIBS A sail arrangement in which two similar jibs are carried, one boomed out to port and the other to starboard, so that the vessel becomes, in effect, almost square-rigged. This is a suitable rig for use when running down the trades.

VEER, TO The wind is said to veer when it changes direction by following the sun, that is clockwise in the northern hemisphere and anti-clockwise in the southern. Opposite to "back."

V.H.F. Very high frequency. A range of radio frequencies.

VOYAGE A series of consecutive passages by sea.

WALKER LOG An instrument for measuring the distance that a ship travels through the water (not over the bottom). It uses a spinning rotor towed astern. Probably the most accurate of such instruments available to yachtsmen.

WARM FRONT Part of a low pressure system; usually associated with deteriorating weather and increasing winds.

WARPS Lines used to secure a vessel to the quay or to an anchor.

WEATHER, TO To pass to windward of, usually without tacking.

WESTING Movement towards the west.

WHITE SQUALL A sudden, strong wind with no cloud or rain to warn of its approach.

WINCH PAWL The ratchet controlling a winch. It can be released to allow the winch to run free.

WIND When steering to put the wind further ahead, one speaks of coming "up" or "into the wind." When putting it further aft one speaks of "falling off," "bearing away" or turning "down-wind."

WINDLASS Similar to a winch, but larger and used for hauling in an anchor line or dock warp.

WING That part of a trimaran lying between the hulls.

WOM A radio station at Fort Lauderdale, Florida, handling telephone calls to and from ships at sea. Until 1970 it also broadcast marine weather forecasts.

YAW To turn erratically from side to side.

YAWL Similar to a ketch, except that the mizzen mast is located aft of the rudder post and is usually smaller.

NUMBERS

2 MHz BAND The radio band used by ships for voice communication.

5.6 MHz A short wave frequency suitable for long range.

12-METRE A type of large racing sailboat, as used in the Americas Cup.

27 MHz A radio band used for walkie-talkie purposes. We refer to it as v.h.f., although technically this band starts only at 30 MHz.

200 kHz A frequency representing 1,500 metres and used by the B.B.C. for both broadcast and marine weather forecast purposes.

2,182 kHz The International Calling and Distress frequency for voice purposes on the marine band.